MOTHER GOOSE
on the Loose

Here, There, and Everywhere

ALA Editions purchases fund advocacy, awareness, and accreditation programs for library professionals worldwide.

MOTHER GOOSE

on the Loose

Here, There, and Everywhere

Betsy Diamant-Cohen

CHICAGO | 2019

Dr. Betsy Diamant-Cohen is a librarian, consultant, teacher, and trainer in the fields of early literacy, children's programming, family engagement, and building twenty-first-century skills. Based on her experiences as a children's librarian in public libraries and children's museums, a preschool teacher, a home daycare provider, and a parent of three children (now grown), Betsy knows firsthand that children learn best through play. Best known as the creator of Mother Goose on the Loose, an award-winning early literacy program, Betsy holds a master's degree in library science and a doctorate in communications design and is a certified "Listen, Like, Learn" instructor. In 2013, she was awarded the Association of Specialized and Cooperative Library Agencies' Leadership and Professional Achievement Award for "revolutionizing the way librarians work with children from birth to age 3." As this book was being published, Betsy received the Alexandre Vattemare Award for Creativity in Libraries recognizing that she "has taken the traditional storytime to an elevated level . . . to reach and connect with educators, caregivers, parents, professionals, and children beyond the walls of the library."

© 2019 by the American Library Association

Extensive effort has gone into ensuring the reliability of the information in this book; however, the publisher makes no warranty, express or implied, with respect to the material contained herein.

ISBN: 978-0-8389-1647-6 (paper)

Library of Congress Cataloging-in-Publication Data

Names: Diamant-Cohen, Betsy.
Title: Mother goose on the loose : here, there, and everywhere / Betsy
  Diamant-Cohen.
Description: ALA Editions. | Chicago : American Library Association, 2019. |
  Includes index.
Identifiers: LCCN 2018031876 | ISBN 9780838916476 (print : alk. paper)
Subjects: LCSH: Language arts (Early childhood) | Nursery rhymes—Study and
  teaching (Early childhood) | Early childhood education—Activity programs.
  | Children's libraries—Activity programs.
Classification: LCC LB1139.5.L35 D52 2019 | DDC 372.6—dc23 LC record available at https://lccn.loc.
gov/2018031876

Book design by Kim Thornton in the Minion, Proxima Nova, and Soft Compound typefaces.

⊚ This paper meets the requirements of ANSI/NISO Z39.48-1992 (Permanence of Paper).
Printed in the United States of America.

23 22 21 20 19   5 4 3 2 1

Contents

Part III   Everywhere

Part IV   Mother Goose on the Loose Resources

Preface

MOTHER GOOSE ON THE LOOSE: HERE, THERE, AND Everywhere is a book meant to inspire you to use your proficient MGOL skills to go out into the community and share MGOL there. Since MGOL is easily adaptable, this book gives many examples and tips for adapting MGOL for programs in schools, parks, Early Head Start (EHS) centers, home daycares, museums, hospitals, prisons, synagogues and churches, and senior citizen centers. It gives tried-and-true tips on how to successfully adapt MGOL for parents of hospitalized NICU babies, for children with a wide array of disabilities, and for non-English speakers, among others. It explains how MGOL can be tweaked to work well with different communities such as rural areas, multiage participants, and huge storytime crowds. It highlights successful practices for using media in MGOL programs and for sharing the MGOL app with older elementary students.

This book is a celebration of many successful MGOL adaptations and the people who have creatively tweaked MGOL, presented it to a wide variety of populations in new settings, and then shared their stories with me. Without these individuals, this book would never have been written.

Enormous thanks goes to the following people: Adrienne Butler (in rural communities), Amanda Bressler (in hospitals), Amy Bluemel (with American Indians), Amy Koester (with digital media), Angel Wilde (Kickapoo Nation), Ann Bakker (in EHS), Annie Calderon (with Spanish speakers), Barb Henschel (in Neonatal Intensive Care Units [NICUs]), Beth Munk (using the app with older elementary children), Dr. Brenda Hussey-Gardner (in NICUs), Carole Schlein (using art), Caroline Chavasse (attending as a parent), Carolyn Brooks (with sensory storytimes and *2s & 3s On the Go!*), Cathy Lancaster (for teen mothers), Celia Yitzhak (bringing illustrations alive), Cen Campbell (with digital media), Christy Estrovitz (for childcare providers), Cork Hardin (in community centers, pop-up storytimes, and teen moms), Dawn Sacks (in NICUs), Deborah Margolis (for children with special needs), Derek Cooper (in children's museums, schools, and daycares), Devon Ellis (using volunteers), Dora Garraton (in home daycares, prisons, schools, and other settings, as well as with foster parents), Dorothy Stoltz (in Judy Centers), Dorothy Valakos (in art museums), Edwin Perez (for Spanish speakers and a multicultural crowd), Elizabeth McChesney (in laundromats), Glennor Shirley (in prisons), Gloria Bartas (for infants, toddlers, and large crowds), Gloria Melchor (for Spanish speakers), Gretchen Wronka (in stores and malls), Haley Downer (for senior citizens), Iris Cotto (for Spanish speakers), Jamie Naidoo (in master's of library and information science [MLIS] classrooms), Jan Fabiyi (in children's museums and synagogues), Jan Simons (in Judy Centers), Janet Shepherd (for children on the autism spectrum), Jason Driver (with sensory storytime), Jeannie Whitehorse (for Navajo tribe), Jenna Nemec-Loise (in public libraries), Jennifer Bown-Olmedo (for Spanish speakers), Jennifer Timmerman (in preschools and kindergartens), Jenny Gallagher (in public libraries), Joanne Browning (during Family Place sessions), Jordan Sachse (for children with developmental delays), Joshua Farnum (with sensory storytimes), and Julie Ranelli (using digital media and in the public library).

Additional thanks to Karin Wood (for teen moms and social workers), Katharine Phelps (with multicultural programming), Kent Gerber (using musical instruments), Keren Joshi (with EHS in prison), Kerry Funari (in Judy Centers), Kim White (for homeless women), Klaus Libertus (as a parent education program), Kristin Williamson (as a citywide school readiness push), Laurie Collins (for connecting community artists with the community), Laurie Willhalm (with First Five program), Linda Squire (using volunteers), Linda Valle (using volunteers), Lisa Eck (at the pool), Lisa Kropp (in LIS classes), Lisa Sensale Yazdian (in malls and stores), Lisa Tyson (with EHS), Lisa Wood (with Smart Start), Lori Guenthner (for children with special needs), Marci Brueggen (with Smart Start), Maricela Leon-Barrera (for children on the autism spectrum), Marilyn Hage (in home daycares, preschools, and Women, Infants, and Children [WIC] Centers), Marisa Conner (in WIC Clinics), Marsha Leno (Pueblo of Zia), Melanie Hetrick (for infants and in rural communities), Melissa Da (for Spanish speakers and in kindergartens), Michele Presley (for toddlers and using digital media), Michelle Guvendiren (using art), Michelle Irvine (using volunteers), Miruna Patrascanu (parent-run MGOL), Nicole Brown (for senior citizens), Nora Thompson (in museums and hospitals and with Head Start programs), Phoebe Bacon (in hospitals), Regina Wade (in libraries and museums, at picnics, as "Jingle Jangle Music Time," and for children with special needs), Roberta Hoffman (building visual literacy through MGOL), Robin Head (for children on the autism spectrum in preschool), Rondia Banks (as a four-week series), Selma Levi (in public libraries and hospitals), Shelley Quezada (with underserved populations), Stacy Dykstra (with Smart Start), Summer Rosswog (in museums, NICUs, preschools, and home daycares), Susan Pannebaker (about MGOL trainings), Susan Sonnenschein (in NICUs), Tamar Kirschner (with First Five program), Tyra LaVerne (in preschools and kindergartens), Valerie Kimble (with American Indians), Terri Wortman (in prison-based EHS programs), and Carmen Slothower (in prison-based EHS programs).

I could not ask for a better publisher than ALA Editions. It has been a wonderful partner in the making of this book, and I would be remiss not to give a special mention to Jamie Santoro, Angela Gwizdala, Jill Hillemeyer, Rob Christopher, Patrick Hogan, and Rachel Chance. Another hearty thank you goes to my terrific assistant, Jennifer Bergantz.

Introduction

What Is MGOL?

MOST CHILDREN'S LIBRARIANS ARE EXTREMELY CRE-ative. Working with children of all ages means they have to be flexible and adaptable. Since 1998, I have had the privilege of introducing Mother Goose on the Loose (MGOL) to children's librarians and educators throughout the United States and Canada. Although MGOL is a program designed for children and their parents, it has had a meaningful impact on adult facilitators as well.

During MGOL training workshops, I have stressed that most important for a successful program is that the facilitators know themselves, be themselves, and share themselves. Once they have mastered the "plain vanilla" version of MGOL, facilitators are encouraged to adapt it for their audiences and make it their own. I have followed this path myself by adapting and presenting MGOL programs in public libraries, in daycare centers, in preschools, at summer camps, in museums, in prisons, for new foster parents, for counselors in a drug treatment program who were helping recovering addict parents learn appropriate parenting techniques, at child-abuse awareness events, in synagogues and churches, in home daycares, for English-language learners, in high school programs for teen moms, in hospitals, and at medical centers.

According to the Association of Specialized and Cooperative Library Agencies, MGOL has "revolutionized the way storytimes are presented to young children at libraries across the country."[1] MGOL workshops train facilita-tors to use and then tailor the MGOL structure, activities, and information to fit programs they are already running at their libraries or the new audiences they hope to work with. Because they can adapt everything and do not need to keep the MGOL name, there is no way to count the number of MGOL or MGOL-influenced programs being presented today. Documented versions of MGOL have already engaged families in Israel, Canada, Mexico, Egypt, Australia, India, New Zealand, and Argentina, but its reach could be much wider.

Unlike typical program models that provide a range of scripts for librarians to follow, detailing precisely which books and fingerplays to use, the beauty of MGOL is that it provides the architecture of a well-designed program and invites facilitators to fill in the blanks with songs, books, and rhymes that they know and like. During training workshops, future program facilitators are taught the theory behind MGOL and given a blueprint for creating successful programs. After becoming comfortable with the plain version, facilitators are encouraged to adapt MGOL to fit their personalities, their communities, and their audiences. The facilitators are encouraged to share themselves with participants by tailoring sessions to match their skills and interests. For instance, some MGOL facilitators play guitar during their programs, others use a wide variety of puppets, some use more book illustrations and fewer flannelboard characters, and so forth.

MGOL facilitators learn that by being themselves, sharing their enthusiasm, finding and implementing comfortable methods of presentation, and interacting with each attendee, the result is a relatively stress-free program for them and an enjoyable one for the participants. A bond grows between the facilitator and participants through the person-to-person connections. The positive, nonjudgmental atmosphere that is established encompasses the facilitator as well, providing a safe place to present the program.

Although content plays an important role, the most important part of a MGOL program is the nurturing, nonjudgmental environment. The welcoming atmosphere that is created, the celebration of each person's individuality, the recognition of achievement for even the smallest accomplishment, and the joy of being together is the magic behind MGOL.

There are no early childhood programs that promote family engagement by strengthening child-parent bonding through nursery rhymes, emphasize the building of musical and literacy skills through song, provide an array of opportunities designed to help children practice and strengthen self-regulation skills, boost children's sense of competence, and assist children's development in all domains of learning exactly like MGOL. It is research-based and uses music, movement, and literacy activities as tools to help children develop school readiness skills. MGOL makes use of a flannelboard, felt pieces, and book illustrations to connect language and music with print. It is designed to be a group experience that builds parenting skills while giving children joyful encounters with language and communication through songs, stories, and rhymes.

Since public libraries have redefined their missions to include family engagement, outreach, and early literacy, children's librarians have been looking for existing programs or creating new programs to reach groups of people who are not yet library users. Each of the contributors to this book has used MGOL in unique ways that might be exactly what other librarians are looking for. Although each adaptation of MGOL has its own distinctive traits, commonalities can always be found. The following examples are meant to inspire readers to create their own adaptations to fit their particular out-reach efforts and audiences. Rather than a show-and-tell piece, this book is meant to illuminate different MGOL programs and offshoots, describe key modifications and features, talk about challenges, list tried-and-true tips for success, and inspire even more adaptations by sharing practical advice and know-how. It is meant to celebrate those adaptations by giving librarians the opportunity to tell their stories, present formulas for replication, and encourage others to make use of this information by adapting their own versions of MGOL.

The Anatomy of MGOL

MGOL follows a format of ten sections, with different rhymes, songs, and activities in each section. Although everything is up for change during adaptations, many programs still follow the same basic structure.

Section 1: Welcoming comments sets the tone for a comfortable place. In addition to welcoming everyone warmly and introducing themselves, facilitators spell out the guidelines and put parents at ease.

Section 2: Rhymes and reads involves introducing rhymes, allowing participants time to get familiar with the facilitator's voice, and reading one book aloud cover to cover.

Section 3: Body rhymes uses songs and rhymes to exercise small muscles while naming parts of the body and their movements.

Section 4: The drum sequence is an activity where the facilitator personally welcomes each participant at the session (by name, if possible). Each person is invited to tap his or her name on the drum to the beat of the syllables.

Section 5: Stand-up / sit-down activities gives everyone a chance to move around and get their wiggles out and often involves a freeze game to help children practice stopping.

Section 6: Animal activities reinforces animal names and sounds by matching them with illustrations, puppets, and photographs.

Section 7: Musical instruments and scarves provides opportunities to experiment with cause and effect (STEM), to practice listening and responding, to use the imagination, and to connect with music as listeners and as musicians.

Section 8: Lullabies is when adults sing a lullaby to their children and experience the calming atmosphere that lullabies can create.

Section 9: Interactive rhymes includes the recitation of a rhyme followed by an invitation for each child to perform an easy-to-do action for which they receive positive reinforcement from everyone.

Section 10: Closing ritual consists of the same songs each week that tell everyone the session is ending and reassures them that the facilitator is glad they came and looks forward to seeing them next time.

A Typical MGOL Session

The standard MGOL session in the public library lasts for thirty minutes. There is 80 percent repetition of material from week to week. Most of the rhymes and activities are associated with felt pieces that are placed on a flannelboard. Each rhyme is repeated twice, giving participants a chance to listen first and then chime in. Adults sit in a circle around the flannelboard with their children in their laps or sitting next to them. This program was originally created for parents and caregivers with chil-

---

Snapshot: MGOL for Parents

Tanya has brought her daughter, Fiona, to MGOL since shortly after her birth. She was interviewed when Fiona was six months old and then again after Fiona had been attending the program on a regular basis for more than two years.

At six months:
I've told all my friends about it, and I'm trying to get them to come too because I love that there are so many things I would never think to do with her. Just the emphasis of the words and then all the tactile stuff. We do the songs at home. I try to remember things that we did here in the library. And I now try to make up some of my own songs and things.

At two and half years:
I think it really helped me as a parent early on to give me confidence in what I was doing and to give me ideas and also to show me what she was capable of. Before I had a child, I didn't understand children, and I think I probably thought of them more as objects. Now I really have an appreciation for what they understand. I really think about everything I do with her and everything she hears and everything she sees, and I'm sure I got a lot of that from coming to Mother Goose on the Loose.

I came here for a little structure and for her to be with other kids—I guess for me to be with other mothers and fathers. But for her, there's so much. I can't imagine what she would be like now if she hadn't come here all this time. The songs are a daily part of our lives. We sing them as we're getting dressed, as we're eating breakfast, as we're going in the car. She recognizes the songs in her books.

She knows that it's something she has known as long as she can remember. And then she'll see them in other contexts. I think that's what got her interested in books. We started her on Mother Goose books very early. Her favorite books are the Mother Goose books from here. She loves books now. I'm sure coming to the library every week was good for her, just to have the chance every week to get new books and to see people reading and to see how fun it was.

I would never have thought that you could teach "loud" and "soft" and these concepts. I would never have known how to teach them. I would have thought they were well beyond her abilities when she was the age to learn them. The way these kids are introduced to these things are so inventive, I think. I really appreciate that it's a little different every time, but there's enough routine in it, and that routine is important.

She definitely has learned without having other children at home how to take turns and just how to be with other kids. She's learned to clean up from being here. She loves doing that!!! I read that article about preparing kids for preschool, and I definitely think that she's ready when the time comes for her to go to school because of all the things she's done here.

dren from birth to age three and follows the "Listen, Like, Learn" approach of Canadian music educator Barbara Cass-Beggs. For more information about the basic MGOL program, see *Mother Goose on the Loose, Updated* (ALA Editions, 2018), and to learn about the variety of wonderful MGOL adaptations for use here, there, and everywhere, keep reading!

Each chapter in this book begins with an overall introduction to the chapter topic. Following these introductions are individual modules that describe different adaptations within the topic, including specific key features and tips for success. Each chapter also includes "Snapshots" by parents, MGOL practitioners, and MGOL participants. These direct quotes contain valuable advice, uplifting stories, and points to ponder.

In all MGOL adaptations, the most important thing you can do is to create a welcoming environment for all families and to remain a positive piece of their lives. This includes parents or children with disabilities, new immigrants, minorities, foster parents, LGBTQ+ families, and grandparents raising grandchildren. A connection with you becomes by extension a connection with all libraries. A positive relationship with a librarian can have a lasting effect on children and the adults in their lives; one caring adult makes all the difference.

NOTE

1. ALA News, "Mother Goose on the Loose's Diamant-Cohen Receives ASCLA Leadership and Professional Achievement Award," ALA, released June 10, 2013, www.ala.org/news/press-releases/2013/06/mother -goose-looses-diamant-cohen-receives-ascla -leadership-and-professional.

Part I
Here

MGOL Programs in Public Libraries

WITHIN THE PUBLIC LIBRARY, MOTHER GOOSE ON the Loose (MGOL) can be adapted to reach different audiences, to bring community members together, and to fill time in a creative way. Children's librarians have adapted MGOL to fit urban and rural settings, large and small audiences, and families with children of a variety of ages. Some librarians present sessions for families with children from birth and up; other libraries divide their sessions into groups for nonwalkers and for walkers using the same rhymes and format. MGOL sessions presented during weekend events provide both learning and marketing opportunities since they often draw in new families. Recruiting retired teachers and librarians to help with MGOL sessions uses their talents and gives them a sense of purpose while providing you with assistance. MGOL programs offered in different languages attract new immigrants alongside native English speakers who want their children to be exposed to other cultures. Talented community members and students become involved when they are asked to make props for your program and for display in the library. Through these adaptations, MGOL extends beyond its young audience and can positively affect everyone who is involved.

MGOL for Nonwalking Babies

Early childhood is a critical time for developing literacy skills, and we live in a period where adults are sometimes uncomfortable with their roles as models and teachers for their babies' development of early literacy skills. Many new parents feel self-conscious about talking and singing with their children. Some state "I can't sing!" Others wonder "How in the world do you 'play' with a baby?" or ask questions like "My four-month-old can't understand me, so why should I talk to him?" Of all the ways that early literacy skills are taught in MGOL, playing, talking, and singing appear to be the most impactful activities for nonwalking infants and their parents and caregivers. Thus some libraries with enough staff to offer

 Snapshot: MGOL in Public Libraries

Jenny Gallagher is the youth services librarian at the Centreville Library in Queen Anne's County, Maryland.

I think Mother Goose on the Loose has so many wonderful effects on the children who come. They calm down a little bit, they are able to sit still and pay attention, and they are able to work on taking turns, which is really important. They learn how to socialize and be prepared for preschool and kindergarten before they even go.

multiple MGOL programs run sessions for adults with babies who have not yet started to walk.

Key Features

At this stage, parents do the activities for their children—the babies will most likely be watching their parents or sucking on the musical instruments. After participating in just a few sessions, most self-consciousness disappears. In the comfort of their own homes, parents can repeat the activities and not worry about making mistakes. Relatively quickly, you will see the same parents talking, singing, and playing with ease with their babies during storytime!

Since new parents often feel isolated, creating community through informal playtime before or after the session is essential.

Snapshot: A Parent's View of MGOL in Public Libraries

Caroline, mother of two-and-a-half-year-old Louis and six-month-old Franny, reflected on the benefits that attending MGOL had for her family.

There is a real feeling of trust about children's energy. There's not a fear that I've run into in other group activities. There's a trust that children want to learn. There's a trust that all hell won't break loose, or the room won't erupt into chaos and utter confusion if a child is left to move and pause and be distracted or pay attention to whatever is going on in the room.

We started coming when Louis was around three or four months old, and he is now two and a half, so there was a break there when I was pregnant with Franny. We have done some of the Terrific Twos, and that has been great. In particular, the tone and environment of the infant/baby Mother Goose has been just great for us as a start out. I'm so thrilled we'll be able to give that to Franny.

A contrast to the generous and very wise feeling of our MGOL experience would be to go to other places where children are supposed to be playing and moving and singing, and there is a lot of fear out there that if you don't reign in those children right away, as soon as they are old enough to listen to direction, then society will crumble from within. Just...we had gone to a movement class, and the kids had to sit in a certain place. No one could do anything until all of the children were sitting. If the children were not absolutely quiet and sitting down, they would be removed from the room. And these were two-year-olds. There was no trust that if children were left to their own devices, great things could happen. It was in such sharp contrast to the wonderful experience we felt at MGOL... When Louis couldn't sit still, I thought, "Oh no, my

child isn't standing on the line, he's not touching the wall." It was so stressful. Lo and behold, the same boy was able to sit while his six-month-old baby sister went through a half an hour of nursery rhymes. Not absolutely still—he wandered a little but was engaged and enjoyed and could take part in the group activity. The result was just spectacular. It socialized him in a way... and we didn't have to force it. It was just a wonderfully natural experience.

The impact on our lives has been great—in terms of informing me as a parent to trust my child and how to provide something to them that is interesting. There is an absolute trust that he will come to it on his own terms and learn from it.

It's just informed our parenting; it's confirmed our best instincts about what children can be and what they can do. I'm so incredibly thankful for it. I wonder where I would be without it. I think I would have had the instincts, but they would not have been supported, perhaps...Raising a child would have been so much more stressful, I think.

The crux of it is that there's a trust in children. There's a confidence in children here—not that you have to change them or teach them, reign them in, shape them, mold them...providing a gentle, trusting, magical environment is pretty much all you have to do. Of course, you have to make sure people are safe and basic courtesy things...But in terms of teaching children to sit and listen; that is so unnecessary...there's just a joy and happiness here that, unfortunately, is hard to find in other places.

Tips for Success

For this audience, focus on new developmental skills every week, with an emphasis on the importance of singing, talking, and playing together.

- Offer developmental tips, share ideas, and demonstrate how to talk, sing, and play with a baby.
- Create community by offering playtime after the session and using questions to spark conversations. Talk with each parent, asking after the well-being of his or her child, discovering what new things the child is doing, and offering additional developmental tips. A great generic question is "What did your child do this week that was new?" For this question, you don't need to remember the child's name or gender. Since babies are always doing new things, parents will certainly have something to say. Other parents will hear the answer and may then pipe up: "My child just started doing the same thing!" A conversation will then ensue.
- Check out Melanie Hetrick's script at https://bit.ly/2wcxOAK and Rondia Banks's script at https://bit.ly/2odrqEY.

MGOL for Toddlers

In addition to her MGOL program for nonwalking babies, children's librarian Gloria Bartas offers adapted MGOL sessions for toddlers. This gives additional program options for parents and caregivers and helps break larger audiences into smaller groups.

To keep the toddlers occupied, Gloria leaves very little time between activities and includes as much movement as possible. Since toddlers have short attention spans, she places extra thick mats on the floor and a low book unit in the back of the room filled with board books, very easy nonfiction, and large picture books. Caregivers whose children need a break during the program can use this area as a time-out, break time, and crying area. Wanderers, shy ones, and those who can't sit still can go to this space, relax, and look at or read books with their adult caregivers.

Key Features

Many toddlers have just discovered their feet and want to move, move, move, so your program must be active. Large body movements help toddlers focus their energy. Use more variation than a standard MGOL session. Include nonfiction books; display their covers, and sing a call-and-response chant based on information in the book. Use scarves, stuffed animals, and puppets as often as possible. End with a movement activity.

Tips for Success

Gloria suggests these tips for success:
- Place wipes, paper towels, and hand sanitizer on a table to be available for emergencies.
- Stock a parents' table with giveaways promoting your library and information relating to babies and toddlers.
- Adapt songs and rhymes to become more active. For instance, lie on your back and kick your legs in the air, or while in a prone position, move your legs up and down to "Cobbler, Cobbler, Mend My Shoe."
- If more physical movement is needed to release the overflow of toddler energy, cut out some passive rhymes during the rhymes and read section and add more movement rhymes during the standing-up section.
- Keep time between activities to a minimum and include as much movement as possible, even if it is movement in place.
- Integrate more new rhymes with the original rhymes, and try adapting the format as the program unfolds, depending on the composition of the crowd and its mood.
- When using nonfiction, bring out a stuffed animal or toy on the same topic as the book. Show the book's cover and then display it in front of you. Create and sing a call-and-response chant using the facts in the book.
- Close with a standing-up activity. Try blowing bubbles to music and invite the toddlers to catch them, or dance in a circle to Hap Palmer's *Rumble through the Jungle.*
- After the program ends, bring out toys to encourage families to stay and play. Large cardboard blocks, balls, dishes, puzzles, and trucks are popular choices. Parents and children can play together with background music.

- Create a Google Groups account with the e-mail addresses of participants. Send them rhymes to do at home, and notify them of program changes or cancellations.

For more information on MGOL-based programming for two- and three-year-olds, try El Dorado County Library's *2s & 3s On the Go! Storytime Manual*. It is available for download at the El Dorado County Library website.[1]

SAMPLE PROGRAM

Toddler Jumps *(for a Very Large Audience)*

Gloria Bartas works at the Enoch Pratt Free Library's Govans Branch. She has divided her MGOL programs into "Baby Time Fun for Under One" and "Toddler Jumps" for walkers between the ages of one and two and a half. She presents this twice a week; her largest group often has sixty to eighty attendees. This sample program was designed with a group of about sixty in mind. Since Gloria creates many of her own routines, looking at the rhymes online is recommended.

When the room is really crowded, Gloria's standing-up rhymes involve in-place activities. She shows nonfiction book covers and creates call-and-response chants out of the facts. She sings a line, and everyone echoes it.

Note: This version lasts from forty-five minutes to one hour! It follows a different order from the typical MGOL session. There is no section 8 with a lullaby or section 9 with an interactive rhyme for each child.

To see a video of Gloria recreating this program, visit https://youtu.be/qP7VBBV2vFQ.

Section 1: Welcoming Comments
Branch, library, and community announcements
"We're So Happy"

Section 2: Rhymes and Reads
"Good Morning Medley" *(call-and-response)*
"Hello, Everybody, Yes, Indeed" *(with a tambourine)*
"Good Morning Song" *(Personally greet each child or family by name.)*
Book: Read aloud the big book version of *Hooray for Fish!* by Lucy Cousins.

Section 3: Body Rhymes
Hands: "Open Them, Shut Them"
Arms: "Two Little Apples" / "Shake My Sillies Out" / "Two Little Red / Blue Birds" *(variation on "Two Little Dickey Birds")*

Tummy Time: "Peter, Peter, Pumpkin Eater"
Legs: "Cobbler, Cobbler, Mend My Shoe" / "One, Two, Buckle My Shoe" / "Wee Willie Winkie" / "Hickory Dickory Dock" / "Ten Horses Galloping"

Section 4: The Drum Sequence *(not done)*

Section 7: Musical Instruments and Scarves
Scarves: "Wind, Oh Wind"
Scarves: "Peek-a-Boo"
Scarves: "This Is the Way We Wash Our Knees"
Scarves: "Abracadabra"
Scarves: "The Wheels on the Bus"
Scarves: "ABC Song"
Scarves: "Scarves Away"

Section 6: Nonfiction Activities *(In the standard program, this is the animal activities section.)*
Show Nonfiction book covers and chant "Bears" (call-and-response facts). Introduce a teddy bear.
Hibernation by Margaret Hall
Sleep, Bear! by Shelby Alinsky
Time to Sleep by Denise Fleming

Section 5: Stand-Up / Sit-Down Activities
"Here We Go Upperty Up"
"The Hokey Pokey"
"Ring around the Rosie"
Move to a recording of "The Elephant" by Hap Palmer *(Circle dance to changing tempos while listening to the song. Participants swing big arm trunks, walk with big feet, and make elephant sounds.)*

Section 8: Lullabies *(not done)*

Section 9: Interactive Rhymes *(not done)*

Section 10: Closing Ritual

(similar to the typical drum sequence)

"Good-Bye Song" *(Each child taps his or her name on the drum.)*

Be sure to offer free play with toys immediately afterward. When it is time to clean up, invite everyone to put the toys in a large plastic storage container. Put on the lid, ask the children to place a hand on the lid, and make choo-choo noises together as you push the "toy train" across the carpet and into its station under the table.

Adapting MGOL for Huge Audiences

Sometimes, MGOL becomes such a beloved program that the community response is overwhelming. This section is dedicated to Gloria Bartas for that reason! Attention must be paid to room occupancy levels and fire codes if your crowd is large. If you have a soft voice, use a cordless microphone or portable voice amplifier. Repeating a welcoming song lets everyone know it is time to get started and focuses the group's attention.

Sitting in a circle is crucial for crowd management; adults are less likely to talk to each other when in direct eye contact with you. Distributing and collecting props, giving puppet kisses, and being able to have eye-to-eye contact is much easier if everyone sits in a circle rather than a clump.

Call-and-response songs force your audience to pay attention. Utilizing recorded music during your program gives your voice a rest. When the room is very crowded, choose stand-up rhymes that involve in-place activities, such as "I'm a Little Teapot." To save time, consider bypassing individual interactive rhymes like "Hickory Dickory Dare" and "Humpty Dumpty," or choose to use either a musical instrument or colored scarves (rather than both). You may decide to extend your program to forty-five minutes or take away some activities to ensure that your program fits the traditional thirty-minute time frame.

Key Features

Programs for huge audiences use more recorded music than a typical program. Stand-up activities allow people to stay in one place rather than moving around the circle. One-on-one interactive rhymes are reduced or eliminated in favor of more group activities.

Snapshot: Revising Words to Songs and Rhymes

While writing this book, I wrote to children's musician and early childhood specialist Hap Palmer asking if I could reprint the lyrics to his song "The Elephant." He responded immediately with a request of his own.

Thank you for your interest in our music. I do have one issue we need to address.

I found out that elephants in the wild actually have very little body fat. Elephants in zoos, however, often have too much fat, which is threatening the species. See article... www.washingtonpost.com/national/health -science/fat-threatens-elephants-with-heart -disease-and-its-hard-to-weigh-them/2014/ 07/21/ffe8c5b2-0ea5-11e4-8c9a-923ecc0c 7d23_story.html?noredirect=on&utm_term =.b4ab27ac8f83.

For this reason, I rerecorded the song with a slight change in lyric replacing the word fat with heavy. You can hear the lyric and view a video here: https://www.youtube.com/ watch?v=xSsDbneWFJ8.

Added to the fact that "so big and fat" is scientifically incorrect are the current efforts against "fat shaming." I hope you can see why this change is very important to me. Thank you for your understanding.

Tips for Success

- Keeping the lights dim and the room cool helps manage behavior.
- If space is too tight, ask everyone to sit in concentric circles. Then walk in the aisles between the circles to distribute and collect props.
- Invite a library volunteer who loves children to help you distribute and collect props. Divide the musical instruments and scarves into two bags each. To distribute them, start at one end of the circle, and ask your volunteer to start at the other end. Continue handing out the props until you meet in the middle. Collect them in the same fashion. Do the same for the drum sequence, using two tambourines.

- Try using a butterfly net with a long handle to collect instruments and scarves.
- If possible, set aside a place for children who need time away from the group.

SAMPLE PROGRAM

Toddler Jumps
(for a Very Large Audience)

See sample program on page 6.

Using MGOL as "Circle Time" for Family Place

Developed by Middle County Public Library in Long Island, Family Place Libraries is an initiative designed to "expand the role of public libraries as community centers and key players in early childhood development, parent and community involvement and lifelong learning beginning at birth."[2] The core components of Family Place Libraries include trained staff; a five-week parent-child workshop for toddlers and their parents or caregivers; special collections of books, toys, music, and informational materials; specially designed play spaces; and collaborations and partnerships with community resources.

Before becoming a Family Place library about three years ago, the West Babylon Public Library in Long Island transformed its children's room to make different centers for dramatic play, movement, and learning that were appropriate for the different stages of children's development. Then they started offering Family Place's five-week parent-child workshop in the redesigned space. Called "1, 2, 3, Play with Me," the hour-and-a-half session begins with an hour of free play. Children's librarian Joanne Browning invites a different specialist to come in each week and talk informally with parents during playtime. These have included a literacy specialist (the librarian), a nutritionist, a speech therapist, a behavior specialist, and a play specialist.

As per Family Place Libraries' guidelines, a fifteen-minute circle time follows the free play. Joanne uses a very short version of MGOL for this circle time.

Key Features

Opening and closing rituals are used. A shortened MGOL format is loosely followed, starting with fingerplays and a quick story, then doing body parts, wiggle rhymes, and stand-up rhymes. Developmental tips explain the importance of talking, singing, reading, writing, and playing. No flannelboard is used. Families are given handouts with lyrics to the fingerplays and rhymes recited.

Tips for Success

- Get to know your audience so you can predict what types of activities the children will enjoy after an hour of free play.
- Go with the flow; if you see that the kids are engaged and able to pay attention, add longer rhymes or use a story longer than the typical ABC or shape books. For instance, try reading a Spot book by Eric Hill.
- Start with "Ring around the Rosie," which is an active rhyme. As soon as the children "all fall down," begin doing the fingerplays. Ease into the quick story, and then get up and wiggle around during the body rhymes.
- Try ending with a movement rhyme such as "Teddy Bear, Teddy Bear, Turn Around."
- At the beginning of the circle time, explain to participants that it is fine if they don't know all the words.

Bringing MGOL to Rural Settings

Bringing MGOL to an area that is unaccustomed to early literacy programming offers different challenges than simply adding MGOL to existing offerings. When Melanie Hetrick began work as the children's specialist at Tillamook County Library in February 2011, there were no age-appropriate programs for children under three in the local community. Her goal was to provide early literacy family engagement opportunities in Tillamook County through MGOL.

In Tillamook, a few families were quite enthusiastic, yet most people had never heard of a storytime for babies. After asking "How does that work?" parents claimed they were hesitant to bring their children because they

Snapshot: Using MGOL as a Family Place Circle Time

Joanne Browning stumbled on the MGOL binder (a how-to book for MGOL) when she first began working as a children's librarian. She used the binder when presenting her first programs, and now as the children's librarian at the West Babylon Public Library, she has adapted the MGOL format for Family Place circle times.

Finding the Mother Goose on the Loose binder with its wealth of information was the best thing to have happened to me when I began my tenure as a children's librarian at the West Babylon Public Library. It gave me the direction I needed to create a wonderful program for the families who attend.

Tips for Success

- Always invite anyone you see with a young child to attend MGOL sessions at your library.
- Be prepared to explain, explain, and explain the value of early literacy programs. But do this tactfully; former classmates may not appreciate being told information about child development by someone they consider a peer.
- Be patient with new audiences, and maintain a consistent approach to marketing your program.
- Create a MGOL Facebook page, and encourage parents to share stories and photos with each other.
- Check out Melanie Hetrick's script at https://bit.ly/2wcxOAK.

Using Volunteers for Public Library MGOL Programs

Baltimore's Hampden Branch Library is physically small, but the MGOL program there has drawn upward of eighty participants. Michelle Irvine, the children's librarian, has successfully integrated her own songs, chants, and rhymes into the sessions. To make attendance as pleasant as possible for families and as easy as possible for Michelle, two volunteers were recruited by the branch manager.

A volunteer greeter welcomes each family and holds the front door open for them, since trying to wrangle strollers through the door can be a struggle. The greeter also takes a head count during the program and assists parents as they exit the library.

A retired elementary school teacher was chosen as the other volunteer. She and Michelle jointly plan and present the sessions. Sitting on either side of the flannelboard, they recite rhymes together. By taking turns for certain sections, each presenter gets a few moments to rest her voice.

Key Features

A greeter verbally welcomes families, assists with their entry and exit from the library, and counts program attendees. A volunteer facilitator helps plan and present the program.

would be noisy and most likely would not sit still or pay attention. Many parents worried about being judged negatively because they did not own the newest gadgets and tech toys for their children. They expressed embarrassment about not knowing the social customs and norms of regular library-goers and were afraid that they wouldn't fit in.

In rural New York, parents became upset when the librarian, who had grown up with them, began adding developmental tips to her programs. Their attitude was "Who are you to tell me what to do with my child? I've known you since kindergarten, and I don't want you telling me how to raise my child." In cases like these, it is better to run quality programs that maintain an inclusive, welcoming atmosphere and to use very generic tips in the language of the community rather than run the risk of alienating your audience.

Key Features

A rural program is more informal than the typical MGOL program. Connections outside of the program should be encouraged in order to create a supportive community. Include developmental tips, but be sure to use understandable language.

Tips for Success

- Make sure your volunteers are friendly people who enjoy their MGOL assignments!
- Ask your volunteer if there are songs and rhymes he or she would like to integrate into your program. If they are appropriate, use them!

Using Digital Media during MGOL Sessions

MGOL is about strengthening connections between children and the adults in their lives, giving parents different tools to assist their child's development and presenting age-appropriate activities that build social, emotional, and cognitive skills through the framework of early literacy programming. Digital media's danger is that it can take time away from the important activities of childhood and distract adults from spending valuable time with their children.

Making a comment about using digital media out of the blue can be awkward. But during or immediately following a digital activity is a perfect time for commenting about the importance of joint media engagement. Remind parents and caregivers of the valuable role they play in their child's development, and explain that using an app *with* their child is much more valuable than using electronic media as a babysitter. Provide information to help them make informed decisions regarding the quality of the apps they use with their children, the amount of time their children spend on electronic devices, and the importance of human interaction.

Digital media that is handled with careful consideration and used in moderation can be a useful tool. Make sure to use technology in ways that fit with a program's intent and don't overwhelm the rest of your content. Digital media should enhance rather than replace elements of your presentation and should encourage parent-child interaction. Since swiping and tapping is part of the modern experience, brief exposure to tablet use is a baby step for helping bridge the digital divide.

App use should fit the context of your sessions by involving nursery rhymes or helping extend an activity that has already been introduced. For instance, sing "I Went to Visit the Farm One Day" and make animal sounds while looking at illustrations of farm animals. Then use an app that shows photographs of farm animals and makes their actual noises when you touch the photo. Since real animal sounds differ from the English words we use for their sounds (e.g., pigs don't actually say "oink"), the addition of photographs and recorded sounds enriches this activity.

Key Features

Use apps to introduce a new rhyme or to expand on a rhyme your group is already familiar with. Choose an activity that allows children to have turns physically interacting with the tablet. Become a media mentor by including developmental tips about joint media engagement, suggesting limited screen time and providing information about good sources for reviewing apps, such as http://commonsensemedia.org or http://digital-story time.com.

Tips for Success

- Use developmental tips such as "Electronic devices surround us, and many apps advertise themselves as being educational, even for our youngest children. But studies have shown that young children benefit most from these types of games when they are played together with an adult and involve human connection and conversation. Remember that your personal interaction with your child is the most beneficial contact of all."
- Limit app use to one or two rhymes per session.
- With very large groups, projecting an e-book onto a big screen may be more practical than reading aloud from a standard-sized picture book and expecting everyone to be able to see the illustrations.
- Read more in Resource B: Using Digital Media.

NOTES

1. Carolyn Brooks and Debbie Arenas, *2s & 3s On the Go! Storytime Manual* (El Dorado Hills: El Dorado County Library, 2014), www.eldoradolibrary.org/wp-content/uploads/2016/04/2s-3s-On-the-Go-Manual.pdf.
2. Family Place Libraries, "Our History," accessed September 17, 2018, https://www.familyplacelibraries.org/about-us/our-history.

MGOL Events in the Public Library

FOR THIS BOOK, ANYTHING THAT IS NOT A TYPICAL program is considered an event. Events usually happen just once or twice a year and are centered on a theme.

Running a Mother Goose on the Loose (MGOL) Weekend Fair

Similar to an early literacy fair, a MGOL weekend fair involves setting up tables and defining spaces for different activities. Teen volunteers, library staff, library Friends, or community partners can be recruited to serve as staff for each activity. A sign with rhyme lyrics should be posted at each table, and the corresponding activity should be named after the character or first line of the rhyme. Below are a few activity suggestions based on successful weekend events:

- At a **1-2-3-4-5 Table** (from "1, 2, 3, 4, 5, One I Caught a Fish Alive"), children can be invited to guess the correct number of goldfish crackers in a bowl. Answers can be dropped into an empty fish bowl. Books can be given away as prizes.
- Children and their parents can be encouraged to write their own poetry at the **Rhythm and Patter Station**. With permission, poems can be put on display. Blank journals make fantastic giveaways for this activity.
- Create a **Craft Cottage**, an arts and crafts area

where children can decorate cutouts from an Ellison machine.

  » **Three Little Kittens' Mittens**—Children can decorate construction paper mittens by drawing and gluing, and then they can hang them on a clothesline to dry.
  » **Twinkle Little Star Wands**—Children can use glitter to decorate construction paper stars and attach them to craft sticks. Dangling ribbons or tinsel is optional.
  » **Mary Had a Little Lamb Craft**—Children can use a glue stick to decorate a paper sheep with cotton balls or pom-poms. A piece of yarn and a bell makes a snazzy collar.

- **How Does Your Garden Grow?** Parents and their kids can make a sprouts pouch by planting a sunflower seed in a little paper pouch of dirt to take home.
- **The Dress-Up Spot** can be located inside of a tent, and a mirror makes a great prop. Invite children to dress up as Old Mother Goose and Old King Cole. Take digital photos, print them, and put them in tagboard frames decorated with markers by the children.

In addition to your regular MGOL session, offer some group programs to complement the table activities.

- Hold a tongue twister challenge using rhymes like "Peter Piper picked a peck of pickled peppers" and "She sells sea shells by the seashore."
- Ask "Who can jump the farthest?" for the "Jack Be Nimble" candlestick jumping contest.
- During "Jack and Jill" races, let children compete with plastic pails filled with balls of tissue or cotton balls overflowing the top, representing water.
- Invite toddlers to "Ride a White Horse to Banbury Cross" using hobbyhorses. As an added bonus, post directional signs for St. Ives.

Of course, create a display of nursery rhyme books and encourage families to find the rhymes related to the activities.

Key Features

Stations with activities related to nursery rhymes can be created at an MGOL fair. A sign with the rhyme lyrics should be posted at each station. Children can be asked to recite the rhyme before, during, or after the activity.

Tips for Success

- Don't rely solely on librarians to staff the tables.
- Ask representatives from other local cultural organizations and educational institutions if they would like to run an activity. In addition to increasing your staffing and expanding the range of activities, it gives them the opportunity to publicize what they do and allows them to reach a wider audience.
- If you provide adult supervision, children as young as eight or nine can learn how to run booths on their own. Children of librarians, who are often already familiar with the library setting, can make wonderful volunteers. They can help prepare by cutting out templates and can be terrific greeters at a welcome booth. This instills a sense of volunteerism in them at an early age, gives you more staff, and provides younger library visitors the pleasure of doing an activity at a booth run by another child.

Making a MGOL Session into a Summer Reading Themed Event

School-age children who do not read during the summer often lose some of their reading skills. This is called "summer slide," and to combat it, public libraries promote summer reading clubs (SRC) across the nation. Although children under age five do not yet attend school, children of all ages (and in some cases, their parents too) are encouraged to read books or participate in other early literacy activities and to keep track of them. In many cases, children report back to their local library by filling out charts, making lists, talking to a librarian, or entering information online. In most areas, each SRC is based on a theme with games and characters that encourage children to read. Promotional materials and programs based on the theme are offered in order to entice children to participate and continue reading even while school is out of session. While MGOL programs don't traditionally follow a theme, they can be modified to do so.

Key Features

Focus on the SRC theme-related content rather than adhering to the 80:20 ratio of old versus new material. Replace many of the "old favorite" activities with new activities related to the theme.

Tips for Success

Most libraries have a summer reading theme; even though MGOL is a nursery rhyme program, it can be adapted relatively easily to fit in with any theme. For instance, in 2011, the Collaborative Summer Library Program theme for children was "One World, Many Stories," and an SRC program was created using the basic MGOL format with a few modifications:

- Substitute songs from around the world as well as a variety of regions and cultures in the United States. Search for "children's songs" along with the name of a country on YouTube. Music Together (www.musictogether.com) has CDs with child-friendly music from around the world that includes suggested activities, such as using beanbags with "Obiswana." Mention the country or place of origin when the song is played.
- Use a variety of newer songs rather than only changing 20 percent.
- Create new flannelboard pieces from foreign language books or from royalty-free images online.
- Use more recorded music than in a typical MGOL

session (including selections from other countries).

- If you are using a YouTube video, you don't need to screen it. Hook your tablet up to wireless speakers. Then simply press "play" on your device and listen to music while ignoring the video!
- Take advantage of the welcoming comments and closing ritual sections to give a quick mention of the SRC. Explain what is available for children of the ages at your program, and invite families to sign up directly following the program.
- Themed SRC MGOL sessions work as well with preschoolers as they do with babies and toddlers.
- Local ethnic restaurants may be a good source of songs. If you are running a program for older children, ask the restaurant owner if that country has a folk costume. If so, invite a restaurant staffer to attend your program in the costume to briefly tell the participants about it.

SAMPLE PROGRAM:

MGOL around the World for a Themed Summer Reading Club (SRC)

Find a sample program online on the MGOL website at https://mgol.net/script-submissions/music-around-the-world-src-script/.

Sharing Live Music through MGOL

Since MGOL facilitators are encouraged to be personal and create programs that include activities they really enjoy, some librarians have brought musical instruments into their MGOL programs. In a few states, public libraries lend out ukuleles and librarians use them during programs. When three of my Baltimore colleagues brought guitars to MGOL and played them during the sessions, many of the children had never seen anyone playing an adult musical instrument and were fascinated. Being invited to touch the guitar and strum some strings after the program was a highlight for them. Another Baltimore librarian uses the guiro to scrape out the beat to rhymes, and another included a rainstick as her musical instrument of choice.

Librarian Laurie Collins from Ipswich, Massachusetts, plays the bodhran (Irish hand drum). When the babies

Snapshot: Using the Guitar during MGOL

Baltimore families still remember how much they loved attending MGOL programs when librarian Kent Gerber, now a digital library manager in Minnesota, brought his guitar.

"Playing the guitar was a way to add another layer to the Mother Goose on the Loose programs I did. Kids not only had fun hearing the rhymes, but they could hear and experience how an instrument produces sound. I enjoyed the chance to use the guitar to be silly or add emphasis to the lines or rhymes we were doing together. It also encouraged me to grow in my own guitar playing so that I could concentrate on engaging the kids during the program and not just trying to hit the right chords. It was such a joy to see the kids' eyes light up when I pulled the guitar out of my case and see them move or sing to the music!"

begin to seem restless during MGOL, Laurie plays her drum to get their attention. During the drum sequence, the babies often try to imitate Laurie's rhythm and her style of hitting the drum. Laurie believes "that is how MGOL stays fresh…with personal input from those who practice it." For a quick demonstration, view Laurie and her bodhran on the MGOL YouTube page.[1]

Key Features

The facilitator brings a musical instrument (in addition to the child-sized percussion instruments) and plays it during the MGOL session. Children see how the music is being created and are encouraged to sing along. With supervision, children are invited to try out the instruments once the session has officially ended.

Tips for Success

- You do not have to be an expert musician to bring in an instrument, but you must enjoy playing it.
- Choose in advance which songs and rhymes to present with musical accompaniment and which to share using only voices. The voice is also a musical

instrument, and it is important to help the children enjoy the sounds of their own voices too.

- Do not leave your instrument(s) unattended. Even with the best of intentions, little hands can sometimes cause damage. If you value your instrument, put it away before leaving the area.

Using MGOL to Show an Artist at Work

My sister Celia is the artist behind the MGOL logo and all of the felt templates. Although we don't live near each other, when she visits, we like to take advantage of the opportunity to present programs together. Called "Instant Illustrations" for preschoolers and elementary school children, the program includes a story I tell while Celia illustrates it. The kids are always fascinated to see the art being created right in front of them. Since this program was such a big hit, we decided to do the same with MGOL. We used an easel with a big pad of paper in place of a flannelboard and felt pieces, and Celia drew cartoons as visual representations for each rhyme. At the end of the program, as Celia began tearing the used pages off the easel, the parents insisted on dividing them up and taking the sketches home.

Key Features

This program features an artist and introduces children to the process of creating illustrations. The rhymes and nursery rhyme characters that they know so well are seen through a different lens, and they are exposed to the wonders of the creative process.

Tips for Success

- Share a list of the rhymes you plan to use well ahead of time, so the artist can practice drawing the cartoons as simply and quickly as possible. Practice together at least twice before you present the program to your audience.
- Using no more than three colored markers will give drawings enough color to stand out but eliminate the extra time needed to switch colors often.
- Play a game that involves the children in the creative process. Choose a well-known character, such as Humpty, and ask the participants to describe

 Snapshot: Using Flannelboard Pieces for Art Literacy

After attending a number of sessions, Roberta Hoffman, a graphic designer and the mother of twenty-seven-month-old Jasper, commented on the visual literacy aspect of MGOL.

I thought the flannel pieces were great. Using the different styles of art through the ages, whether it's modern or very way back, is very important. It introduces young children to art culture.

I'm speaking from experience. I grew up with a lot of books about art in the house, and both my husband and I are actively interested in art. I like introducing young children to very basic visual concepts by showing them to them. Because then, once you have been introduced visually to something like that, the door is opened, and it continues to be open throughout your life. And in America, we really need this sort of thing! I think in Europe there is more emphasis on this sort of art training. Visual literacy is very important. Not just verbal. Art really opens your brain, both mentally and verbally. It sort of makes the synapses more fluid and makes you more creative. It makes it easier for you to solve problems or come up with ideas.

him. Your artist will listen to the comments and draw accordingly. Alternately, the artist can draw a character before you recite the rhyme and ask the participants to guess who it is.

- For "If You're Happy and You Know it" with older children, the artist can draw five circles. Ask for volunteers to come up to the easel and demonstrate different emotions (e.g., what it looks like to be happy [smile], sad [frown], angry [grimace and hands crossed], surprised [eyes and mouth wide open], puzzled [mouth closed, finger in front of mouth]). As each child demonstrates a different facial expression, the artist draws it in the circle and the group sings a verse of the song, substituting the name of the new emotion and the action that goes along with it. This is a great way to build communication skills.

Using MGOL to Build Community Connections through Art

If you want to expand the artistic side of MGOL and build community connections, follow the example set by children's librarian Laurie Collins at the Ipswich Public Library in Ipswich, Massachusetts. Laurie applied for and received a grant to invite local artists to create props to go along with her MGOL programs, focusing on soft sculpture, felt pieces for the flannelboard, and finger puppets. Once all the work was created, she hosted a display at the library. She lauds this project as a wonderful outreach effort, explaining that the local artistic community felt that it played an important part in establishing MGOL for the library's youngest patrons. Also, the contribution was valuable because it was concrete, beautiful, and long-lasting. Plus, it provided many beautiful pieces for use in MGOL sessions.

By getting to know community members through these types of projects, wonderful partnerships can arise. For instance, because of this project, Laurie got to know Caldecott-winning illustrator Ed Emberley, who lived in her community. He authorized the library to base some flannelboard pieces on illustrations from his book Chicken Little! After her library was awarded a local cultural council grant, Laurie built on this connection and hosted an "Ipswich Celebrates Ed Emberley Week!" during the April school vacation.

Key Features
Instead of actually presenting a MGOL program, MGOL can be used as an impetus to support community involvement (and even apply for grants).

Tips for Success
- Focus on something that has a direct connection with your library's MGOL program.
- Publicize the project to get as much participation as possible.
- Use the opportunity to get to know community members and then build on those connections.
- Go to the MGOL YouTube page to view a video

interview with Laurie that includes many of the beautiful works of art created by community members.[2]

Celebrating Holidays with the MGOL Community

A great way to welcome families in your community into American culture and rituals is by holding a Thanksgiving celebration. When I began presenting the first Spanish language MGOL program with my colleague Annie Calderon, our audience consisted of immigrants from different Spanish-speaking countries. During the program's second year, the original group of parents was joined by other Spanish speakers, English speakers who wanted to learn Spanish, and immigrants from countries that did not speak either English or Spanish. Just before Thanksgiving, after some moms told us they had never celebrated Thanksgiving before, we arranged to hold a MGOL Thanksgiving Celebration. The resulting event was memorable for the families as well as the librarians.

We explained that Thanksgiving Day is a feast and arranged a potluck lunch. On the celebration day, we

 Snapshot: The Ripple Effect

Laurie Collins, children's librarian at the Ipswich Public Library in Massachusetts, has been facilitating MGOL programs for about five years. She uses MGOL as a springboard for community collaboration.

The inclusion of Mother Goose on the Loose in our library programming has opened us up to so many new people and ideas! Very exciting. We are a small town and a relatively small library, but we had 776 participants in children's programs last month.

Sharing the growth of the program with the schools and the community at large has offered a great opportunity for collaboration. There is a children's service agency in town called the Birth to Three Center, and this has opened the door for us to operate cooperatively.

placed a large pumpkin next to the flannelboard. At the other end of the same room (it was a *huge* room), we set up chairs and a long, decorated table where families were asked to place their covered dishes with labels.

The MGOL session included themed holiday rhymes. For instance, a turkey illustration was used with "I Went to Visit the Farm One Day" and a turkey puppet with the animal songs. Bells were rung and scarves waved to a recorded version of "Over the River and Through the Woods."

Luckily, we had extra musical instruments and scarves, since many families brought relatives. When the session ended, everyone was thanked for participating and invited to join the holiday feast. Folks shared something they were grateful for. We took a group photo, sent it to everyone who provided an e-mail address, and wrote an article that was published in *American Libraries*.[3]

Key Features

Expect a larger crowd with many relatives attending at holiday events. Match your rhymes and illustrations with the holiday when possible. Display holiday-related decorations. Present a shortened program since people will want to eat while the food is still hot.

Tips for Success

- Starting a few weeks before the holiday, mention Thanksgiving during your sessions and use simple rhymes that highlight traditions such as eating turkey, being thankful, and eating popcorn. Create felt pieces, and practice these rhymes so everyone will be able to recite them with you at the holiday celebration.
- Try to find a local merchant to donate paper goods (plates, cups, forks, knives, spoons, napkins, and plastic tablecloths).
- Encourage people to bring whatever they are comfortable making; emphasize that it does not have to be traditional American food. A wide array of foods from different countries makes the feast even more extraordinary!
- Ask everyone to label their dish, listing all the ingredients. It is imperative for people with food allergies or restrictions and vegetarians to know what they can and can't eat.

- Assign a library staff person to keep track of what each family says it will bring. Look at the list of foods, and ask library staff to supply some of the traditional dishes or see if you can get a local supermarket to donate some classic holiday foods. Make sure to have these, even in small quantitates.
- Prepare plates with very small portions of the traditional holiday foods in order to ensure that everyone gets a taste.
- Having spare plastic serving utensils on hand is always a plus! Families often bring relatives.
- Be aware that not everyone who signs up will attend, families may turn up with other family members (e.g., spouses, grandparents, aunts, uncles, and cousins), and someone who signs up to bring a certain dish may end up bringing something totally different.

SAMPLE PROGRAM

Thanksgiving MGOL

This is a script that I used with Annie Calderon and Kit Bloom during our Thanksgiving MGOL at the Southeast Anchor Branch of the Enoch Pratt Free Library in Highlandtown, Maryland.

Section 1: Welcoming Comments

Section 2: Rhymes and Reads
"Old Mother Goose"
"Mrs. Turkey Went Out One Very Fine Day"
Read-Aloud Book: *Spot's Thanksgiving* by Eric Hill
"We Hit the Floor Together"

Section 3: Body Rhymes
Face: "My Face Is Round"
Fingers: "Five Little Pumpkins"
Clapping: "If You're Thankful and You Know It"
    (adaptation of "If You're Happy and You Know It")
Knee Bounce: "Popcorn"

Section 4: The Drum Sequence
"Rum Pum Pum"

Section 5: Stand-Up / Sit-Down Activities
"We're Marching to the Drum" *(Use "Gallop.")*
"Over the River and Through the Wood" *(Play a recording and gallop like a horse.)*
"Handy Spandy"

Section 6: Animal Activities
"I Went to Visit the Farm One Day" *(Use a turkey prop.)*
"When the Turkey Gets Up in the Morning"

Section 7: Musical Instruments and Scarves
Bells: "We Ring Our Bells Together"
Bells: "A Pumpkin Ran Away" *(Ring bells to the beat. Show illustrations from* A Pumpkin Ran Away *by Anne Meeker.)*
Bells: "Bells Away"
Scarves: "Wind, Oh Wind"
Scarves: "The Wind Is Singing in the Mountains"
Scarves: "Scarves Away"

Section 8: Lullabies
Sing along to a recording of Raffi's "Thanks a Lot."

Section 9: Interactive Rhymes
"Little Jack Horner" *(Invite children to come up to the flannelboard and pull the felt pie off the felt table.)*

Section 10: Closing Ritual
"Can You Kick with Two Feet?"
"We're So Happy"

Presenting Jingle Jangle Music Time

Designed to create an unexpected literacy break for parents and their children, Jingle Jangle Music Time (JJMT) is a pop-up program that was created from MGOL activities. First developed and used inside a children's museum, JJMT is a spontaneous way to bring families together. Singing and playing together in a group activity breaks down social barriers for parents and caregivers, and participating adults find it easier to approach each other. Additionally, families intimidated by structured programming enjoy this informal approach.

When the children's room suddenly gets very crowded and chaotic, an impromptu JJMT session can calm things down while providing a quick but meaningful family activity that can be adapted for families with children of all ages. The beauty of JJMT is that it can take place anywhere and anytime. It does not need to be scheduled ahead of time and does not have to tie into a theme. It offers music for the sake of bringing families together, creating community, building vocabulary, reinforcing listening skills, exposing children to new experiences, and having fun.

Key Features
JJMT is a group of short musical, literacy activities (utilizing MGOL props) that provides shared, fun, age-appropriate activities for families. Children are introduced to a variety of songs, rhymes, and musical instruments, and positive interaction between adults and their children is encouraged. This pop-up program can last between five and thirty minutes depending on the interest of the audience. Not scheduled in advance, JJMT is designed to take place when the need for an impromptu program is felt and staff are available. JJMT does not use the flannelboard and relies heavily on recorded music. JJMT facilitators use multiple developmental tips, giving parents valuable information while modeling ways that parents can play with their children at home.

Tips for Success
- Be willing to customize the program for the people who are present since you can never know ahead of time how many people will be attending.
- March through the children's department while tapping on a tambourine and announce "Jingle, Jangle Music Time will be starting in three minutes in the program area."
- Introduce new songs and include old favorites that everyone knows. When reciting rhymes, repeat each rhyme twice as done in MGOL, and invite participants to listen and repeat or join in both times.
- Create a CD or playlist of songs to use for a short, interactive musical program. Combine a few well-known children's songs (e.g., "The Wheels on the Bus") and a few MGOL activities (e.g., scarf songs or the drum sequence). Two JJMT examples are provided at the end of the chapter.

- In addition to musical instruments, use clapping, tapping, and snapping to provide musical accompaniment to the rhymes.
- Prepare a tote bag filled with scarves, a bag with musical instruments from your MGOL program, and a bag with "kitchen instruments." Children love using wooden spoons to tap on empty plastic juice bottles, banging plastic plates together, and shaking a sealed water bottle with lentils inside.
- As children watch, invite them to come and play. For children who seem wary or shy, make eye contact and say, "You may play too."

- It often helps to say to a dad or mom, "If you begin to play, the child will feel more comfortable joining in."
- Because recorded music is heavily used, play different types of music such as children's songs, klezmer music, rock and roll, folk songs, and so on. Any song with a steady beat will do. However, watch for content! Do not use songs that reference sex or violence, negatively single out a specific group of people, or use any derogatory language.

Snapshot: JJMT Partner Perspectives

Regina Wade, a retired children's librarian, facilitated MGOL and JJMT programs at Port Discovery Children's Museum. She remained in the museum's infant and toddler space for a few hours in between and after the programs and interacted with families there.

Retired librarians make wonderful JJMT presenters! Inviting them to stay for an extra hour to talk to families is valuable too. Retired librarians can often offer commonsense advice while sharing knowledge of child development, the importance of early literacy, and fun ways to help develop school readiness skills. Their presence can increase both the popularity and the value of visits to the library. Some families plan more frequent library visits because of the JJMT facilitator's presence. Regina describes JJMT:

Because interpreting moving in space and perceiving where the body is in space occur mostly in the right hemisphere of the brain and in the cerebellum, the left-hemisphere seat of language awareness and speech is not involved. In fact, in some of the Jingle Jangle Music Time classes I facilitate, I make it a point not to speak aloud. I want the families with their infants and children to be experiencing being in "music brain," and "body brain" without the interference of language processing.

Two weeks ago, I had a large group of toddlers and their teachers from a Korean preschool. The children did not speak English, but they completely understood, responded to, and imitated everything we did to music—the universal language. It was satisfying to be able to communicate so directly to the little ones' limbic systems (the emotional center) and to have each one imitate everything I did.

Whenever possible, as I observe a child doing a certain movement, I immediately try to imitate that child. It is so affirming for the child to have an adult value what he is doing enough to imitate it. This is valuable modeling for the parents—to see that whatever the child is able to do, it is delightful and it is enough.

One more adaptation I am aware of is sensing and providing for the various levels of social development within each group. Shy children can quietly observe from a parent's lap while the parent participates in the activity. Very friendly, curious tots who want to hold what I have or find out what is in the bin behind me can be accommodated with a kind request to wait (they can be given a substitute object to hold) or with an invitation to sit beside the teacher and "help" with the book.

Jingle Jangle Music Time Playlist

"Let's Go Fly a Kite" from Georgiana Stewart's *Musical Scarves and Activities* (Wave colored scarves.)

"Popcorn" by Gershon Kingsley (Tap clackers or dance.)

"Mexican Hat Dance" (Use castanets, but put them on the floor and tap them shut to make sounds.)

"The Itsy Bitsy Spider" by Little Richard on *From Our Children* (Use plastic spiders or yarn pieces.)

"Love Me Tender" by Elvis Presley (Wave scarves or dance.)

"Ariang," a lovely song from Korea, by Music Together (Dance or use bells.)

"Turkey in the Straw" by Phil Rosenthal, on his CD *Turkey in the Straw* (Ring bells, shake maracas, or tap tambourines.)

"Rig A Jig Jig" by Sharon, Lois, and Bram (Shake maracas and dance.)

"Shake My Sillies Out" by Raffi (Dance!)

"My Little Bird" by Elizabeth Mitchell (Cuddle together during the lullaby.)

"My Grandfather's Clock" by Carole Peterson on *Sticky Bubble Gum* (Use with egg shakers.)

"Sally the Swinging Snake" by Hap Palmer (Use with a set of jointed plastic snakes from a party store.)

"Walter the Waltzing Worm" by Hap Palmer (Waltz with worms made of yarn.)

"Listen to the Horses" by Raffi on More Singable Songs (Hold your scarf like reins, and ride to the fair.)

"Little Red Caboose" by Music for Little People, from the *Toddler Sings* CD (Shake Chickitas to the beat.)

"Bobby Shaftoe" from *Step by Step: Skipping Songs* (Ring bells.)

"Bellybutton" by Heather Bishop (Shake Chickitas, and walk slow and fast.)

"I Know a Chicken" by Laurie Berkner (Sing this call-and-response song with egg shakers.)

"Playing in the Kitchen" by Music Together (Use kitchen instruments.)

SAMPLE PROGRAM

Jingle Jangle Music Time Step-by-Step Directions

by Regina Wade

1. Play recorded music and empty a duffel bag full of "kitchen instruments" (consisting of clean and empty juice bottles, pie tins, cardboard oatmeal "drums," plastic plates, plastic lids, wooden spoons, and spice bottles filled with uncooked lima beans and sealed with hot glue) onto the floor.

2. Pick up a juice bottle and a wooden spoon and begin tapping along to the beat. Children and adults who hear the music will come over to see what is going on. The children will instinctively pick up their own instruments and start tapping along to the rhythm also.

3. Give each person a warm welcome, but provide no instructions whatsoever. After a short time, put down your juice bottle, pick up two plastic lids and begin gently banging them together. Your audience will follow your example and begin trying out different "instrument" combinations. The recorded music can last for three to four minutes, so people have plenty of time to come and join the circle.

Alternately, you can run the program this way:

1. Before beginning your program, choose a lively, rhythmic piece of music (e.g., a John Philip Sousa march, a preschool song with a steady beat, or

something you might like, such as "Love, Love Me Do" by the Beatles).

2. Dump out some instruments, bells, sticks, or tambourines on the carpet.

3. Turn on the music, and begin to play to the beat. Families will begin to approach, children will turn to watch, and some will come over and begin playing. (The *music itself* is the drawing card!)

4. Introduce yourself and make a brief comment about early literacy and the connection to keeping time along with music. Mention the correlation between musical rhythms and reading rhythms, explaining that household items can be used as instruments. Comment that children need to move when learning, and tie the activity in with the importance of early literacy, encouraging parents to replicate it at home.

5. Play one more song with the freestyle musical instrument playing, and then collect the first instruments and hand out other instruments like egg shakers.

6. Play another recorded song ("I Know a Chicken" by Laurie Berkner has a slow beat in the verses but a fast chorus). Encourage everyone to participate in the call-and-response song while shaking their shakers to the tempo.

7. During the songs, ask children's names and give a personal hello to each participant.

8. Do a few more shaker songs together and then collect the shakers.

9. Hand out scarves, and sing scarf songs. Collect the scarves as part of your good-bye song.

NOTES

1. Mother Goose on the Loose, "MGOL Rhymes: Rum Pum Pum & We're Marching to the Drum (Tips for Using the Bodhran)," YouTube, published on September 7, 2018, https://youtu.be/rfpNNPgVc_A/.

2. Mother Goose on the Loose, "MGOL Projects: Interview with Laurie Collins," YouTube, published on September 7, 2018, https://youtu.be/b0L46YkSC9k.

3. Betsy Diamant-Cohen and Anne Calderón, "A Warm Home at the Library: Baltimore's Outreach to Spanish-Speaking Families," *American Libraries* 40:12 (2009), 41–43.

Snapshot: MGOL Training Workshops

Susan Pannebaker, youth services advisor for the Pennsylvania Department of Education, Office of Commonwealth Libraries, always arranges for a different group of children to pop in during MGOL trainings to participate in a session. Librarians attending the workshop sit or stand behind the children and observe them in their first program with a facilitator they have never met before.

The first time I participated in a MGOL training, a group of children from a local childcare center came to the library so workshop participants could see what a session of MGOL looked like. Children were with an adult they didn't know, but in less than five minutes and two activities, they were captivated and engaged in the activities. We were all amazed. The Barbara Cass-Beggs music is gentle, but most pieces of the program were very active; the mix was captivating even for the older children in the group. The hit of the show had to be each child so happily grabbing Humpty Dumpty off the felt board. The expression on each face was ecstatic! I knew then that when I would provide trainings across Pennsylvania, I had to have a group of preschoolers attend to show how engaging the pieces of the program are.

I have provided a number of trainings over the years, and I always do them where a preschool group can walk to the library or in a library where participants in a toddler time are available. Everyone sees not only the techniques in action but the way kids react. I have seen kids come in crying, jostling, and wired, but each time the magic of the program has reached them and they leave with a smile on their face. I really think that seeing a session has given many people who have not done programs for toddlers the confidence to start.

Part II

There

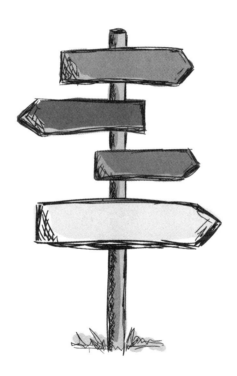

Chapter 3

Taking MGOL to Museums

MOTHER GOOSE ON THE LOOSE (MGOL) SESSIONS and activities can be modified for museum settings in order to make the museum experience richer for families with young children. Sessions can enrich visits to a children's museum or any museum that has a designated space for infant or toddler programs. MGOL activities for children ages eight and under provide a museum experience that is developmentally appropriate and thus meaningful to them. Activities are designed to use purposeful play to enhance parent-child bonding while also providing fun enrichment. MGOL sessions in children's museums are similar to those offered in public libraries and can be presented with a minimum of modifications. Individual MGOL activities can connect children with paintings, mosaics, and sculptures in art museums; they can be used to highlight specific areas and exhibitions in other types of museums.

Key Features

Museums are unique places with rich resources. MGOL in museums is meant to complement collections and enhance visits for families with children, not to steal the limelight! It is also an important opportunity to attract new audiences.

Tips for Success

Always consider the museum contact person your partner and make sure they know and approve of all the activities you will be doing ahead of time. Be sure to visit the museum where you will be presenting MGOL before even starting to plan. Looking for the conditions below will help you prepare for a successful program.

- Although many museums charge admission fees, don't let this deter you. As a public library representative, negotiate with your museum contact. Ask if admission fees can be waived for families preregistering for MGOL in the Museum. Check if there are certain days or times each month when the museum offers free admission, and plan your tours, sessions, or scavenger hunts for that time. Ask if the museum will donate some family passes to the library; encourage families to borrow them in order to attend the program. Or simply limit the number of library programs presented at the museum and use them as opportunities to inform families about free library services.

- If presenting a MGOL session, be sure there will be enough open space for families to sit in a circle around the flannelboard. You don't want to worry about dancing around freestanding exhibit pieces or sitting huddled under computer terminals.

- If you are planning on doing a series of sessions, see if you can get access to a locked closet or other storage space, which allows you to leave bulky items at the museum rather than carrying them back and forth weekly.

- Choose a location strategically placed near electrical outlets if you plan on using a CD player or other equipment that needs plugging in.

On the day of your programs, keep this in mind:

- Wear fashionable but comfortable clothing—you may be doing lots of walking!
- Use baskets, tote bags, a mobile folding cart, or an AV cart to easily transport musical instruments, scarves, and any other equipment. Be sure to collect all props before moving from one exhibit to another.
- At museum programs, always mention that you are from the public library. Describe the free services offered, and if possible, arrange to give out library cards on the spot. Be sure to bring brochures about upcoming events at the library, and describe the ones that are most relevant for the families attending your museum program. This will help you extend the early literacy activities beyond the museum and into the library as well.

Presenting MGOL in Children's Museums

Since most children's museums encourage visits by families with children of all ages, the traditional MGOL program for parents with children from birth to age two can be easily used with a minimum of modifications. When programs take place within an exhibit area, there are plenty of kid-friendly, safe distractions for the children. Use welcoming comments to remind parents of age-appropriate behavior: "Children this age don't sit perfectly still, especially in this stimulating environment! It is fine for them to wander around, but if they come within the invisible circle, please pick them up and physically take them back to the circle with you. Since this is a kid-safe room, children can explore the exhibit while you continue here with us. Or you can feel free to join them at the other spaces around the room and to return with them when they wander back. More often than not, children will explore and return, and that is fine. They learn by doing; even if they don't seem to be paying attention, they are absorbing everything."

Key Features

Although the content is very similar to MGOL in the public library, the context is totally different. Presenters must keep in mind that the space is open to the public and plan accordingly, not taking it personally if everyone leaves and adapting if a large group of parents and children sits down to join in when the session is halfway over.

Tips for Success

- When toys and manipulatives are in the area, arrive well beforehand to clear up. Place the distracting objects out of reach for the duration of your session.
- After setting up for your session, stay there until it ends! Leaving the items unattended even for just a few minutes may result in their being strewn all over the room or disappearing completely.
- Because exhibits are open to the public, crowds will likely be walking in and out of the space while your program is taking place. Don't let the constant flow distract you.
- Don't worry about interrupting your session a number of times to welcome room newcomers and invite them to join in.
- Try to include newcomers as much as possible—for instance, bring them musical instruments even if they are not sitting in the circle.
- The stand-up / sit-down activities (section 5) can be interpreted by adults as an opportunity to leave the session and return to exploring the museum. You may be suddenly left marching around the room on your own! If this happens, use standing-up rhymes that involve staying in one place and not moving around in a circle (e.g., "The Hokey Pokey"). You can also eliminate the standing-up rhymes from your sessions.
- Keep an eye on children who wander away from the circle while holding a musical instrument or scarf. To prevent your props from disappearing, ask parents to return them when the program ends or to drop them in a box strategically placed at the door when exiting the exhibit.
- Other families may be playing in the exhibit space while your session is taking place, so be prepared

for a high noise level. If you have a soft voice, use a portable voice amplifier.

- Be aware that there are tempting things to do all around and do not take distractibility personally!

SAMPLE PROGRAM

MGOL in a Children's Museum

by Derek Cooper, early childhood and performing arts coordinator at Port Discovery Children's Museum

Note: This version is similar to public library programs. However, since the audience is constantly coming and going, standing-up rhymes (if used) may involve staying in one place and not moving around in a circle. Newcomers who have entered the exhibit after the session has started will often join the group when everyone starts playing their instruments. The same rhyme is used in more than one section but repeated differently (e.g., "Jack-in-the-Box" below).

Section 1: Welcoming Comments

Section 2: Rhymes and Reads
"We Hit the Floor Together"
"Old Mother Goose"
"The Itsy Bitsy Spider"
"Two Little Puppy Dogs"
"Rain on the Green Grass"
"Baby Shark"
"The Eency Weency Spider" / "The Great Big Spider" (*with puppet kisses*)
Book: Row, Row, Row Your Boat by Jane Cabrera
"How Does the Busy Bee"

Section 3: Body Rhymes
Fingers: "Fingers Like to Wiggle Waggle" or This Little Piggy Went to Market (*Choose one*)
Hands: "Open Them, Shut Them"
Knee Bounces: "Way up High in the Banana Tree"
Knee Bounces: "Zoom, Zoom, Zoom"
Knee Bounces: "Row, Row, Row Your Boat" (*fast and slow*)

Snapshot: MGOL at Port Discovery Children's Museum

Early childhood and performing arts coordinator Derek Cooper has been facilitating MGOL sessions at Tot Trails in Port Discovery Children's Museum since 2012. One of Derek's MGOL sessions is featured in the MGOL Mission Statement video at https://bit.ly/2jea6gM.

I like doing MGOL in children's museums because there is an expectation that a museum visit is going to be a combination of education and engagement, and MGOL combines those two elements very effectively. Both children and their parents enjoy it. It can be challenging to equally engage both of those demographics simultaneously within a program, but MGOL is one program that accomplishes that goal very well.

MGOL is purposeful play; it is playtime with an educational, deeper component. The program encourages experiences between the parent or caretaker and the child. In "Baby Shark," children learn sequencing by the order of when things appear, which is actually learning about math. They develop motor skills and coordination by using their fingers, clapping and using their hands, and then moving their whole arms. We use the whole upper body for Papa Shark. It also opens the door for parents to have conversations with their children about baby versus mommy versus grandpa.

Presenting MGOL sessions helps me create connections with children and their family members. I follow the basic guidelines of MGOL, but I add my own energetic stuff to it. It's a great structure with a solid foundation that allows us to add our own style and our experiences. Parents and children get so much out of it—it inspires people to come back. There is so much to do in the museum that there is always a battle for attention. But the fact that they are coming back to this program is a testament to the merit of MGOL.

Section 4: The Drum Sequence
"Rum Pum Pum"

Section 5: Stand-Up / Sit-Down Activities
"The Hokey Pokey"

"Jack-in-the-Box" (*Show a real jack-in-the-box before doing the rhyme.*)

"Handy Spandy"

Section 6: Animal Activities
"I Went to Visit the Farm One Day" (*Sing the animal sounds with Eric Carle's illustrations for* The Very Busy Spider.)

"Old MacDonald" (*Give children one felt animal each. Ask them to place their pieces on the flannelboard when the animal's name is mentioned.*)

Section 7: Musical Instruments and Scarves
(*Newcomers who have entered the exhibit after the session has started will often join the group when everyone starts playing their instruments.*)

Bells: "We Ring Our Bells Together"

Bells: "Grandfather's Clock"

Bells: "Jack-in-the-Box" (*Because this rhyme was demonstrated during the standing-up rhymes, you are showing that the same rhyme can be used for multiple purposes.*)

Bells: "Bells Away" (*Parents often comment, "I wish I could get my child to clean up so easily at home!"*)

Scarves: "Wind, Oh Wind"

Scarves: "Peek-a-Boo" (*Play peek-a-boo with each child individually.*)

Scarves: "Jack-in-the-Box" (*Children should ball the scarves up in their hands and then throw them up in the air.*)

Scarves: "Scarves Away"

Section 8: Lullabies

(Lead into the lullaby before collecting the scarves, and ask the children to pretend that they are their blankets.)

"Twinkle, Twinkle"

Rather than moving from object to object to expose children to as many items as possible, you may want to highlight one piece and attach a wide range of activities to it. For instance, sing "BINGO" together and then search through the museum galleries for a statue of a dog. When you find it, ask questions about the statue's size and color, name the material it is made of, mention the name of the sculptor, and then clap while singing "BINGO" to the statue. Wave bye-bye to the statue, and look for the next item on your list. These kinds of interactions can spark children's interest in museum collections and encourage parent-child conversation.

Section 9: Interactive Rhymes
"Humpty Dumpty"

Section 10: Closing Ritual
"Can You Kick with Two Feet?"

"We're So Happy"

(*If the children have held onto their scarves, you can say, "Take your scarves and we're going to throw them up in the air!" The program thus ends with a beautiful display of color.*)

Giving Museum Tours with MGOL

Art museums can offer visual treats for children, but kids have to look at the artwork in order to enjoy it. In our fast-paced world, young children may need to learn how to get pleasure from looking at a watercolor painting, a statue, an illuminated manuscript, or an installation. This can be done by giving a MGOL tour of the museum, which creates connections between the children and the artwork via MGOL activities. In addition, looking at a picture of someone in a rowboat, singing "Row, Row, Row Your Boat," and understanding that a rowboat is a real object that can be rowed builds literacy. Just as the printed word *boat* means boat, a picture or sculpture of a boat means boat as well. Understanding that pictures can represent real things is a prereading skill. Interacting with an object or a piece of art using different senses also activates multiple intelligences, providing a much richer sensory experience for children. For instance, a display of teacups connects with "I'm a Little Teapot," a sculpture of a car can lead to "I'm Driving in My Car," and an oil painting with birds fits perfectly with "Two Little Pretty Birds."

Key Features

This mobile program is created around the museum's artwork. Familiar nursery rhymes connect children with art on display and extend the experience from simply looking at art to interacting with it using different senses and building visual literacy skills.

Tips for Success

- To prepare, visit the museum ahead of time and look for different types of art that can relate to certain activities. Walk through the museum with a willing curator, educator, or exhibit interpreter, and look for one or two connections in a few different exhibit areas.
- Note if there is enough space to sit or only room to stand in front of the art pieces, and decide which puppets, musical instruments, or scarves to use. Prepare a few sentences about the artwork that smoothly lead into the activity.
- When giving a museum tour to families and using MGOL activities to highlight different areas in order to expose children to a wide variety of art styles and mediums, quiet adult museum visitors may look warily in your direction and treat your noisy activities as unwanted interruptions. Make sure the museum understands that your MGOL activity tour is going to be noisy and may interrupt the quiet atmosphere expected by other museum visitors. For instance, an exhibit of Brian Pinkney's original illustrations for *Max Found Two Sticks* can lead to some frolicking percussion activities! To keep this from spoiling the fun, discuss your activity plan with your museum contact and ask for support ahead of time. This can include posting a sign stating that a family program will be taking place between certain hours inviting museum visitors to join in with the songs and rhymes.
- Ask for a museum representative to accompany you as the group walks from gallery to gallery to take care of any necessary troubleshooting while you remain engaged with your group of families.
- Arrange a date and time for the tour, and let your MGOL families know about it. Be sure to tell them that there is a connection with the rhymes that you share weekly and the museum tour. Be aware that the museum may also want to open up the tour for museum member families or the paying public.
- Use a wheeled carrying case, such as a mobile folding cart with a lid (look for dimensions around 16"H × 18"W × 15"D—I found mine at Office Depot), to carry your props around the museum with ease. The open top means that your bags of instruments and props will be easily accessible.
- It's often impossible to know ahead of time how many participants you'll have, so plan for the maximum number allowed. Being part of a lively group, seeing everyone else get bells to ring, and then being told "I'm sorry, but I don't have any more bells" can ruin the program for some children.
- In the event that a full thirty-minute tour is not possible, try creating a MGOL Scavenger Hunt (see the following section).

Creating MGOL Museum and Library Scavenger Hunts

Scavenger hunts based on rhymes used in MGOL offer age-appropriate ways to encourage children to observe and explore their surroundings. Read the "Giving Museum Tours with MGOL" module above for preparation suggestions. Once you have matched rhymes with objects, create written or online scavenger hunt clues to lead children and their parents into different spaces to find targeted objects.

After your MGOL session, hand parents a printed scavenger hunt, give them the online address, or tell them where they can download the app. Then ask them to search with their children for objects mentioned in the rhymes. As a family activity, this encourages talking,

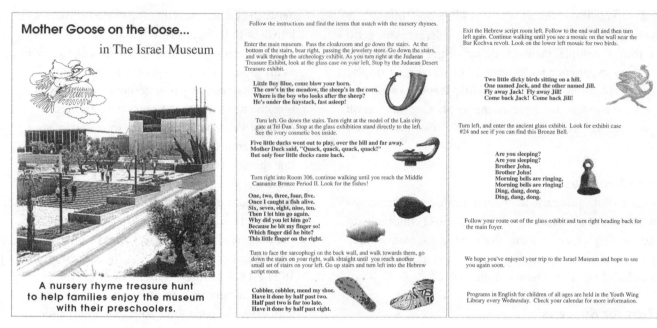

An example of a scavenger hunt I created at the Israel Museum in Jerusalem.

reading, singing, and playing together in a joyful way. If there is funding for prizes, offer to give a sticker, book, or something else to each child who presents evidence of a completed scavenger hunt.

To make your hunt more interactive, add activities similar to those described in "Giving Museum Tours with MGOL."

Key Features

A printed or online scavenger hunt is a game based on the rhymes used in your MGOL sessions. It encourages parents to use early literacy behaviors to interact with their children. The children see and hear them reading the clues aloud, they respond by talking, together they chant or sing the rhyme, and they play detective while looking for the objects.

Tips for Success

- Base your clues on rhymes already used in your sessions so the children are already familiar with them.
- Pinpoint objects that young children can easily see. If the object is at an adult's eye level, put those instructions into your scavenger hunt.
- In addition to focusing on objects, scavenger hunts can also be about shapes. For instance, if you are

creating a scavenger hunt for your library, try asking about something in a diamond shape and sing "Twinkle, Twinkle," or ask about a square shape and then recite "Jack-in-the-Box."

Presenting MGOL Sessions That Highlight Museums' Collections

To highlight collections at local museums, you can present MGOL sessions either in the museum or at your home library.

Presenting a traditional thirty-minute MGOL session in any type of museum brings families into spaces they might otherwise not enter. Art museums, history museums, and science museums often are based around collections of objects. MGOL felt pieces can be used to familiarize your audience with the museum's collection. For instance, photos of objects on display in a space museum might make good accompaniments to "Zoom, Zoom, Zoom," and a steering wheel from a transportation museum might work for "The Wheels on the Bus." Once children have seen objects as flannelboard pieces, they will become excited about finding them in the museum.

Key Features

MGOL sessions held inside museums of all types rely on felt pieces used on the flannelboard to be visual representations of objects on display as well as representations of rhymes and songs. The same pieces can be used during your library sessions to introduce those unfamiliar with the museum to some of its delights.

Tips for Success

- Museum sessions should be presented in the museum library or another room separate from the exhibits where random people aren't constantly walking in and out.
- Ask the museum staff to supply you with a catalog or photographic replicas of specific artwork and objects. Turn them into felt pieces by cutting them out and sticking them to felt with Tacky Glue.
- This same process for creating felt pieces based on a museum's collection can be used for the regular MGOL sessions in your library. Use the same rhymes your audience is familiar with, but substitute photos of museum objects in place of your traditional felt pieces. Mention that these objects can be found at the museum (and if you know something about the object, feel free to give a bit of history or explanation!).
- You may want to invite a local curator to bring one of the objects highlighted in your MGOL session and talk to the group about it informally once your session has finished.
- For help finding rhymes to go along with an eclectic collection of items, ask fellow librarians for suggestions (the Association for Library Service to Children [ALSC] electronic discussion list is a great resource!). Or you can do an online search. The connection doesn't have to be in the title. For instance, a rhyme to match a photo of a Victorian chair may be "Kitty Cat, Kitty Cat, Where Have You Been?" since the lyrics mention the cat who went to London frightening a little mouse under a chair.
- View a script for a MGOL session with a focus on book illustration at the Israel Museum's Ruth Youth Wing Library in Jerusalem at https://bit.ly/2P9cwLp.

Taking MGOL
to Public Spaces

ALTHOUGH EARLY LITERACY PROGRAMS HAVE VALUE for children as well as for the adults in their lives and public library services are free to everyone, a large number of people do not visit the library. Because of the easily adaptable nature of Mother Goose on the Loose (MGOL), it has been used in outreach programming in some obvious and unusual places such as Women, Infants, and Children (WIC) centers, clinics, and laundromats. Families who otherwise might not be exposed to rich, skill-building early literacy activities are given the opportunity to talk, sing, and play together, ultimately helping their children to practice social, emotional, intellectual, and literacy skills while strengthening the bonds between them.

Key Features

Presenting programs in public spaces means that attendance is not guaranteed or limited. It is impossible to restrict attendance to children of a specific age, and it's rare to find an enclosed, dedicated space for your program. Each program brings new surprises and challenges, but it is incredibly rewarding to see the joyful outcome of exposing new families to MGOL and drawing them into your community.

Tips for Success

Find the module that fits your outreach audience, and use those tips to plan and present your programs!

Pop-Up MGOL

Pop-up programs have been happening all over the country, but what is a "pop-up"? Google's definition is "denoting a store or other business that opens quickly in a temporary location and is intended to operate for only a short period of time."[1] Pop-ups were first seen in the late nineties in California when retailers wanted to test a market before moving in permanently. The pop-up trend eventually extended to restaurants, concerts, and even theaters. They have now become popular "go-to" events for organizations and businesses. Pop-up MGOL allows families to discover new outdoor and indoor spaces and to explore the city around them; it gives children more freedom to wander around, and it creates a community of parents and caregivers working together to raise their children.

Since the MGOL location is only announced shortly before the pop-up session takes place, finding a way to advertise and ensure that people know about the event can be a challenge. Free online resources should be utilized to help you reach a large audience quickly.

Key Features

While the program time and day of the week remain the same, social media is used to maintain contact, informing families about all relevant information regarding the upcoming MGOL session.

Tips for Success

- To start successfully, ask storytime families questions such as "Where do you like to hang out?" "Do you meet up with other parents or nannies during the day?" "Is there a park or green space where you notice a lot of young children?" and "Would you attend a session in the park, at the playground, or at a farmer's market? If so, how often?" Analyze the answers, visit locations around the neighborhood, and choose the most popular location for presenting your first program.
- Parks are ideal for pop-up MGOL. Each week, select a new park (or create a rotation) and hold a pop-up MGOL session there.
- Give parents a sense of consistency by keeping the same program times and days of the week, but change locations to allow families to explore different areas.
- Although the first session will be attended by families who already come to storytime at the library, each group will continue to grow as families stumble on the session and join in the fun.
- To keep track of all attendees, use a tablet with an app such as Remind (www.remind.com) for storytime sign-in. Continue using the app to

inform families of the varied locations from week to week. The website was created for teachers by teachers, offering a simple text service. Individuals often subscribe to the text service. Although users provide their contact information, it is kept private. As the subscribed user, you can send mass texts to a large group of people, but everyone's phone number remains hidden. This wonderful website enables weekly location updates and reminders for upcoming events to be sent to parents. Remind is continuing to grow; new services including e-mail and phone call services are being added.

- Using social media enables you to notify attendees of program times and locations, inform them of last minute changes, and keep track of statistics.
- Review the resource section "Marketing Your Program Using Social Media" for more tips on how to manage and expand your program.
- Check out a pop-up script at https://bit.ly/2wpQjRQ.

Presenting MGOL Sessions Outdoors: Parks, Playgrounds, Farmer's Markets, Festivals, and Fairs

An outdoor space can be crowded and chaotic, so follow the typical MGOL format when planning, remember to stay calm and always be flexible. Speak with the venue's coordinator to learn about guidelines, and obtain permission before beginning any sessions.

The beauty of presenting MGOL at weekly farmer's markets (in season) is that it can draw a diverse audience. Because of the quest for healthy food, farmer's market visitors include people who do not live in the neighborhood, new immigrants who might be unaware of public library services, and families from a variety of income levels. Held within view but out of earshot of the food stalls, the session can take place on an expanse of lawn or under shade trees.

Key Features

Because of the loud and distracted nature of presenting an outdoor program, quiet activities like the lullaby may be removed. Competing noises often force short breaks in the sessions. A portable, smaller flannelboard is used.

Setting up for pop-up MGOL.

Snapshot: Pop-Up MGOL at Reservoir Hill

Cork Hardin, an urban educator with Sprocket, has run MGOL programs in child-care centers, children's museums, and community-run libraries. Cork developed a pop-up MGOL as a passport to urban exploration and community building in order to involve more families in early learning programs by bringing the programs to them.

Presenting circle times at a local library for several years gave me an appreciation of the wonderful community created around MGOL. After hearing adult attendees express the desire for quality outdoor educational experiences that would provide opportunities to see the city around them with their children, I started a pop-up MGOL. In addition to giving children a chance to see a new part of the city and enjoy a wonderful storytime, a community of caregivers and parents who can work together and learn from each other has slowly formed.

As the group organically grew into something larger than I had anticipated, I asked for ideas about how to proceed in future weeks—specifically for suggestions regarding continuation during the winter months. Amazingly, through this network of parents and caregivers, several location opportunities opened up. A local bookstore, a restaurant, a theater, a church, and a synagogue are all locations that we have now used in addition to the local library.

Before starting to work with social media, I did some research and discovered that tweeting with hashtags is a great way to spread the word about pop-up events. Google offers wonderful free resources for any small business or small program project. Google Forms can be used to create a simple form for capturing information from the parents and caregivers who attend your pop-up programs. It can record their names, e-mail addresses, ages of their children, and so on. Google can also be used to create a QR code to print out and bring to your programs. Simply scanning the QR code directly with their phones takes parents directly to the form. Google Forms can also be used for feedback surveys. This wonderful product stores all the information in an easy-to-read spreadsheet that can easily be downloaded to other systems or programs.

Currently, I present five pop-up MGOL sessions in five neighborhoods each week, rotating between two and three locations per neighborhood. Now that we have moved indoors for the winter, pop-up MGOL averages 200 attendees per week. When the sessions were held outdoors, attendance increased to 250 attendees per week. I visit diverse neighborhoods and find that pop-up MGOL serves as a melting pot, drawing people from all walks of life including Baltimore natives, Baltimore transplants, immigrant families, African Americans, Orthodox Jewish families, and families from varying socioeconomic backgrounds. MGOL is the thread that weaves everyone together.

Each week, these families gather to create positive educational experiences for their children while also creating connections with each other. One week, someone suggested bringing a picnic meal and staying together after the session to talk and play together. Almost everyone brought a picnic meal the next week, and the gathering has grown since then. The families have become friends, and they now spend each week sharing food, laughter, and ideas in addition to the MGOL sessions. Though they all come from different walks of life, they have found common ground and community while creating a better future together for their children.

One of my pop-ups is in the Reservoir Hill neighborhood, adjacent to Sandtown/Winchester, where Baltimore's Freddie Brown riots took place. Parents who belonged to a neighborhood Facebook group approached me and expressed concern about their local park being used for drugs, gangs, and violence. They asked if MGOL could be used as a tool to bring families into the park, to shift what was happening in the playground from something destructive to something positive.

The weekly pop-ups began drawing thirty to forty families regularly. According to police statistics, during that first month, crime was cut in half. The families now consider MGOL their anchor. The adults have started going door-to-door, asking, "Do you have children? If so, come to our Sunday group at 4 p.m. in the park."

I don't think it is just the rhymes, the puppets, or the flannelboard. It is the whole atmosphere of MGOL that has made a difference. I'm just creating a space where community happens.

Tips for Success

- Wear comfortable clothing to enable sitting on the ground easily.
- Because MGOL includes a collection of program materials (bells, flannelboard, colored scarves, etc.), it can be a challenge to transport materials from one location to the next or from the car to the playground. Preparing a packing list of the essentials and investing in a cart with the ability to be pulled through the grass will help ease the transition from your vehicle to the program space.
- If you don't have carpet squares, ask parents to bring old towels or blankets to sit on.
- For successful outdoor programming, use equipment that is easy to carry, set up, and take down, such as a portable, smaller flannelboard.
- Prepare for people eating snacks during the session.
- You may want to remove the lullabies since playgrounds are not conducive to restful and calming lullabies. Also, you can't compete with a fire truck, so don't even try! Simply wait for the siren blares to fade away and then continue with your program.
- Enlist attendees as your allies by asking families to invite their friends to join in and requesting recommendations of other nearby locations that would work well for a MGOL session.
- Be prepared in case it begins to rain before a scheduled outdoor MGOL session by reaching out to local businesses and organizations and asking if they would host MGOL sessions in their spaces during inclement weather. This benefits everyone; it can bring newcomers into community centers, theaters, bookstores, churches, children's boutiques, and many other exciting places.
- Use social media such as the Remind app to update the location if the weather becomes rough or a snowy winter sets in. The library can provide a fallback space in the event of unforeseen bad weather or send a message to cancel the session for that day.
- See "Marketing Your Program Using Social Media" for more tips.

MGOL in WIC Clinics

Parents often find that waiting is one of the most difficult activities for small children. Waiting becomes even harder when parents are tense and there is no space specifically designed for children. WIC, a special supplemental nutrition program for women, infants, and children that is run by the Food and Nutrition Services of the US Department of Agriculture, targets the health care and nutrition of low-income women, pregnant woman, nonbreastfeeding postpartum women, and infants from birth to age five who are at nutritional risk. It is common for adults without childcare to bring children with them to their WIC appointments.

Libraries have begun sending outreach staff into WIC offices and other public places where children and parents can be subjected to long waits without much to do. Instead of presenting group sessions, librarians share individually selected MGOL activities with children and their adults, using them as a springboard to talk about child development and library services.

Key Features

Instead of presenting a full session, librarians choose selected activities with matching developmental tips to share with the children and their adults.

Tips for Success

- Tell families in the WIC waiting room that you are from the library. If the adults appear totally uninterested and uninvolved with their children or in what you have to offer, tell them that you have brought a fun book and some exciting activities for young children. Ask if it is OK for you to ask the child if he or she wants to hear a story and play with some musical instruments and scarves. The adult might be grateful to have something for the child to do and may even become involved in the activities too. However, if the adult declines, you must respect those wishes.
- Try singing "This Is the Way We Wash Our Knees" using colored scarves and then talk with parents about using songs to ease transitions and to help children through an activity that they don't usually enjoy.

• Talk about early literacy, and give out brochures regarding library services. Invite the families to come to programs at the library, where they can meet other parents and children for learning and fun. When possible, sign families up for library cards.

MGOL in Laundromats

In recognition that families with children come to laundromats and have plenty of waiting time, many laundromats now house a "play area." These play areas are often a bit removed from the noise and action of the washers, dryers, and folding areas and have space for sitting in a circle and presenting programs. Laundromats can be great places to "drop in," meet the unserved and the underserved, read a book aloud, and share some MGOL activities (fingerplays, musical instruments, and books) with everyone.

Unlike the typical library programming space, the laundromat is loud, and people often talk through the programs. In such a lively environment, children's attention easily can be lost, so sessions must be loud and invigorating.

Key Features

A shorter program that eliminates the more passive activities but includes extra developmental tips for adults can be presented in laundromats. Information regarding free library services is shared, and everyone is invited to visit you at the library. Songs with water and cleaning motifs are highlighted.

Tips for Success

For a successful program, planning ahead is essential.

• Find the manager or owner of the laundromat, and secure approval for your visit. Ask permission to create a library bulletin board that promotes library events as well as a bookshelf of free books that laundromat users can read while waiting for their laundry or take home and keep.
• Display a sign or pop-up banner advertising "Laundromat Storytime."
• Create fliers because advertising works! Putting your library logo on the flier will remind people

MGOL at a laundromat.

when to come for your programs. Fliers also give credibility when recruiting families; handing them a flier explains where you are from and what you are doing.
• When planning your program, cut down on the number of passive rhymes done in the rhymes and reads section.

On the day of your program, do the following:

• Bring quilts to place on the floor to define your storytime space.
• Be outgoing; walk through the laundromat on arrival, and invite everyone with children to join in. Encourage seniors to stand along the periphery and clap out the rhymes!
• If possible, use a visual schedule (felt pieces that that indicate progression between the sections) similar to those used in sensory storytimes. Following a visual menu keeps people engaged.
• Expect people to get up and down to check on their laundry.

- The welcoming comments are critical; they reassure parents or caregivers that young children will not sit still, particularly in a highly engaged environment such as the laundromat. Setting everyone's expectations is important in this environment!
- When the audience is large, omit the drum section.
- Do not bring colored scarves; they somehow tend to end up going home with the clean laundry! Instead of scarves, use two types of musical instruments.

- Accept that not everyone will pay attention all the time. Don't feel you have to keep going for a full thirty minutes. If fifteen seems enough, finish the program. Remember that even fifteen minutes of early literacy programming is more than many families have had in their day!
- Use fairly loud musical instruments that can be heard over the washers and dryers, such as bells and maracas. Be flexible and adaptable to the circumstance.

Snapshot: MGOL in Laundromats

Elizabeth McChesney, the director of children's services and family engagement for the Chicago Public Library's (CPL) eighty library system, has been a children's librarian with CPL for thirty years.

Laundromats are loud and busy with a lot going on for parents. Many now have a play area in a corner of the laundromat, sometimes with some communal toys, oftentimes not. We use this space and sit in a circle, a bit removed from the noise and action of the washers and dryers and folding areas. Because laundromats are also often a community meeting spot and a sort of gathering place, we see the numbers grow when we hold consistent programs (hold fast to the date and time).

The format of MGOL works really well in the laundromat, particularly in those that have a play area. MGOL's welcoming comments emphasize that young children do not sit still for long. And this is great to reiterate in your laundromat opening messages; it's very important in this setting. The nursery rhymes and flannelboard rhymes and stories work in this environment, as does the repetition of the rhymes and songs. The "Listen, Like, Learn" approach is wonderful here: many of these young children are being exposed to songs and rhymes for the very first time. Because it's new, listen-like-learn is played out each and every time. In fact, repetition is critical because of the noise and distraction in the environment. We often show animal images from a book without reading the book, another MGOL tip that helps parents with a wide degree of print facility understand how showing pictures can bring a book to life!

Given the complexity of the laundromat environment, the content of MGOL is perfect! The emphasis on short, rhythmic nursery verses allows for learning in a highly changeable environment. Moms or dads, aunties and uncles, or abuelas and abuelos will jump up and run to the dryer in the middle of a picture book or story, but they will stay and finish out a nursery rhyme or song with no worries about taking up a valuable machine or wrinkles forming in newly dried clothes!

We have adapted the MGOL format to present a shorter program. We may focus on four rhymes and do some quick flannelboard nursery rhymes or even act out a nursery rhyme in the middle of the program. We tend to open with "Scrub a Dub Dub" to tie a connection to soap and cleaning at the laundromat. Because the MGOL songs are so developmentally appropriate, they are wonderful for the variety of ages we see in the laundromat. Typically, we cut the scarves section because we have found it isn't practical in this setting. We always use the song structure: it really works here. Because we may have a caregiver with a three-month-old baby and a five-year-old, the rhymes are welcome because they are particularly appropriate for such a wide age range.

Most of the families who have joined us in these programs have no familiarity with the library. This is a great way to start your program: tell folks about the public library and its services. Hand out library card applications, and if you can issue them remotely, do so!

- Body rhymes help children focus their physical energy and are always good for caregiver-child interaction.
- Tailor your program to fit the environment of the laundromat. Pay attention to what is going on around you, and switch your activities accordingly. What works one day will not necessarily work the next.
- Be sure to close the program with a developmental tip and the reminder that just like we always seem to have laundry to do, language is important and "piles up" in a child's brain. The more you use it, the stronger the child's brain becomes!
- Pass out fliers for library programs along with a handout that includes lyrics to the rhymes and songs used in your session.

MGOL at Community Events

MGOL sessions are perfect for celebratory events such as foster parent appreciation picnics, chili cook-offs, and Fourth of July fairs. These outdoor MGOL sessions are similar to the pop-ups and can include children up to age five with their important adults. If taking place in a park, invite families with children at the playground who are not associated with the specific event to also join in.

Key Features

Replace passive rhymes with more active rhymes at community events. Treat this session as if it is a child development class, and use more developmental tips than the standard two tips per session.

Tips for Success

Since this is a onetime event and not a series of sessions, don't feel wed to your standard rhymes.

- Choose rhymes that are easy to follow and that have exciting accompanying activities. For instance, reduce the rhymes and reads section and add a second (and perhaps even a third!) musical instrument.
- You may want to create a handout to give to participants at the end of the session, so they can repeat the songs and rhymes at home. At the bottom of the handout, provide information about the time and

location of the regular MGOL programs at your library.

MGOL in Stores and Malls

If you receive requests to present MGOL sessions in malls or large stores, it may be best to decline. Although not always the case, many businesses want children's programs presented in order to lure shoppers in rather than to provide quality experiences for children and their families. Acoustics in malls are not ideal for programs, and a high-quality portable sound system will most likely be needed. Parents may think it is safe to leave their children to participate in "childcare area" programs while they shop and become huffy when told they are expected to remain. Librarians are not meant to simply be entertainers or babysitters; they are early literacy specialists who offer ongoing, in-depth literacy programming.

Key Features

If hosting MGOL at a mall or large store, adults must be reminded to stay with their children during the program. Some type of voice amplification will be needed. A wide variety of ages should be expected no matter what age the program has advertised as its target.

Tips for Success

- If you are eager to create goodwill in the community, consider requests to "perform" but ask the following questions first:
  - » Does the retail facility have a separate program room?
  - » Is the facility requesting the program going to promote it as an opportunity for parents and caregivers to learn more about how to incorporate literacy activities into their daily routines, or is it using the program as entertainment and advertisement of its goods?
  - » Can the facility establish a direct link to the more intensive and ongoing services available at the library?
  - » Will the library be reimbursed for the time the librarian spends out of the library?

- Use a portable sound system.
- Be prepared to "give a show" rather than to facilitate parent-child interactions.
- Bring a helper to ensure that instruments and scarves don't leave the area if families choose to depart while you are still presenting the program.

NOTE

1. Google, s.v. "pop-up," n.d., https://www.google .com/search?q=what+is+pop-up%3f&oq=what +is+pop&aqs=chrome.0.69i59j0j69i57j0l3.2149j0j7 &sourceid=chrome&ie=utf-8.

Snapshot: MGOL in Stores

In response to an invitation from the Babies "R" Us local marketing specialist, Lisa Sensale Yazdian, the youth services manager for outreach, arranged for the Boone County Public Library in Kentucky to bring its Tiny Tots program to the store once a month on Saturdays. The program was marketed as Baby Time, but they were prepared for anything.

The play center was a corner of the store partitioned off for classes. The environment was fairly sterile with a linoleum tile floor and no soft seating. Different library staff signed up to cover each program; they had to bring all the supplies with them, which meant lugging the portable flannel/magnet board, books, instruments, a radio, and rhyme sheets. Chairs set up in rows had to be removed to create floor space.

Although the sessions were offered for free, attendance was low and sometimes nonexistent. The majority of people attending the sessions were already library users, but one parent from another county shared that she had never been to a storytime before. Based on low attendance, the sessions were discontinued after seven months.

Bringing MGOL to Childcare and Educational Settings

IN HOME DAYCARES, CHILDCARE CENTERS, PREschools, and schools, Mother Goose on the Loose (MGOL) empowers caregivers and teachers by modeling useful activities that can be used in day-to-day routines. While the children learn rhymes coupled with physical actions, their providers learn new activities to use during circle times, to ease transitions, and to build early literacy, along with social and emotional skills. They observe different ways to share books with young children in addition to simply reading them aloud.

Educational settings that require parental involvement can use MGOL during "family time." Parents living in poverty may not feel they have the education, time, or energy to interact with their children because of obstacles faced in their daily lives. Attending MGOL sessions or even being exposed to some MGOL activities in their children's home daycare, preschool, or school gives them easy ways to talk, sing, and play with their children.

Being exposed to MGOL also increases awareness of the library and its services. It perfectly fits in with Family Place Libraries' vision statement that "public libraries will become vital centers for early learning, parent engagement, family support and community connectivity ensuring children get the best start in life."[1]

Key Features

The same MGOL session used at the library can be brought to other educational settings. There will not be a one-to-one ratio in most of these settings since parents are not typically present.

Planning Ahead for Daycares and Childcare Centers

1. Make a list of home daycares or preschools interested in hosting a MGOL program, and contact them. Because many daycares take some sort of summer break and reopen in September, call each interested daycare in August and confirm that they are still interested.
2. While on the phone, interview the caregiver to get information about the number of children, the classrooms, and special needs, and fill out the daycare intake form (provided in the resources section), adding information regarding transportation to the home or center.
3. Once your list of sites to visit is complete with addresses, plot each one on MapQuest or Google Maps. In addition to suggesting routes, both programs list travel times and mileage. Use the maps to set up a schedule for visiting sites that are close to each other in order to save gas and time.
4. When setting up your schedule for monthly visits, assign a day rather than a date, such as the first Friday or the second Wednesday of the month. The date may change, but the day will always stay the same.
5. After creating your schedule, call back the sites to tell them their assigned days.

6. Send a welcoming letter introducing yourself and describing your MGOL program. Put your expectations, such as the need for caregivers to stay in the room and participate during MGOL, in this letter.

Planning Ahead for School Visits

1. Send an e-mail to the school librarian and the principal requesting a meeting to discuss setting up class visits for the upcoming school year. If you don't get a response to your e-mail, call!
2. Decide which age group(s) you want to target, and create a sample program.
3. Bring a list of research-supported reasons why monthly classroom visits would benefit the school.
4. At the end of your meeting, ask for the e-mail addresses of all teachers of the grades you plan to visit, and get in touch with each teacher individually.
5. Send a welcoming letter introducing yourself and describing your MGOL program. Put your expectations, such as the need for teachers to stay in the room and participate during MGOL, in this letter.
6. E-mail each teacher (and carbon copy the librarian and principal) with the dates for the sessions.

Tips for Success

- The typical wooden flannelboard with the shelf in the middle is heavy and not easy to move. If you can convince the school to buy a flannelboard, recommend the Best-Rite Magnetic Flannel Easel with a steel frame and wheels, because it is easy to wheel from classroom to classroom. If you are going to be bringing one without wheels and prefer not to carry any weight, purchase a cart such as Custom Craftwork's "Solutions Table Cart" for carrying massage tables. You can also invest in a tabletop flannelboard rather than the traditional standing one with a shelf in the middle. One librarian uses a homemade portable flannelboard that she wears around her neck!

According to Dora Garraton, the staff "Mother Goose" at the Vigo County Public Library in Indiana, the most important ingredient for a successful outreach to home daycares, preschools, and schools is a supportive library that values community collaboration and encourages programs that think outside the box.

- Since you will be reading the same book aloud in numerous places, type out the words ahead of time, print them out minimized so they will fit on one piece of paper, and tape them to the book's back cover. While holding the book open directly in front of you and closer to the children, you can flip the pages without having to tilt the book by reading the text off the back cover.
- Overplan! Although you are targeting specific ages, the children may not be developmentally where you expect them to be. They may not be able to sit for the longer rhymes you have planned, or they may have much better attention spans than you predicted. With extra rhymes and related materials, you can tweak your program on the spot to fit your audience's capabilities.
- Use (and modify if needed) the intake form in resource C. Peruse all local school calendars. Check the dates before calling the school and suggesting a visit. Note school closing policies due to the weather or holidays.
- Provide a booklet with lyrics to all songs and rhymes for teachers so they can reinforce the activities between sessions.
- In order to effectively evaluate and tweak your program, consider giving teachers evaluation forms to be administered prior to the first MGOL session and after the last session. An example form is included in resource C.

Bringing MGOL to Home Daycares and Childcare Centers

Bringing MGOL to home daycares and childcare centers provides a learning experience to children as well as their adult caregivers. Home daycares are typically housed in informal settings where the caregiver has little or no specific training. When providers lack formal early childhood training, MGOL developmental tips and modeling of activities provide substantial professional development. In informal environments, the ages and numbers of children can vary greatly. Some caregivers provide care only for infants, some only for toddlers, some only for preschoolers, and some for children of all ages. Some home daycares simply consist of a living room area with a sofa, while others have larger playrooms. MGOL has been presented in daycares and childcare centers for six-month-old babies who sit in bouncy chairs or on the provider's laps. Although it is impossible to do a complete MGOL program for babies under age one without a one-to-one adult to child ratio, when babies are twelve months and older, a regular MGOL program can be presented.

Key Features

Modifications can address the lack of a one-to-one adult to child ratio at daycare and childcare centers. Interactive rhymes are brought to the children who are not yet walking rather than expecting them to come up to the flannelboard. Space is often very tight, so activities requiring children to move around are limited or eliminated.

Tips for Success

Preparing for your program:

- Make a list of home daycares or childcare centers interested in hosting a MGOL program, and contact them. Because many daycares have a summer break and reopen in September, call in August to confirm that they are still interested.
- While on the phone, fill out the MGOL intake form (found in resource C).
- A useful resource for locating sites to visit in "high-risk areas" is ChildCare Aware (go to http://childcareaware.org or call 800-424-2246 for more

information). In order to visit childcare centers located in the highest-risk areas, the Enoch Pratt Free Library's Book Buggy looks at census districts with the highest infant mortality rates. If you have a local rating system, look there. For instance, the Vigo County Public Library in Indiana relies on the Paths to QUALITY rating system for early care programs to determine sites for visitation.

On the day of your program, make sure to do the following:

- Bring fuzzy socks with you! Some daycares request that shoes be removed, so always come prepared.
- You may want to make a masking tape circle on the floor around the flannelboard to delineate the "invisible circle" that children are asked not to cross during the session.
- Present a modified or shortened version of MGOL for infants under age one by using rhymes with pictures and pointing to key points in the picture, singing songs with shakers, and playing peek-a-boo with the scarves.
- During the first few MGOL sessions, a child might watch everything but not participate. Tell the caregivers that this is fine; the children are still absorbing everything. Caregivers often happily share that their students sing the rhymes to themselves when they are at home or in the car. It is reassuring to caregivers when their children absorb these rhymes even if they do not participate during the sessions.
- Provide a booklet with lyrics to all the songs and rhymes for home providers and center staff so they can reinforce the activities between sessions.
- Use the intake form in resource C to keep track of the different locations.

SAMPLE PROGRAM

MGOL in Home Daycares

by Dora Garraton, MGOL, Vigo County Public Library

While MGOL was originally designed to be a program for parents with children, it is equally effective in settings where there are more children than adults. When running programs in childcares, the activities build on what

Snapshot: Dora Garraton, Mother Goose on the Loose

In 2009, a partnership between the Vigo County Public Library in Terre Haute, Indiana, and United Way via the Success by Six Program established a library outreach position for MGOL. Dora Garraton is the full-time "Mother Goose on the Loose" for the library and drives her Goosemobile to selected low socioeconomic locations.

Vigo County is a high poverty area, and my mobile outreach targets daycares that have low ratings because their providers don't have a background or training in childcare or because they are just starting their services. I visit county daycares once a month for a year to expose the children to activities that develop school readiness skills and to aid caregivers by demonstrating activities that promote learning these skills while having fun. The Goosemobile currently serves thirty-two daycares and preschools for a total of fifty-five sessions with approximately 470 children.

We recognize that patrons have difficulties developing early literacy skills because of the barriers of an at-risk population. Vigo County has a median income of $31,817. Indiana doesn't have a comprehensive pre-K, kindergarten isn't mandatory by law, and children don't have to be enrolled into first grade until age seven. We have geographic barriers due to rural pockets that are not easily accessible because of lack of transportation.

MGOL incorporates the five early literacy practices (talk, sing, play, read, write) in a way that is not intimidating and is very doable. It reinforces again and again the importance of nurturing young developing brains so that the child will have the best chance of succeeding in school. It demonstrates that putting these practices to work in parents' daily lives is easy and doesn't involve thought beyond "playing" with their children.

One daycare that I visit is home-based, and we do MGOL in the living room. The children are eighteen months to two years of age. When I walk in, the children arrange themselves on the sofa and sit all in a row.

When reading aloud, I don't use big books. I print out the text on a single sheet of paper that I tape onto the back cover. I feel more comfortable not having to look at the words. I tend to memorize the book after a few reads, so this serves as my cheat sheet. Of course, I point things out in the pictures, but I like looking at the children's captivated faces as I read rather than the pages in the book.

The children *love* the program and are excited when they see the Goosemobile pull up. The pro-

Dora in her Goosemobile.

viders happily anticipate my visits as well. I believe that the childcare providers benefit greatly from the MGOL outreach. They often ask for the lyrics to the songs I use and then continue using them in their classes.

A provider who ran a disability class e-mailed me a picture of one of her kids sitting in a bean bag chair "reading" a book to himself that we had used a few days before during MGOL. It was a Pete the Cat story with lots of repetition and some singing, so he retained it well. The provider was happy and proud to see this boy repeating the book-reading behavior that he had seen modeled at MGOL.

Typically, we serve each daycare for one year, then move on to those that have been on the waiting list. I have providers begging to stay on and even willing to have afternoon sessions even though morning is usually the preferred time.

Initially, parents or caregivers may be hesitant with unfamiliar songs or feel a little silly, but they warm up quickly. It's great to stress how important early face-to-face talk is for little brains and that these informal interactions are extremely valuable. Parents and caregivers feel pride that they are doing something that will aid their children's development.

the children can do on their own instead of focusing on adult interaction with the children. Because of limited space in home daycares, standing-up activities can be eliminated. If you are working with children who are too young to sing on their own, be sure to use lots of recorded music!

Section 1: Welcoming Comments

Section 2: Rhymes and Reads *(The book is read aloud later.)*

"[Name of Child] Has a Pig on [His or Her] Head" *(Name whatever stuffed animal is used that month.)*

"Old Mother Goose"

"Goosey, Goosey Gander"

Section 3: Body Rhymes

Hands: "Five Fat Sausages"

Knee Bounces: "Mother and Father and Uncle John" *(with babies)*

Hands: "One Yellow Fish Swimming in the Water" *(change colors each time and do motions with hands)*

Section 4: The Drum Sequence

"Rum Pum Pum"

Book: Emergency, illustrated by Cocoretto

Section 5: Stand-Up / Sit-Down Activities *(not done)*

Section 6: Animal Activities

Section 7: Musical Instruments and Scarves

Shakers: "We Shake Our Shakers Together"

Shakers: "Pitter, Patter"

Shakers: "Popcorn" *(play recorded music)*

Shakers: "Milkshake" *(with babies)*

Shakers: "Shake!" *(from the We Kids Rock—Every-body Clap Your Hands album)*

Shakers: "Shakers Away" *(Do a second book, if applicable.)*

Scarves: "Wind, Oh Wind"

Scarves: "Popcorn" *(recite rhyme)*

Scarves: "Balance a Scarf" *(from Never Mind the Bobbins—Rainbow Stripes)*

Scarves: "I Put My Scarf on My Head" *(from I Am Happy! with Sukey Molloy)*

Scarves: "Wiggle It High, Wiggle It Low"

Scarves: "Scrunch Your Scarf into a Ball"

Scarves: "Scarves Away"

Section 8: Lullabies

"Baa Baa Black Sheep" *(Insert other colors too.)*

Section 9: Interactive Rhymes

"Humpty Dumpty" or "Hickory Dickory Dare"

Section 10: Closing Ritual

"Can You Kick with Two Feet?"

"It's Time to Say Good-Bye"

Presenting MGOL in Preschools

Preschool for children from ages three to five is often a child's first great adventure into the larger world; it is a time when they explore the world with and without their parents or guardians. Play is the real work of childhood,[2] and preschools can use play to build on children's natural curiosity while strengthening their budding social and emotional skills. Learning to wait patiently, to take turns, to share, to listen, to follow directions, and to "say it with words, not with hands"—a phrase commonly used in preschools and daycares—are important skills to practice repeatedly.

Based on findings that "read-to-learn" children have distinct advantages and are more likely to do well in school, pre-K classes have been added into many elementary schools. Parent engagement is often encouraged, and children in these pre-Ks are exposed to activities that build readiness skills. Students often gather with their teacher(s) on a colorful rug for "circle time," and this is when they participate in group activities such as MGOL.

Preschool MGOL without parents works well. Rather than being bounced on parents' outstretched legs during knee bounces, children extend their own legs and bounce them to a variety of tempos. They love lifting and lowering their legs to rhymes such as "The Grand Old Duke of York."

While preschoolers still learn through ritual and repetition, the 80:20 repetition model should be adapted to allow the introduction of more new material for each session. Repetition of 50 or 60 percent of the material from session to session is a good framework. Rhymes can be longer as well. Although songs like "The Wheels on the Bus" are limited to one or two verses in MGOL sessions for infants and toddlers, preschool children enjoy singing all the many verses. In addition to building language awareness and general knowledge, MGOL sessions in preschool classrooms help children practice self-regulation skills, build up their self-confidence, and set a strong foundation for kindergarten.

Key Features

In preschools, expect the children to do the activities themselves rather than with a parent or caregiver. Use about 50 percent repetition from session to session, read longer books with more involved plots, reduce the number of rhymes recited, and sing more verses of songs. Try to include nonfiction books, and if possible, extend your session to forty-five minutes.

Tips for Success

- Plan your preschool program with the assumption of independent child participation, unless you are told otherwise. Direct your welcoming comments to the children, introducing the program and reminding them of the invisible circle.
- Expand the repetition rate to fifty-fifty.
- Consider extending the session to forty-five minutes.
- Children who are accustomed to hearing books read aloud can listen to the entire story; for children without developed listening skills, introduce the book by reading part of it at first and then expanding the read-aloud selection during following sessions.

Snapshot: Bringing MGOL to Family Education Centers

Dorothy Stoltz, director for community engagement at the Carroll County (MD) Public Library, arranged for four consecutive weeks of MGOL for parents with children from birth to age two at a local Judy Center.

Maryland's Judith P. Hoyer Early Child Care and Family Education Centers, known as "Judy Centers," are located in every jurisdiction and offer a wide range of services for children from birth through kindergarten and their low-income families. Based at or close to a Title I school, a Judy Center focuses on school readiness and uses the "whole child" approach to address the variables that can impact a young child's readiness for kindergarten. Judy Centers provide a holistic family engagement approach with early childhood education, family activities, health care, adult education, childcare, parenting classes, identification of special needs and early intervention, and family literacy.

Carroll County Public Library and Carroll County Public Schools have had a long, vibrant collaboration with their Judy Center, receiving the support and expertise of Sue Mitchell [Judy Center director] during the library's successful research-tested study on early literacy training. Expanding this partnership to offer Mother Goose on the Loose at the Judy Center was a natural step in working together. When I walked into the classroom during the MGOL session, I was struck by the high energy, playfulness, and respectfulness of adults and children alike. It was positive family bonding time in a setting without the many interruptions of daily life—but it was more than the lack of outside distractions. Betsy's program offers a fast-paced, how-to-have-fun-*and*-learn-together time for adult and child, where they both can easily transfer the joyful activities to the home setting. However, MGOL offers more. A captivating sense of excellence, enchantment, and goodness is in the air.

- Include nonfiction books, such as *All the Water in the World* by George Ella Lyon and Katherine Tillotson.
- Consider bringing handouts with lyrics for preschool teachers and participating adults so the songs and rhymes can be practiced.
- Some schools have preschools with lots of parent involvement, but many family members have difficulty with English or simply do not know the songs and rhymes. They may not participate at all during the first session. Don't worry; this is normal! Simply repeat more than 50 percent of the material from week to week. During your welcoming comments, inform the adults that they are their child's first and best teachers, that children learn best by imitating the adults that they love, and that children get the most out of the program when their adults participate joyfully in all the activities.
- Ask that preschool teachers stay in the room because it has benefits for them too.
- Be sure to arrive early to deal with all types of situations. The most important step for ensuring a smoothly run program is to have everyone sit in a circle. I once presented a series of five MGOL programs in the school cafeteria of Campfield Elementary School in Baltimore County for two combined preschool classes, a daycare group without parents, and a program similar to Early Head Start with parents. I rearranged the cafeteria tables to form a big semicircle with my flannelboard facing the audience. Everyone sat backward on the lunch table benches, facing me rather than the table. The five-week MGOL program in the cafeteria was a bit chaotic, but it worked. To see a short montage of the program, go to https://youtu.be/uNY3j0g9eR8.

MGOL for Preschoolers and Their Parents

by Betsy Diamant-Cohen

Section 1: Welcoming Comments

Section 2: Rhymes and Reads
"Alligator, Alligator"
"Zoom, Zoom, Zoom"
"I'm Driving in My Car"
"Two Little Penguins"
Book: *Eat Your Peas, Louise!* by Pegeen Snow *(Show a photo of peas and ask if they know where peas come from.)*
"Five Fat Peas" *(Show the toy pea pod.)*
"Grey Squirrel" *(Give puppet kisses.)*
"We Wiggle Our Fingers Together" *(Add a verse for tapping your toes.)*

Section 3: Body Rhymes
Fingers: "Put Your Fingers in the Air"
Hand: "Baby Shark"
Hands: "Five Fat Sausages"
Whole Body: "Chewy Bubble Gum"
Knee Bounce: "Row, Row, Row Your Boat" *(preschool version)*

Section 4: The Drum Sequence
"Rum Pum Pum" *(no flannel piece)*

Section 5: Stand-Up / Sit-Down Activities
"The Grand Old Duke of York"
"Here We Go Upperty Up"
"Jack-in-the-Box"
"Handy Spandy"

Section 6: Animal Activities
"I Went to Visit the Farm One Day" *(Developmental Tip: There are many ways to use books. In addition to reading them, you can simply talk about them or sing songs about the illustrations.)*
"When the [Cow] Gets Up in the Morning" *(three farm puppets)*

Section 7: Musical Instruments and Scarves

Bells: "We Ring Our Bells Together"
Bells: "Grandfather's Clock"
Bells: "Hurry, Hurry, Drive the Firetruck"
Bells: "Jack-in-the-Box"
Bells: "Bells Away" (*no flannel piece*)
Scarves: "Wind, Oh Wind" (*no flannel piece*)
Scarves: "The Wheels on the Bus"
Scarves: "Jack-in-the-Box"
Scarves: "Scrunch Your Scarf into a Ball" / "Scarves Away" (*no flannel piece*)

Section 8: Lullabies

"You Are My Sunshine" (*Share a developmental tip about the limbic system.*)

Section 9: Interactive Rhymes

"Humpty Dumpty"

Section 10: Closing Ritual

"Can You Kick with Two Feet?" (*one piece for all three*)
"We're So Happy"
"It's Time to Say Good-Bye"

Bringing MGOL to Kindergartens

Although rolling, crawling, and scooting are the norm during MGOL, it is different in school settings where children are introduced to "circle time" to learn how to participate in group activities. While occasional MGOL sessions are fun, kindergarten teachers often find that MGOL activities can be extremely helpful for classroom management. Developmental tips are thus directed toward teachers rather than parents, pointing out that lyrics such as "toys away, toys away, put your toys away today" encourage everyone to participate in classroom cleanup. Since children often get antsy and may start bothering each other while waiting in line when they have nothing to do, teachers can keep them occupied by reciting "Two Little Dickey Birds" or the faster version, "Two Little Penguins."

Modeling goes a long way! Teachers learn to incorporate the "Rum Pum Pum" technique of tapping out the syllables on the drum when introducing new words to

Snapshot: bringing MGOL to Preschools

Kerry Furnari and Jan Simons, resource teachers at ABC Preschool / Judy Center, reflect on a five-week MGOL outreach program held at their center.

I just think I've never seen a program that incorporates language development, motor skills, bonding with parents, socialization, cooperation...all those getting ready for school skills. And prekindergarten skills. It's all there. It's all in the whole program.

And it's fun. It's showing parents that children are learning through fun and that they don't have to sit down and do worksheets to learn.

their students. And after observing the calming effects of lullabies when energy levels climb into a danger zone, teachers can use "lullaby time" and ask children to sit cross-legged on the floor, close their eyes and hug themselves, rock slowly back and forth, and gently sing a lullaby.

Key Features

For kindergarteners, a formula of only 20 to 40 percent repetition rather than 80 percent is used. More than one book is read aloud, including nonfiction and longer stories. All verses in long songs, such as "The Wheels on the Bus," are sung rather than limiting singing to one or two verses.

Tips for Success

- Kindergarten teachers may prefer that their students sit in chairs during MGOL rather than on the floor. While respecting teachers' preferences for a more structured environment, compensate for the limited movement by adding more programmatic opportunities to march, hop, and wiggle. Standing up and moving balances the time children are seated. Additionally, extra flapping or waving while seated helps release physical energy.
- When introducing a new rhyme, try reciting it

more than two times. Demonstrate it, teach it, and then have everyone do it together once or twice. Kindergarten children connect to the rhymes used in that fashion and often ask for them on other visits.

- Rhymes that are fairly uncomplicated but include the use of American Sign Language (ASL) signs or other hand and body motions work well with school children.
- To encourage imaginations, ask the kindergarteners to make up their own versions of rhymes. Explain using an example, such as replacing the lyrics of "Two Little Dickey Birds" with "Two little knapsacks sitting on a desk, one was neat and the other was a mess."

SAMPLE PROGRAM

MGOL for Kindergarteners

The program lasts for forty-five minutes rather than thirty minutes. It involves reading more than one book.

by Summer Rosswog, early childhood and literacy manager at Port Discovery Children's Museum

Section 1: Welcoming Comments

Section 2: Rhymes and Reads
"Old Mother Goose"
"Can You Clap with Two Hands?"
"Open Them, Shut Them"
"The Wheels on the Bus"
"Fee, Fie, Fo, Fum"
Book: Hello by Rachel Isadora

Section 3: Body Rhymes
Hand: "Pizza, Pizza, Hot"
Whole Body: "I'm a Little Teapot"
Hands: "Pat-a-Cake" *(Choose a friend and do the rhyme together.)*
Fingers: "Dance Your Fingers Up"

Section 4: The Drum Sequence
(This does not take place here.)

Section 5: Stand-Up / Sit-Down Activities
"Jack Be Nimble" *(Clap while kids take turns jumping over a candlestick; use the children's names.)*
"We're Marching to the Drum" *(Do adventure version with a drum and a lion puppet.)*

Section 6: Animal Activities
(This is a part of "We're Marching to the Drum.")

Section 7: Musical Instruments and Scarves (Set 1)
Tambourines: "We Shake Our Tambourines Together"
Tambourines: Things by Eloise Greenfield
Tambourines: "ABC Song"
Book: Z is For Moose by Kelly Bingham and Paul O. Zelinsky

Section 7: Musical Instruments and Scarves (Set 2)
Castanets: "Tick Tock, Tick Tock, Where's That Cuckoo Bird?"
Castanets: "No More Monkeys" *(CD song by Asheba)*
Castanets: "Jack-in-the-Box"

Section 8: Lullabies
"Twinkle, Twinkle" *(with individual felt stars)*

Section 9: Interactive Rhymes
(There are no interactive rhymes.)

Section 10: Closing Ritual
"With My Little Hands I Go Clap, Clap, Clap"
"We're So Happy"
"It's Time to Say Good-Bye"

Using MGOL Activities in First-Grade Classrooms

Tyra LaVerne and Jennifer Timmerman from Boone County, Kentucky, used MGOL in first-grade classrooms of Title I schools. Monthly visits follow the traditional MGOL outline but with more frequently varied rhymes. One chosen rhyme is introduced by simple repetition, and more parts are slowly added to it at each visit. For instance, when using "Pease Porridge Hot" with first graders, the rhyme was taught while tapping hands on knees to the beat. When presenting it the second time, the more complicated motions of tapping knees and then clapping hands was done. During the third visit, after a short practice, the students were invited to turn to their neighbors and do the traditional clapping and tapping alternative hands while reciting the rhyme. According to Jennifer, the enthusiasm inspired by the slow adding of more complicated movements to this rhyme caused a first-grade teacher to comment to her, "We love doing the Mother Goose rhymes!"

Key Features

While the usual MGOL format is roughly followed for first-grade classes, multiple books are used and more new material is introduced each week. One rhyme is chosen and expanded on by adding new verses or actions during each following visit.

Tips for Success

- Feel free to delete entire sections to make room for additional books and longer verses.
- Choose a rhyme that you *really like* to be the one you will build on.
- A good resource for different multicultural rhymes is the book *Over the Hills and Far Away* (2015), collected by Elizabeth Hammill and illustrated by more than seventy artists.
- Nina Crews's *The Neighborhood Mother Goose* (2003) and *The Neighborhood Sing-Along* (2011) are illustrated with photographs of children from different backgrounds in urban and rural settings.
- More selections can be found in Patricia McKissack's *Let's Clap, Jump, Sing and Shout; Dance, Spin and Turn It Out!: Games, Songs, and Stories from an African American* (2017), illustrated by Brian Pinkney.

Talking about MGOL at PTA Meetings

One way to inspire adults to talk, sing, share books, and play with their children is to present a MGOL session at school events such as PTA meetings. Many parents don't have much spare time; they are busy trying to make ends meet and may feel that they don't have enough time to spend with their children. They may have to frequently make difficult choices, such as choosing between going to work when their child is sick or staying at home. If they don't have an understanding manager or enough sick days, staying home can mean a loss in pay or loss of a job. Because these parents already struggle, it's important to convey that even little changes can make a difference. During PTA meetings, back-to-school nights, and other school programs, visiting librarians can encourage parents to talk and sing with their children while grocery shopping (it's a great time to play *I Spy*), to sing during bath time, or to recite rhymes while tucking them in at night. When added to normal everyday routines, little additions like songs and rhymes can foster adult-child bonding and encourage brain development.

Key Features

One-time presentations to parents can use a few selected songs and rhymes accompanied by simple developmental tips to encourage parents to talk, sing, read, and play with their children.

Tips for Success

- Keep it brief; the less you say, the more your audience will remember.
- Select a few unique rhymes or songs and well-known ones such as "The Wheels on the Bus" or "If You're Happy and You Know It" to present.
- If possible, bring books to give away.
- Always invite families to visit you at the library and mention that library cards and library services are free.

MGOL as a Citywide School Readiness Program

What do you do when the diversity of the community is not reflected in attendance at library activities? Since early literacy programs are a key factor in school readiness and child development, getting programs and resources to families who might have barriers preventing them from visiting libraries becomes critical. Barriers can be caused by transportation restrictions, language differences, or lack of information about program offerings being communicated to all neighborhoods.

Snapshot: Bringing MGOL to Elementary School

Jennifer Timmerman, youth services manager at the Boone County Public library, visits Title I first-grade elementary school classes with MGOL.

When I travel to schools, I usually see about four to five first-grade classes with about 100–120 students. When I visit the first-grade classes, I take fewer props than for a normal MGOL. Usually we sing and use our hands for rhythm by tapping and clapping. On occasion, I have drawn prompts—for example, when singing "There's a Hole in the Bottom of the Sea." When I first started bringing in a MGOL rhyme to first grades, I wondered what the reaction would be. It has been really positive from both the teachers and the children.

Librarians can reach these families by going out into the community and offering services inside institutions that are located inside the neighborhoods lacking library access. A 2003 citywide initiative consisting of the public library, the public schools, and Success by Six by Smart Start Central Oklahoma (SSCO) was tasked with promoting school readiness initiatives over a larger area and supporting community-based efforts to increase the number of children ready to succeed by the time they enter school. The project involved research, partners, funding, and teamwork and is now serving children from birth to five years old and their caregivers throughout Oklahoma County.

Key Features

To create a citywide early literacy program, the initiative must have investment from multiple stakeholders in the community. Key partners include school systems or other organizations that can host programming inside their communities; early childhood educators and trainers, including librarians and teachers; funding support from foundations, the government, or local businesses; and the families you want to serve.

Tips for Success

- Partner with organizations that are physically located in the community you want to serve.
- Start small if needed, but aim for program growth.
- Build a working relationship with education leaders who value and support early learning.
- Ensure there is adequate funding.
- Find partners who are as committed to the success of the program as you are.
- Look at the entire plan, and only commit to what you can reasonably handle.

SAMPLE PROGRAM

Smart Start Central Oklahoma

SSCO is an early childhood initiative serving families with kids from birth to five years old in Oklahoma County. The Smart Start in the Schools program serves thirty-two schools in Oklahoma County. Families with babies and young children living in elementary school neighborhoods are invited to participate in play, storytime, exercise, and art activities. With support from health department presenters, teachers, local artists, musicians, SSCO staff, and volunteers, young children not yet in school and their parents participate in developmentally appropriate experiences at their future school.

Six early literacy activities are offered in two school districts with demographically diverse populations of children and families:

- *1, 2, 3, Play with Me i*s an Oklahoma City version of Family Place, where children are encouraged to learn through play.
- The standard thirty-minute *MGOL* program is offered.
- *Toddler Aerobics* is based on the *Preschool Aerobics Fun* CD by Georgiana Stewart.
- *Reading Ready* starts with a little storytime where a very simple concept book or picture book is read aloud. Then children and parents are instructed to make their own book. Once the book is created, parents are encouraged to "read" the book aloud to their child by talking about the picture (and not actually reading printed words).

- *Play Dough Power* is an early childhood playdough program created and taught by artist Kiona Mil-lirons. Via homemade salt dough, children use their powers of observation to verbalize their thoughts and use different words. Parents and children are encouraged to converse and are given opportunities to follow directions and to create on their own. Fine motor skills are exercised, engaging play goes on between parents and their children, and praise and positive feedback are freely given.

- *Scribbling to Writing* focuses on the importance of writing and drawing as a preliteracy skill. The facilitator hands out crayons, chalk, markers, and paper and allows the children to draw. While the children are scribbling, the facilitator walks around the room and points out some of the common patterns in the children's art and how they relate to their emerging reading skills. The program ends with a short storytime with books focused on shapes, colors, or drawing.

- More information is available at http://smartstart centraloklahoma.org.

Taking MGOL to Early Head Start and Head Start

Early Head Start (EHS) is a center- and home-based visitation early childhood / parenting education program for low-income families. EHS programs serve infants and toddlers up to age three. Services can begin during a mother's pregnancy, while Head Start serves preschoolers and their families. Some EHS programs must leave a percentage of their enrollment for children with disabilities.

Because MGOL has so many developmental components—fine and gross motor skills, social-emotional skills, communication, language and literacy, pretend play, and fun connection with books—Lisa Tyson, youth services coordinator at Tazewell County Public Library in the Appalachian Mountains of Southwest Virginia, brings her MGOL program to Head Start. She visits an EHS center that serves children from sixteen months to three years and a Head Start center for children from ages three to five. During the first few visits, the young children carefully observe everything and everyone but might not clap hands or attempt fingerplays. To put their

Snapshot: How to Reach Underserved Families

A social worker by trade, Lisa Wood wanted to reach everyone with the early literacy message, especially families who might have barriers to coming to the library, like transportation or language. After investigating why some families were not coming to programs, Lisa concluded that the only way to reach these families was to go out into the community. The Smart Start in the Schools program now serves thirty-two schools in Oklahoma County.

I discovered that some families did not know the library was free because going to the public library had never been a part of their daily lives. They didn't grow up in families that used the library. For others, the concerns that they had to face daily consumed so much effort and energy that they did not feel there was room to make library visits a part of their weekly habit. Furthermore, many immigrant families in the Oklahoma City community came from countries that did not have public libraries or had libraries that were similar to a country club, requiring a recommendation letter or sponsorship by an existing member to join and requiring membership fees. Finally, some did not realize that reading to their children and playing with them was an important thing to do. They did not understand the value of talking, singing, reading, writing, and playing with their children; no one had ever explained the importance of these activities to them. Their parents had not read or played with them, so it was not in their realm of experience.

caregivers at ease, she includes a word in her welcoming comments about children observing and absorbing, telling the adults not to be concerned if the children don't participate during their first few Mother Goose experiences.

Teachers look at MGOL as a way of introducing children to "circle time." The EHS teachers at the site Lisa visits prefer for the children to sit in chairs rather than on the floor. They want their children to learn how to participate in group activities following the classroom structure of sitting in chairs. This can be hard for children under age three, who don't find it easy to sit still. For all ages, the MGOL rhymes and songs help build vocabulary and increase narrative skills.

Key Features for EHS

Parents may or may not be present for the programs. Teachers often prefer that their students sit on chairs; to compensate for this more limited movement, more opportunities to march, hop, wiggle, and move are built into the program.

Key Features for Head Start

Choose a developmental skill, and use the nursery rhymes to help preschoolers master that skill. Repeat fewer rhymes, continually introduce new rhymes, and use more complex fingerplays. For instance, if focusing on fine motor coordination, use "Old King Cole." Take time to practice holding up three fingers for "He called for his fiddlers three." Talk about how to hold up three fingers, and use the thumb to hold down the pinky. Older preschool children will want to imitate the movements exactly. Although it seems like a small detail, the children want to master this skill. You may notice them staring intently at your fingers and comparing them to their fingers! This is why the Mother Goose program promotes repetition. By sharing the rhyme twice, children have another opportunity to practice the words and accompanying movements.

Tips for Success

- Respect teachers' preferences for a structured environment; if they require children to be sitting in chairs, add lots of movement opportunities to keep them engaged.

 Snapshot: Taking MGOL into Head Starts

Tazewell County Public Library's youth services coordinator, Lisa Tyson, regularly presents MGOL sessions at EHS and Head Start centers in her rural Southwest Virginia community.

Music is a terrific tool for interacting with kids, as few can resist ringing bells or shaking maracas. Even the most reluctant child won't be able to pass up the joy of making music. I always try to hand the instrument directly to the child, to create that personal connection.

I changed the wording to "Old Mother Goose" because the traditional rhyme didn't feel right to me. I feel a bit bold changing the wording of something hundreds of years old, but this flows well for me and is easy to sing (to the tune of "One Little, Two Little, Three Little Pilgrims").

> Old Mother Goose when she wanted to wander
>
> Flapped her wings into the wild, blue yonder.

I discovered that lullabies were not as useful for this group, so I decided to extend the scarf activity instead. Our scarf songs are followed by "Peek-a-Boo," then wearing the scarves as hats and noting the colors and whose matches whose. This is fairly quiet and provides the slowdown that children need after noisy bells. Sometimes, if I want to include a lullaby, I'll work it into the beginning rhymes and reads.

I have a plush barn that I absolutely love. The animals are all stuffed inside, and they come out and dance on the roof while we sing and make animals songs. I also have a homemade, portable flannelboard that I wear around my neck.

- Having two or three opportunities to stand up and move will balance the time the children are seated. Additionally, extra flapping or waving while seated will be helpful.
- When running a program with parents present, try to hand the instruments directly to the children.

Adults are used to being intermediaries between their children and the world. Think of MGOL as a great way to facilitate children interacting with adults outside the immediate family in a safe, responsive, and stimulating environment.

SAMPLE PROGRAM

MGOL at an EHS Center

by Lisa Tyson

Key Features

Expect children to sit in chairs, so add plenty of seated movement activities. Omit the full version of the welcoming comments if parents are not present because the same teachers attend every week. Instead, begin with a welcoming song that has simple movements, allowing everyone to join in. Use the adapted version of "Old Mother Goose."

Instead of singing a lullaby, use a scarf activity to help children calm themselves. As a part of your opening ritual, try something like "Wave, wave, wave your hands. Wave them in the air...wave them up high, wave them down low, wave in the middle, wave hello" (at the end, change this to "time to go") sung to a slow "Row, Row, Row Your Boat."

Section 1: Welcoming Comments
(Keep this very brief.)

Section 2: Rhymes and Reads
"Old Mother Goose" *(adapted version)*
"Jack and Jill"
"If You're Happy and You Know It"
"Zoom, Zoom, Zoom"

Section 3: Body Rhymes
Fingers: "The Itsy Bitsy Spider"
Hands: "Two Little Dickey Birds"
Book: Count with Maisy by Lucy Cousins

Section 4: The Drum Sequence
"Rum Pum Pum" *(names and syllables)*

Section 5: Stand-Up / Sit-Down Activities
"We're Marching to the Drum"

Section 6: Animal Activities
Book: I Spy on the Farm (sung to "I Went to Visit the Farm One Day")
"When the Duck Gets Up in the Morning" *(sung to the tune of "Here We Go Round the Mulberry Bush," with stuffed animals and fabric barn)*

Section 7: Musical Instruments and Scarves
Play a color matching game with the scarves.

Section 8: Lullabies
(Quiet activities with the scarves are used instead.)

Section 9: Interactive Rhymes
"Humpty Dumpty"

Section 10: Closing Ritual
"Can You Stomp with Two Feet?"
"We're So Happy"

NOTES

1. "About Us," Family Place Libraries, accessed June 16, 2018, https://www.familyplacelibraries.org/about-us.

2. Fred Rogers, *You Are Special* (Pittsburgh: Family Communications, 1994), 47.

Part III
Everywhere

Chapter 6

MGOL in Special Settings

RATHER THAN ONLY OFFERING SERVICES TO THOSE who physically come to the library, outreach programming enables us to reach a much wider group, often including both the underserved and the unserved. Outreach Mother Goose on the Loose (MGOL) serves families and individuals who may not have easy access to travel and may have limited experience with libraries. It touches special audiences such as teen moms, foster parents, inmates and their families, hospitalized children and their families, and children of all ability levels. It can be used as an intervention by home health visitors or as prevention for child abuse. It can also celebrate and unite families who speak other languages while celebrating traditions from different cultures and religious groups.

MGOL can also be used with adults for providing parent education, training parents to become facilitators, mentoring pre-K and kindergarten teachers, and showing teachers how to use MGOL to ease transitions. And senior citizens can enjoy their own brand of MGOL!

MGOL for Teen Moms and Their Children

According to the most recent figures published by the Centers for Disease Control and Prevention (www.cdc .gov/teenpregnancy/about/index.htm), the US teen pregnancy rate is higher than in other Western nations, with babies born to 22.3 out of 1,000 women between ages fif-

teen and nineteen. Teen moms are children themselves. They often lack basic parenting knowledge, which surfaces during MGOL programs for teen moms.

For instance, in Oakland, California, a teen parent said she was afraid of doing knee bounces with her baby because she did not want to be the cause of shaken baby syndrome. A reassuring explanation by the librarian enabled the parent to begin enjoying bouncing rhymes with her baby. In Traverse City, Michigan, a pregnant teenager told me that no one had ever sung to her, and she had never thought of singing to her baby until attending a MGOL session with a developmental tip about singing to your baby. Evenstart is a program through the

 Snapshot: MGOL by the Pool

Lisa Eck, librarian at the Roseville Public Library, combined MGOL programming with other fun activities in her community. Here is an e-mail she sent me (the author):

"Just finished MGOL with a Parent Tot swim time afterward! It was at the indoor pool here at the City of Roseville, CA. It was great—79 people for storytime, but I'm not sure about doing a storytime that requires me wearing a bathing suit in January, lol."

Flint Community Schools in Michigan that educates and trains teenage mothers who do not know how to interact with their children. During a 2007 MGOL workshop, teen moms were invited to join librarians for the full day of training. At the end of the day, one mom said in addition to learning new songs, she also learned how to play with her child, commenting, "I never realized how important it was to play. Now I can't wait to go home and play with my baby!" A new exciting pilot program in Baltimore, Maryland, brings MGOL into a school with pregnant and teen moms with a childcare center on-site. At the first session, the moms were told that the program would like to hire at least one participant at the end of the year to become a MGOL facilitator to lead a group in her own neighborhood. Those moms exhibited exceptional interest, enthusiasm, and participation. Hopefully at least some of the moms will be able to bring their enthusiasm back into their neighborhoods while also growing a skill that brings them financial compensation and self-esteem.

Key Features

MGOL for teen moms sometimes involves reciting rhymes and songs three times each rather than two. In addition to developmental tips and nursery rhymes, popular songs are incorporated into the program. Informal conversations with participants both before and after the session are essential.

Tips for Success

- Some schools have special classes for pregnant teens and teen moms; many of them have childcare on-site. These are the best places to offer programs for the teen moms—and dads too, if possible.
- In some teen parent programs, the participants are not there of their own free will but because they have to do the program (or another like it) to get free clothing and diaper vouchers. Do not be intimidated by hearing that your audience only attended reluctantly; if you make the program as fun as possible, they will enjoy it despite themselves.
- Invite pregnant teens to also participate even though they have not yet given birth. It is never too early to learn songs and rhymes.
- Prepare yourself mentally for an audience that is not automatically primed to enjoy your program. Teens often like to act cool and may not seem at all interested in what you are doing. Don't demand their attention; expect it.
- Arrive early, set up early, and be sure to take time before the session starts to engage parents in conversation. Ask nonjudgmental questions about their babies (e.g., "What new things has your child started to do recently?"), and listen more than you talk. This informal conversation helps everyone feel comfortable with each other before the program starts.
- Building a rapport with your audience is the most important ingredient for a successful program.
- Don't force anyone to participate. The parents will see after just a short period of time how much fun it is to participate.
- Include songs from popular culture (when ringing bells to a recording or clapping to a song) so there is some material with which the moms are already familiar.
- Since many teen moms are unfamiliar with nursery rhymes, speak slowly and repeat each rhyme three times instead of two during the first session to make it easy for participants to repeat it along with you.
- For the drum sequence, ask the moms to tap out their names too. Many of these adults might not have had the opportunity to play when they were kids, and being able to experience the play part for themselves can become a powerful learning opportunity.
- Make sure your developmental tips are conversational and not condescending or judgmental. Model the good practices associated with the tip. For instance, make sure to do "When the [Cow] Gets Up in the Morning" using a picture book without reading the words, and follow it with a tip about the benefits of looking at illustrations and singing about them with babies.
- Make sure there is also time after the session for informal conversations. Without being judgmental, try to discuss practices such as singing and playing with babies.

MGOL for Foster Parents

New foster parents are often keen to learn positive ways to interact with their children along with loving ways to direct behavior. Because MGOL provides all this, I (Betsy) have occasionally presented introductory sessions presented to foster parents. The developmental tips accompanying the rhymes explain the usefulness of cleanup songs for teaching cooperation in putting toys away, the value of freeze games for teaching stop, and the soothing quality of lullabies for calming agitated children.

Key Features

This adapted program for foster parents uses more developmental tips than usual, which means fewer rhymes in order to keep the length of the session to thirty minutes. Developmental tips about ways to build social and emotional skills must be included along with the early literacy tips.

Tips for Success

- Choose developmental tips that are short and easy to understand.
- Touch on all domains of school readiness with your tips; do not limit yourself to only focusing on language and literacy. For instance, use tips about learning to listen, pay attention, and follow directions.
- Scan current research on children's behavior and self-regulation skills to look for practical tips to share with parents.
- Emphasize the role played by the lullaby in calming a seemingly inconsolable child.

Using MGOL Activities during Early Head Start (EHS) Home Visits

MGOL works well in EHS because it fulfills Head Start regulations requiring regular home visits that include some type of music and movement with families. MGOL activities encourage parents as well as children to participate in music and movement activities, wordplay, and imagination play. MGOL provides the home socialization connection required by EHS standards by encouraging one-on-one, face-to-face conversations between parent and child, which improve attachment and bonding. It also fits well with the "Parents as Teachers" curriculum; by helping parents appreciate age-appropriate behavior and by promoting the social and emotional well-being of children, EHS staff aims to prevent the maltreatment of children. MGOL fits naturally into the environment and doesn't feel forced. Because it allows silliness and play to happen, it is easy for home visitors to use. The nursery rhymes make language learning easy because of their rhyming words, tone, and repetition.

Most EHS staff visit families in their homes in addition to seeing them on-site. MGOL activities for use during these EHS home visits were pioneered by Anne Bakker at the Venango County Families First EHS in Pennsylvania. Invited to a MGOL training at the Butler, Pennsylvania, library, Anne won a copy of the MGOL curriculum. She began adapting and implementing it immediately. In the six years since her home visitors have been using MGOL activities, literacy scores of the families have gone up significantly.

Home visitors come with a plan but vary it to fit the needs of the child, depending on the attitude or the emotions of the child that day. MGOL allows this by enabling nursery rhymes to be turned into opportunities for helping children develop self-esteem, self-regulation, and school readiness skills across all developmental domains. Children are often given the opportunity to lead the visit. Home visits are developed to incorporate age-appropriate child development activities and parent education components that align with EHS standards and the curriculum used.

Parents who require home visits may not spend much face time with their babies, preferring to give them something electronic. Due to depression, they may sit on the couch during an entire visit and refrain from interacting with their baby. Bringing out the colored scarves and musical instruments and singing songs often gets these parents involved. Since EHS incorporates all family members in a home visit, when older siblings are present, an extension of the activities for the younger child can be created. For instance, if a baby has been asked to tap on the drum, the older children can be asked to march around the room to a tambourine's beat. What child does not want to play with a tambourine and march around the room?

If your role as a children's librarian involves doing home visits, try using these adaptations. (For more information about MGOL and Head Start, see "Taking MGOL to Early Head Start and Head Start.")

Key Features

MGOL activities are expanded to include sensory activities that target the development of specific skills. Instead of a full session, specific activities are chosen ahead of time to be used with a small audience of one or two parents with one or more children. MGOL materials can be used in a variety of ways with parents and children, depending on the child's age and interest. Activities can vary by using different instruments, changing the tempo of the rhyme, and encouraging children to play with soft and loud sounds. Along with the activities, devel-

Snapshot: MGOL and Home Visits

Anne Bakker is the program supervisor / educational coordinator for community services of Venango County Families First EHS in Pennsylvania. Her home visitors use MGOL activities during home visits and carry them into socialization activities that are held twice a month with their families as well.

Home visits for each enrolled family take place one day each week, with a total goal of forty-six visits per family for the entire program year, so the possibility of MGOL being utilized in the home on a weekly or semiweekly basis is quite high. Because home visit staff members are experienced in this work, they are quickly able to adjust the activity for the temperature of the visit and the mood of the child.

Programs, schools, and agencies can utilize the basics of MGOL and individualize for the needs of the families they serve to assist parent-child attachment and bonding, which is so important for keeping families and children safe. MGOL has shown itself to be extremely beneficial to the EHS program, as we have seen parents who were previously subdued and resistant to singing out loud or simply being silly with their child become quite engaged and interactive. We are noticing an increase in the language and literacy skills of the children whose families are embracing the program and who were previously slower to develop these most important language skills.

MGOL activities can be used during home visits and carried into socialization activities held twice a month with families. In Venango County, each home visitor receives a MGOL canvas bag filled with a variety of musical instruments, scarves, dance ribbons, a nursery rhyme songbook, and a damage-proof book (such as a board book or one made with Tyvek). This bag is taken to each home, and the items are incorporated into every visit.

One rhyme can be chosen and used repeatedly for a month; it can also be incorporated into the two group socializations held each month for EHS families. By the end of the month, children are quite familiar with the rhyme they have practiced and played with. After using rhyme activities during home visits, the children are instantly engaged when EHS staff uses variations of MGOL as a gathering activity at the beginning of the socialization time. They understand that they are about to experience the fun they have been having during their home visits with that same rhyme. However, there's no need to stick to a specific activity each week since every family visit is individualized.

Choose developmental tips for use agency-wide, and share them with parents while emphasizing the importance of talking, singing, book-sharing, and playing with their children.

After just one MGOL training, home-based Families First EHS began using the activities in their home visits and socialization events. It assisted in enriching the bond between the parent or caregiver and the child, and in many cases, it brought a level of attachment into family units that was previously lacking. MGOL is a viable and easily accessible tool in assisting families to form secure attachments and bonds, which are vital to the development and well-being of the child.

opmental tips about the importance of talking, singing, book-sharing, and playing with their children are continually shared with parents.

Tips for Success
- Before starting a series of home visits, read through the MGOL curriculum and choose a few rhymes to use.
- Select tips from the MGOL curriculum that target common issues for families, encouraging certain types of behavior or responses. Print these tips on cards, laminate them, and put them on rings that can be attached to a diaper bag. After using a particular developmental tip with parents, give them the card with that tip on it.
- Try making musical instruments out of materials that can be found in the home, and model different things to do with them. A dance wand, for instance, is lots of fun and only requires a big Popsicle stick and some ribbon. With that, you can sing a song, march around the room, and then skip around the room.

SAMPLE PROGRAM

Using and Extending MGOL Activities during Home Visits

by Anne Bakker, program supervisor / educational coordinator for community services of Venango County Families First EHS in Pennsylvania

Key Features
Choose one or more MGOL rhymes, and present them in a variety of ways to stimulate different senses.

Example Rhyme
"Humpty Dumpty"

Example Activity
Recite the rhyme as a knee bounce. Show an illustration of Humpty Dumpty to emphasize the shape of an "oval." Incorporate a fine motor activity such as tracing an "egg," lacing string around the oval, coloring the inside of the shape, and so on. Then play a game with a collection of oval-shaped items, such as playing a matching or

sequencing game for cognition or using sensory materials such as shaving cream and food coloring to "paint" the egg. Play with sound by chanting the "Humpty Dumpty" rhyme with the parent and child or using musical instruments.

Using MGOL with Homeless Women and Children

Speaking about library services whenever you attend local coalition meetings or serve on boards can open doors to new opportunities. Kimberly White, a former children's librarian at the Otis Library in Norwich, built trust by serving on the citywide school readiness council where she made it a point to talk about programming at the library.

After Kim spoke about MGOL's success, the director of Thames River Transitional Housing (TRTH), an outreach and housing program for homeless women, asked Kim to bring MGOL there. TRTH provides a "safe space" lockdown facility with a series of at least fifty apartments. Residents are moms who have suffered some kind of traumatic experience and their children of varying ages (with quite a few newborns).

Kim focused on creating an environment where moms and kids would be comfortable using rhymes and songs. MGOL's repertoire of rhymes and its ready-to-go program format with early literacy tips made her job easier. The sessions took place in a play space with toys everywhere. Although "it's hard to compete with rocking horses," Kim let people play if they needed to. Going rapidly from one activity to the next, she kept the session moving but did not leave much time for reflection or conversation. In retrospect, Kim wishes she had encouraged more conversation, using fewer rhymes. She believes that sharing stories and helping people build connections is vital.

Key Features
Sessions at shelters don't use felt or flannel pieces but always start with gentle MGOL knee bounces like "Old Mother Goose" and "Goosey, Goosey Gander." The basic MGOL format with scarves, puppets, and a tambourine is followed. By paying attention to the energy of the group, the facilitators may shorten the session in favor

of more talk. Cardboard books for children to play with before and after the program are provided.

Tips for Success

- Serving on committees can not only help you become a respected part of the city but also open the door for participation in programs like this.
- To make traveling easier, eliminate the flannelboard and felt pieces.
- Take time to build up trust with program participants.
- It is fine to shorten your program. Your main goal is to spend quality time together and give a few tips that could prove valuable.
- Use a rhyme such as "Hickety pickety bumble bee, won't you say your name for me?" to learn everyone's name.

Taking MGOL
to Prisons

UNITED STATES PENAL INSTITUTIONS HOUSE APPROX-imately 2 million inmates, who are parents to more than 1.5 million children.[1] That means that 1 in 28 children have a parent in the penal system. According to the Casey Foundation, the average age of a child with an incarcerated parent is eight, while 22 percent are younger.[2] Along with losing family ties and parental rights, adult family members who are incarcerated can no longer contribute to their child's upbringing. This impacts the community because 95 percent of inmates who eventually return to society experience great difficulty reintegrating with their families, getting a job, and accessing community resources.[3] The result is a high rate of recidivism among formerly incarcerated individuals.

According to the Begin to Read website (http://begin toread.com), 60 percent of incarcerated adults and 85 percent of juveniles in the US penal system are functionally illiterate. Various reports also state that two-thirds of children who are illiterate by fourth grade will end up in the penal system.[4] Thus early literacy programs in prisons should have multiple goals: to work with adult inmates to improve their literacy skills, to let the adults know that they can have a powerful influence on the literacy of the children they care about, to teach playful activities that boost loving connections as well as literacy skills, and to encourage adult inmates to talk, read, play, and sing with their children.

Key Features

Inmates are treated like parents attending a typical Mother Goose on the Loose (MGOL) session, but facilitators should always be aware of safety concerns. Props must be chosen carefully; anything that could be used as a weapon will not be allowed into the prison.[5]

Tips for Success

- In order to get permission to bring MGOL into a prison, share information on the correlation between illiteracy and incarceration and the negative effects on children who lose a parent to the prison system to provide justification for your program. Use local statistics to make your case.
- Be aware of safety concerns.
- Create detailed schedules ahead of time and stick to them. To avoid any compromise of security and safety issues, expect the administration to scrutinize every action and interaction. An administrator will need to approve the date, time, location, participating inmates, outside guests, and number of attendees for each event.
- Look at the prison's website to find out the rules for visiting. Read about the intense entry search procedure so you know what to expect, look over the list of the types of materials that are not allowed in the prison to make sure that you are not bringing in

anything that could be considered contraband, and be aware of stringent dress codes.

- Treat the inmates like any other adult library visitors. Because of the intense screening that takes place before inmates can participate in your programs, the troublemakers have been weeded out. The people you are meeting are eager to learn and want to spend loving and productive time with their children. They are most likely thirsty for knowledge and will be grateful that you are sharing MGOL with them.

- Be respectful; don't ask questions about why the inmates are incarcerated and how their child is related to them. You are not there to find out about them; you are there to help strengthen their relationships with the children in their lives and to help their children reap all the benefits possible from attending MGOL sessions.

MGOL in High-Security Prisons for Men

Librarians in maximum security institutions work with inmates convicted for murder, drugs, and rape, among other offenses.

The inmates serve long sentences, some including life. According to Glennor, prior to incarceration, many inmates had no interaction with their children and had never visited a public library. In prison, however, the library becomes their sanctuary for peace and quiet and for seeking information to help maintain communication with family members on the outside. Presenting a tough image in the prison environment is important, so initially, these inmates are reluctant to openly ask for information dealing with family matters. Inmates gradually gain trust in their nonjudgmental information providers (librarians) and eventually share concerns about not wanting their children to end up in prison like themselves. These inmates often pass on the information they receive from the prison library to family members on the outside.

Snapshot: Bringing MGOL to Prisons

Glennor Shirley, a former library coordinator overseeing all the Maryland prison libraries, developed the program "Family Literacy @ your library" to allow inmates and their children to read together.

When I wanted to bring MGOL to the Jessup Correctional Institution, I pointed out that more than one-third of the children of inmates lived in Baltimore City areas where schools scored below performance standards and emphasized that an early literacy program would be a benefit to them.

Any program brought into the prison will require funding for additional staff. This includes ensuring the safety of outside guests, maintaining an environment that would not provide opportunities for an inmate to escape, preventing any harm to children, and eliminating opportunities for inmates and visitors to engage in contraband exchanges while entering or exiting the institution. While focusing on safety and security, prisons' management staff can also be sensitive to negative public reaction to what might be considered "benefits to criminals."

After months of negotiation and armed with facts, patience, and persistence, the library finally got permission for implementation, with a caution about strict adherence to the prison procedures and guidelines. Once the program was running, I made participation in MGOL an incentive for improved inmate conduct, as those with infractions would not be allowed to participate.

The aim of "Family Literacy @ your library" was to help bridge the illiteracy gap of parent and child, create more direct interaction between the inmates and their children (which might also include nephews, nieces, and cousins), and encourage the use of local public libraries. The success of this program, which began with help from Enoch Pratt Free Library and the MGOL coordinator, can be measured by the comments of inmates: "I never knew my child could read" and "I am no longer afraid to be silly with my children" (names withheld for legal reasons).

Before incarceration, many inmates were involved in serious crimes and did not consider their families a top priority. Instead, their lives revolved around their gangs or businesses. But after being sentenced to many years in a maximum-security prison, their thoughts turn inward. According to Glennor Shirley, the former library coordinator overseeing all Maryland prison libraries, men in maximum-security prisons think about their children, their nephew and nieces, or their cousins. After incarceration, family becomes the most important thing to them. While experiencing the anguish of life behind bars, these men begin hoping that their children will not follow in their footsteps. Their passion for drug deals and violence is often replaced by concern for family members. Many inmates focus on the younger family members, hoping to help them avoid behaviors that might land them in prison. But although there is a desire for connection, it is hard for inmates to create a warm relationship with the children they have ignored before entering prison. In addition, in most maximum-security prisons, visiting rooms consist of carrels with a glass wall between the inmate and his family members, limiting any kind of physical contact between children and their incarcerated relative.

Many inmates' children do poorly in school and have emotional issues. Glennor believes these children display a tendency to badness when there is no parenting support. While looking for a way to help the children get the adult support that they need and to give inmates a way to connect to the children in their lives in a productive way, Glennor heard about MGOL and decided to use it to turn inmates into mentors who could teach their children and encourage them to read. She envisioned a set of early literacy workshops to teach about the value of early literacy and to inspire the inmates to talk, sing, read, and play with their children. She also envisioned a MGOL session on visiting day, where inmates could physically interact in a positive way with their children.

The goal of MGOL in a prison setting is to share information about the importance of early literacy, gleaned from research, in order to prompt the inmates to interact with their children in literacy-enriching ways. To enable these interactions, I (Betsy) facilitated a MGOL program on visiting day. The inmates participated enthusiastically and shared positive connections with their children.

Key Features
Lots of information about early literacy is shared in prison programs, leading up to a visiting day MGOL session. The importance of "enthusiasm breeds enthusiasm" is emphasized when encouraging inmates to learn the rhymes before the program with their children. The importance of loving early literacy interactions between children and the important adults in their lives is consistently reinforced.

Tips for Success
- Keep track of the number of instruments you bring into the prison and the number of instruments you take out with you.
- Remember that although your program attendees are in prison, they still share many of the same concerns that your library parents have.
- Work with inmates ahead of time to ensure that they know the words to the nursery rhymes before your family session begins.
- Because there is no way to accurately know how many children will be coming on visiting day or what ages they will be, bring extra rhymes, books, and related materials for your MGOL session. Flexibility is key; for instance, prepare to turn MGOL into a preschool storytime if some of the children are under age six!
- Encourage use of the local library to the visitors and their children.
- Be prepared for disappointed inmates whose expected family visitors never arrive. Invite them to join in the circle and do the rhymes with you; tell them that it is good practice for them and that it enhances the program when more people participate. However, if they prefer to leave, reassure them that leaving is fine.

In Daycares at Women's Prisons

Some Early Head Start (EHS) programs are housed inside minimum-security prisons. MGOL activities can be used to encourage bonding and physical closeness there. With guided directions and modeling, the mothers participate in rhymes that go along with cuddling, rocking, bouncing, and hugging. Mothers or grandmothers

Snapshot: MGOL at the Men's Maximum-Security Prison in Jessup, Maryland

When I (Betsy) was the children's programming specialist for the Enoch Pratt Free Library in Baltimore, Glennor Shirley asked me to come to the maximum-security prison in Jessup to meet with inmates and run a few instructional classes, followed by an extended MGOL session for the inmates along with the children in their lives.

Since children sit on their parents' laps for MGOL, Glennor got special permission for the participating men to spend the visiting day in a larger room along with their families rather than on the other side of a glass partition.

In September of 2003, I presented three early literacy classes for inmates at the Jessup Maximum Security Prison. About thirty-six men in grey sweat suits attended the first class. An introduction to brain research mentioned that the architecture of the brain is formed in the earliest years of life and emphasized the importance of those years. I spoke about children looking to the adults in their lives as their first and best teachers, pointing out that children often learn by trying to imitate what their adults are doing. We discussed the upcoming visitor's day MGOL program, and I stressed the importance of participating enthusiastically rather than just sitting with the child and being a passive listener. Then I taught two fingerplays and asked everyone to repeat them with me over and over until we could recite them with gusto. Most of the inmates joined in reciting Barbara Cass-Beggs's rhymes "Two Little Dickey Birds" and "Fingers Like to Wiggle Waggle." They were a very receptive and attentive audience.

When I arrived the next week for the second class, an inmate came running up to me, excitedly calling out, "Miss Betsy, Miss Betsy, 'Two Little Dickey Birds' was the jailhouse hit this week!" The men had been practicing the rhymes as often as they could and recited them perfectly. Although it seemed silly to them at first, the idea that their enthusiastic participation could make a difference had taken root. The men not only had learned all the words and all the motions but also

asked for more rhymes to learn before the family session!

During the family visiting day MGOL program, all the inmates were actively engaged and seemed to enjoy what they were doing. Along with their children, they enthusiastically recited "Two Little Dickey Birds" and other nursery rhymes. Refreshments for the men and their children followed the session while I spoke with the caregivers (who were not in prison), explaining the value of singing and playing with their children and the importance of positive reinforcement. Each caregiver was handed a page-long list of positive words that had been used during the session and was asked to reinforce some of the MGOL early literacy practices at home. Glennor presented T-shirts and certificates to children who had finished the summer reading club.

The next week was my final meeting with the Family Literacy Committee men. We talked about the MGOL session, discussing programming techniques and theory put in action. We brainstormed ways to translate MGOL into the reality of their lives in prison with the challenges of a lack of materials, a difficult space (the visiting room had long narrow tables that could not be moved), once a month family visits, the difficulty of never knowing who would show up and who would not, and the wide variety of age groups.

I gave a brief presentation on good books to use with older children and asked the inmates to fill out evaluations. They were all positive, with many requests for similar workshops dealing with older children. One man, who kept making jokes about the adults doing fingerplays, wrote "NO MORE DICKEY BIRDS!"

and their children benefit from the direct interaction; the inmates appreciate not being outsiders watching someone else play with their child. Rhymes that end with a kiss or a great big hug are particularly useful. In addition, the use of music and "fun" objects such as egg shakers and colored scarves livens up the atmosphere.

When she worked at the Wilsonville Public Library in Oregon, youth services librarian Keren Joshi set up an early literacy program at a local minimum-security prison that housed EHS programs for children of incarcerated women. She utilized a flannelboard, books, musical instruments, and scarves in a program similar to MGOL and incorporated the first version of Every Child Ready to Read. She and another librarian worked with the EHS staff and presented storytimes for children from birth to three years old and their incarcerated parents. "Going in and having relationships with the babies and their mothers was really great, but it can be intimidating, so you have to treat it like a baby time at the library," she said. "Don't expect them to all know the books and songs. Assume that every time you visit, you are starting from the beginning. These women may not have been read to as kids, so they may not have that shared memory of curling up on their mom's lap. They are learning how to relax with books and they are getting to know their own kids too."

Dora Garraton (mentioned in chapter 5) brings her Goosemobile to female inmates as well as to schools and home daycares. According to Dora, women with extended sentences have limited time to spend with their children. Contact may be awkward since they are not in physical proximity with their children regularly. Sharing MGOL activities together provides a comfortable way for them to interact playfully.

Key Features

Activities are used to encourage bonding and physical closeness. Rhymes that promote positive physical interaction take precedence over the more passive rhymes. Parents are encouraged to informally share books with their children.

Tips for Success

- Before your first visit, contact the prison staff and ask what programs are already available for incarcerated parents. For instance, if the only contact parents have with their children is on visiting day, find out what is difficult about those visits and provide structure, such as an early literacy parent education seminar or giving parents books that they can share with their children. If there is an EHS, contact their staff and see if you can arrange a visit.

- Find out what details need to be worked out ahead of time. For instance, special permission must be granted from the prison administration for librarians to present the workshops and sessions. There will be background checks and restrictions on what can be brought in. Also, prison participants must be granted time away from their cells to attend the parent education classes, to be part of their children's EHS, and to participate in the visiting day MGOL sessions. Participation often requires inmates to remain infraction free.

- In order to ensure safety and value for this program, participants must be specially selected. The prison librarian can work with staff specialists, who handle files and the cases of each inmate, and the security staff, since their support and cooperation for the implementation of the program is needed. Criteria such as GED completion, a record of no prison infractions, and ensuring that the reason for incarceration was not for harm to children or sexual offenses can be applied.

- Treat visits like a baby time at the library, and don't expect mothers to all know the books and songs since this may be a new experience for them. You may need to start from the beginning each time you visit.

- Bring books to give away! Prison baby time programs are designed to introduce literacy and early literacy ideas and to publicize libraries and let inmates know that libraries exist to serve *everyone*. Bringing books to give away to children, inmates, and on-site daycares creates early literacy environments. Inmates can choose which books to read to their children while in prison, and on release, they can return home to a library of books they are already familiar with.

- Routinely carve out time during your programs for the adults to share a book aloud with their children.

- Don't assume that the inmates are literate. The adults might be illiterate or find reading uncomfortable. They may have never used the public library and might feel awkward having a librarian "outsider" come in.
- Look at each individual as a library visitor rather than as an inmate. Interact in the here and now, and do not judge anyone.

NOTES

1. Lauren E. Glaze and Laura M. Maruschak, "Parents in Prison and Their Minor Children," Bureau of Justice Statistics, 2008, https://www.bjs.gov/content/pub/pdf/pptmc.pdf; Steve Christian, "Children of Incarcerated Parents," National Conference of State Legislatures, March 2009, https://www.ncsl.org/documents/cyf/childrenofincarceratedparents.pdf.

2. Annie E. Casey Foundation, "Children of Incarcerated Parents Fact Sheet," Child Abuse and Neglect Technical Assistance and Strategic Dissemination Center, 2017, https://cantasd.acf.hhs.gov/wp-content/uploads/2017/02/aecf-childrenofincarceratedparents factsheet.pdf.

3. National Reentry Resource Center, "Facts and Trends," Council of State Governments, 2018, https://csgjustice center.org/nrrc/facts-and-trends/.

4. TROYATLMS, "The Relationship between Incarceration and Low Literacy," *The Official Blog of Literacy Mid-South* (blog), March 16, 2016, https://literacy midsouth.wordpress.com/2016/03/16/incarceration -and-low-literacy/.

5. *Maryland Division of Correction Inmates Handbook* (Towson: Department of Public Safety and Correctional Services, 2007), https://www.dpscs.state.md.us/publicinfo/publications/pdfs/2007_Inmate_Handbook .pdf. "The warden can deny a visit from anyone on an inmate's visiting list if there is good reason. Visitors may be denied entrance if they might be a threat to security, staff, inmates or the prison operations. Visits also may be denied where there has been a violation of visiting rules. *Visiting privileges shall be suspended for six months the first time an inmate is found guilty of certain rule violations*" (23).

Snapshot: Parenting Programs for Incarcerated Mothers

Terri Wortman, children's services librarian at the Wilsonville Public Library, started presenting programs at Coffee Creek Correctional Facility in Wilsonville, Oregon, about nine years ago and has continued to serve the moms and their children to this day.

We visit once a month, providing a short circle time (15–20 minutes) in the morning and a mom's literacy info group in the afternoon. During the afternoon portion, we do the following over the course of an hour:

- We recount and review how the circle time went for the babies/preschoolers. The moms share what is happening with their children in relation to reading, literature, or their relationship. Lots of sharing and learning happens in this part!
- The librarian shares a simple teaching point about literature.
- During craft time, we devise a craft that relates to the teaching point or story we shared during circle time. We bring craft materials to make something that the moms then use during the following month. The next month, the moms report how it worked out. There's a lot of learning with this. Moms love to make things with their hands, and time to be creative is a rare activity considering their living environment.
- Each mom picks out two books to keep. This is fun for them as they look through the new board and picture books we've purchased.
- We often sing our good-bye song with them, as it is full of sunshine and hope.

The women express much appreciation for our time with them. Carmen Slothower, the current Head Start teacher at Coffee Creek, is looking into how to reproduce the Head Start program in other correctional facilities throughout the United States.

Snapshot: Teaching Prisoners to Share Books with Babies

Keren Joshi, a youth services librarian formerly with the Wilsonville Public Library in Oregon, designed an MGOL-like program for the Coffee Creek Correctional Facility, a minimum-security prison that provides EHS programs for children of incarcerated women. Children from birth to age three attending the program were either born inside the prison or were born shortly before their mothers were incarcerated. Some lived with relatives or were in foster care.

The in-house EHS program at the Coffee Creek Correctional Facility hosted children of incarcerated mothers for three and half hours, twice a week. Mothers who were accepted into the program spent two mornings a week with their children in a typical early childhood center decorated with brightly colored rugs and furnishings. Participating mothers also attended parent education sessions without their children once a week to learn more about parenting topics such as nutrition, literacy, child development, and childcare.

Once a month when parents and children were both present, the library offered an on-site storytime involving music and books. In the afternoon, after the children left, the librarians spoke with the incarcerated moms about early literacy skills, explaining why they chose particular books and songs and presented them the way they did. For instance, during one parent session, I explained what print awareness was and why the specific book used in storytime had been chosen. Then I suggested that parents try holding books upside down while sharing them with their babies to see if their babies would notice that the print was facing a different way. When I returned the next month and asked about the experiences parents had had with their children, many of them responded that they had tried the exercise and their babies flipped the books right side up again!

We also gave away free books, some for the classroom and some for the children and their mothers to keep. During the first six months of the program, we saw incredible changes. The moms went from not being comfortable reading to their kids to sprawling on the floor and sharing books happily. They learned what reading with babies looks like and saw that it does not mean reading every word and turning every page. Because

Moms select books for their children.

of this, we saw a huge improvement in the way parents read with their children. It was exciting to see the moms go from thinking that reading with babies was hard and silly to thinking that reading with babies was easy and could be done all the time. It was just another way to play.

Once an ease with using books developed, the parents and the EHS staff passed it on to new mothers entering the program. Sharing books joyfully and informally with children had become part of the culture.

Just before being released, each mom received a package with information about her local library in order to encourage her to go to their public library and take advantage of its resources. One mom lived on a reservation and was incensed to learn there was no library there. On her release, she stated, "We need a library!" A year later, the EHS staff reported to me that the woman had begun to work to open a library on the reservation.

Taking MGOL
to Hospitals

OUTREACH TO HOSPITALIZED CHILDREN TAKES MANY forms and can reach a wide variety of ages. Direct programs or early literacy activities for children include storytime on the unit, bedside storytimes and play, family services center storytimes, and clinic visits. Programs for adults include early literacy programming in NICU lounges for parents or caregivers of hospitalized babies and programs for hospital staff and volunteers.

Children may be hospitalized and isolated for a few days, weeks, or months. Adults spending time with their hospitalized children may feel isolated in addition to being consumed with worry. Outreach programming can include these adults as well as their children. Involvement in Mother Goose on the Loose (MGOL) activities gives them a sense of normality; enables them to interact with their children in safe, nonmedical ways; adds some joy into their lives; and gives them incentives for practicing good early literacy behaviors with their children.

Hospital users include people from all economic, racial, and cultural backgrounds. Many families you meet may not be familiar with the public library. Use the opportunity to publicize library services. If possible, allow people to sign up for library cards using e-cards. Give out fliers advertising library events or services. Be sure to talk to the adults as well as the children, letting them know that the public library is a space open for free to everyone.

Key Features

The wide range of outreach opportunities in hospitals includes early literacy kits, clinic waiting room activities and crafts, library card sign ups, hospital television or radio stories, circulating book collections, book giveaways, and storytimes. MGOL programs include bedside storytimes, inpatient and family center storytimes, NICU family lounge programs for parents, and staff and volunteer literacy training. Be prepared for distractions, and think carefully before selecting the items for use in your program.

Tips for Success: Setting Up Your Program

Remember that your top priority must always be health.

- Meet with your supervisor before contacting anyone at the hospital. Together, look at the library's outreach mission, the available funding, and the time you can realistically be away from the library. The process of becoming a hospital volunteer or storyteller is very time consuming, often requiring many visits for blood tests and paperwork, so it is essential to have your supervisor's support.
- In order to create a hospital outreach program, you must first find a hospital near you that serves children. Search http://childrenshospitals.org for local children's hospitals serving children from birth to age eighteen. Check if a nearby university has a

medical school with a teaching hospital for children by Googling "hospital" and your zip code.

- To bring MGOL into a hospital, it is easiest to contact someone you already know who is affiliated with the hospital. Since most hospitals with services for children have a "child life department," try contacting the child life specialist if you don't already know someone. Call or e-mail to set up a meeting, and don't get discouraged if you don't get a response right away. Emergencies can distract anyone from their to-do list. If no one responds, wait a fair amount of time and try again—and again. If need be, call the switchboard operator, explain what you are looking for, and ask to be put in contact with a different professional who may be more amenable to the program you are proposing.

- Once there is someone to talk to, describe the type of program you would like to offer, and ask if the hospital's child life representative would be willing to meet with you. If that doesn't work, try speaking with the volunteer coordinator, the department social worker, or the hospital librarian (especially if there is a children's collection!). Or if you hope to target a specific department, find out who works there ahead of time and ask to speak to the person you think would be most likely to want to partner with the library. The person you eventually find will become your champion. Because there are so many hoops to jump through in order to present hospital programs, having a champion on the inside can make all the difference.

- When dealing with fragile populations, ask a medical professional to check your program before you present it. Rhymes and song choices matter.

- Before doing any kind of work in the hospital, be prepared to complete one or more trainings on hospital safety practices. You may be asked to take an exam to show you understand the material. Presenting immunization records, taking TB tests, and providing proof of yearly flu shots are standard procedures for becoming a hospital volunteer or employee. This takes time and often must be done during working hours, which is another reason why having your supervisor's support is so important.

- Once you have a hospital contact person, check out the space where you will be presenting your program. Will it be in a dedicated playroom, a family lounge, or a standard hospital room? Will you need to move furniture or bring in special equipment to present your program? Will you be able to store program items at the hospital, or will you need to bring them in and out each time? Ask if there is storage space within the hospital for your equipment; if you need to transport everything each time, consider investing in a cart for toting all your materials.

- To convince hospital staff to direct patients to your programs, their approval is essential. If possible, present your proposed program to them by talking about mutual goals and soliciting feedback; taking into account what the hospital wants to accomplish leads to a more equitable collaboration. What is glaringly obvious to staff members might have been unknown to you, so their feedback can take your program off the path to disaster and steer it toward success. Having a say in the formation of the program builds their sense of partnership, which results in more encouragement for patients to participate.

- Come with ideas regarding what you can do and what the library can offer, but make sure you listen to the ideas of people you meet.

- Patient advisory boards can also provide useful feedback and support.

Tips for Success: Presenting Your Program

- Because keeping hospitalized children away from germs is of monumental importance, restrict flannelboard use to noninfectious children and don't use anything soft that can hold onto germs. Check with the medical staff; puppets and scarves can sometimes be used if children are not allowed to share them and they are washed after every use.

- Be prepared for distractions! Children may be hooked up to beeping monitors or machines. Hospital staff may interrupt to take children's vital signs. Very sick children may not have energy to participate even though they enjoy being part of the session. Children most likely will be sitting on chairs, in wheelchairs, or on mobile beds rather than sitting on the floor on their parents' laps. Medical staff attending your program may need to exit abruptly if they are called out for an emergency.

- Be aware of the rhymes you plan to use, and make sure they will not exclude any children in your program. For instance, children with limited mobility or range of movement will not be able to dance or play freeze games. Body normative songs, books, and rhymes won't work well for children who are disfigured or disabled. For instance, do not sing "Head, Shoulders, Knees, and Toes" or read books such as *Ten Little Fingers, Ten Little Toes* to children missing digits. Children in wheelchairs will not be able to perform activities that involve standing up.
- It is imperative to always disinfect everything! Sanitize instruments after use and again in the twenty-four hours before the storytime. Keeping everything clean and sterile should be of utmost importance.
- Library books in circulation must not come into contact with anyone but the program facilitator. When planning your program, keep in mind that you can never let children see the books up close or touch them for contamination reasons.
- Be sensitive to the families' situations while selecting lullabies. Avoid any lullabies that imply harm or a child being "taken away" ("Rock-a-Bye, Baby" and the traditional words to "You Are My Sunshine" are two examples).
- It is best not to use songs, books, or rhymes that allude to death or harm.
- Magnetic boards can be used in place of flannelboards; laminate the characters so they can be wiped down after the program, and attach magnetic strips to the back.

Bedside Storytime

Rather than running an entire MGOL program for children who are confined to bed, a short storytime or a few select MGOL activities work well. Always introduce yourself to the bedridden child (and adults, if present) and say you are from the library. Present a shortened storytime with one story and one song for preschoolers. Use a few MGOL activities for younger children, and read aloud from a board book or an "indestructible" book (made from Tyvek) that can be washed and sanitized after use. Leaving the books you've used with the caregivers gives them something constructive to share with their child during the long hours at the hospital while also building language and literacy skills.

Key Features

Selected activities from MGOL are chosen to fit the age and capabilities of the hospitalized child. When possible, include caregivers in the activity or model how to talk, sing, read, use fine motor skills, and play with the child.

Tips for Success

- Don't present an entire program. Just choose selected activities to use with bedridden patients.
- Only use brand new books, not library books. Plan to bring enough books so that you can leave one with each patient.
- Do not wake a sleeping child! Sleep is the best medicine of all.
- Be prepared for noise and interruptions; children may be hooked up to beeping equipment or hospital staff may interrupt to take vital signs. Very sick children may not have energy to participate but can still enjoy the interaction.
- Expect to interact with children who are sitting on chairs, in wheelchairs, or in mobile beds rather than sitting on their parents' laps.

Storytime in Inpatient Units

Storytime in inpatient units often takes place in communal areas. The audience may include children of all ages; parents may or may not attend. While following the typical structure of a MGOL session works well, since it is hard to know in advance the ages of new patients, extra read-aloud books should be available in case mostly older children attend. Preventing germs from spreading is of utmost importance; only props that are easy to clean and disinfect should be used. For the same reason, scarves and puppets are eliminated. When children are not mobile, the stand-up/sit-down activities section is skipped.

Key Features

This program follows the typical MGOL format, but adaptations for health reasons are required. To keep germs from spreading, nothing soft is used, and nothing is passed from hand to hand. Only new books are used; library books that have been handled by others are off-limits. When children have physical limitations, exercises that require movements like standing up are skipped. To avoid creating situations where children with missing or paralyzed limbs feel self-conscious, review the "Tips for Success" from the introduction to chapter 8, "Taking MGOL to Hospitals."

Tips for Success

1. Eliminate rhymes that involve touching the same objects (e.g., "Hickory Dickory Dare" and "Humpty Dumpty").
2. Discard stand-up / sit-down activities if space is tight or children have mobility issues.
3. Revise the order of the sections; do the drum sequence *after* handing out the musical instruments, and invite the children to use their instruments as drumsticks. Keeping hands off the drum helps the patients avoid multiple points of physical contact.

SAMPLE PROGRAM

MGOL in Hospitals

by Amanda Bressler

This is an example of a storytime that Amanda Bressler presented twice a month on an inpatient unit at Boston Children's Hospital, where most of the children were birth to age five.

Section 1: Welcoming Comments

Section 2: Rhymes and Reads

"Old Mother Goose"
"Hey Diddle Diddle"
Book: Where's Spot? by Eric Hill

What to Bring

Items to bring to hospital programs for children include the following:

- new books
- easy-to-clean instruments or props
- materials for library card sign-up
- library information, including a map, a list of locations, and how-to information regarding e-books

Items not to include in your programs include the following:

- library books that have already been in circulation
- puppets
- flannelboard and felt pieces
- instruments with little crevices
- anything that could be a choking hazard
- anything to be passed around or touched by more than one child

This list was compiled by Amanda Bressler.

Section 3: Body Rhymes

Hands: "We Clap Our Hands Together"
Body: "Alouette"
Knee Bounces: "The Grand Old Duke of York"
Knee Bounces: "Zoom, Zoom, Zoom"
Knee Bounces: "To Market, To Market"

Section 4: The Drum Sequence *(done later)*

Section 5: Stand-Up / Sit-Down Activities *(not done)*

Section 6: Animal Activities

"Old MacDonald" *(with book)*
"Five Little Speckled Frogs"
"Elephants Have Wrinkles" *(This can also be a body rhyme.)*

Section 7: Musical Instruments and Scarves

Bells: "We Ring Our Bells Together"
Bells: "Ring Your Bells Today"

Bells: "Do You Know the Ice Cream Man?"

Bells: "Horsey, Horsey on Your Way"

Bells: "Are You Sleeping, Brother John?" / "Frère Jacques"

Bells: "Miss Mary Mack"

Section 4: The Drum Sequence

(Have children use bells as drumsticks.)

"Rum Pum Pum"

"Bells Away"

Section 8: Lullabies

"I Love You, You Love Me"

Section 9: Interactive Rhymes *(not done)*

Section 10: Closing Ritual

"The More We Get Together"

Family Support in Neonatal Intensive Care Units

A recent shift from open rooms in Neonatal Care Units (NICUs) to private rooms has many benefits, including family-centered care and greater privacy. However, it has brought a new challenge; a 2014 article by Pineda et al. in the *Journal of Pediatrics* shows that premature babies who stay in private rooms often show lower language and motor scores at two years of age than those who stay in an open ward.[1] MGOL Goslings is a new program created to provide medically appropriate interventions to enhance infant language and literacy, especially in NICUs. Goslings combines MGOL rhymes, songs, and props with empowering parents in their roles as their baby's caregivers by teaching them how to interpret their premature baby's signals. Parents participate in activities for lovingly interacting with their babies, and songs are tailored to increase bonding. For instance, a slow "Since I love you very much, I'll make a heart" replaces the peppy "If you're happy and you know it, clap

Snapshot: MGOL at Boston Children's Hospital

Before becoming the supervisor of youth services at the Newton Free Library, Amanda Bressler was the sole youth outreach librarian for the Boston Public Library. She started a partnership with Boston Children's Hospital in 2014 as a single storytime for children waiting for surgery or postsurgery on a single unit and then expanded her programming to include the Boston Medical Center and Massachusetts General Hospital as well. She brought library services into clinic settings, providing books, presenting programs, and offering trainings to staff and volunteers.

I think singing with a book—using a book with farm animals to do "Old MacDonald"—was most surprising for the audience, which is the case in almost all the storytimes I do. I find it gives parents' permission to play around with books and illustrations rather than just read over and over, and when they carried that over into the other parts of their hospital stay, that was a success for me. This was particularly important because Boston Children's Hospital has patients from around the world and many don't speak English well or at all. I hoped using the book for activities other than reading would encourage them since they didn't have to read English to interact.

The instruments were always the favorite part of the program no matter what we did with them! "The Grand Old Duke of York" was always a hit when we did it at different speeds. Most classic songs—"Twinkle, Twinkle," "The Wheels on the Bus," "Old MacDonald," and so on—were successful as well. In the hospital setting where things can be unpredictable and people are far from home, familiar songs are very comforting.

your hands." Learning how to interpret signs and signals and interact appropriately with their medically fragile babies is combined with fostering early language and literacy skills. Parents who cannot yet have physical contact with their babies are empowered as caregivers when shown how to lovingly build their literacy skills from the very first days of life.

My original idea to form MGOL Goslings, a program for parents of premature babies, blossomed due to a successful collaboration between children's librarians, a children's museum, early literacy specialists, a child development specialist, medical personnel, parents of premature babies, researchers, and funders. Its design was guided by feedback from a NICU advisory board, medical professionals, researchers, and parents, and it incorporates research showing the health benefits when caring adults share music with premature babies,[2] the importance for NICU babies to hear their parent's voices,[3] and the positive influences that lullabies have on premature babies' cardiac and respiratory functions, vital signs, feeding behaviors, and sucking patterns.[4]

Premature babies need different kinds of interactions than healthy, full-term babies; song choices and rhymes are adapted to model best practices. For instance, the original version of "Open Them, Shut Them" tells you not to let fingers into your mouth. However, developmental

Snapshot: MGOL Goslings

MGOL Goslings was developed collaboratively by Betsy Diamant-Cohen, Port Discovery Children's Museum, and the University of Maryland Children's Hospital (UMCH). It is now in its second year in the Drs. Rouben and Violet Jiji Neonatal Intensive Care Unit, a level 4 NICU at the University of Maryland Medical Center Children's Hospital. The University of Maryland, Baltimore County (UMBC), has been researching the impact of the program. Dr. Brenda Hussey-Gardner, associate professor of pediatrics at the University of Maryland School of Medicine provided medical oversight and guidance. The program uses Dr. Hussey-Gardner's easy-to-understand guide for parents, a booklet called "Understanding My Signals." Large photographs and simple-to-understand descriptions of the signs that preemies give are accompanied by suggested responses for parents. In her words:

Research shows that babies born prematurely are at high risk for language delays, and early interventions need to be developed to ameliorate this. Goslings is one such intervention and so much more! Goslings shows parents how to tailor interactions based on their baby's medical status and behavioral signals. It helps parents determine when it's OK to talk quietly, talk and touch their baby, or talk, touch, and show toys. It coaches them to talk, sing, and read in a soft voice and provides them with the words to songs and nursery rhymes that were specifically written to foster feelings of love and attachment. It provides parents the opportunity to practice talking and singing to their baby while showing him or her books, rattles, and other toys in a developmentally supportive manner. Goslings also helps parents understand that sometimes it's best to simply let their baby sleep. Goslings does all this in a group setting that allows parents to realize that all NICU babies need special interactions, not just their baby, and that all NICU parents need to learn these strategies, not just them. It allows parents to practice these skills in a warm and supportive environment with dolls and pretend isolettes. By the time parents are done with the seventy-five-minute session, they are able to go to their room and immediately begin implementing what they learned. Research findings show that parents love the program, recommend it to other NICU parents, and implement the strategies they are taught. They learn to read their baby's signals and talk and sing more to their babies. In addition, nurses report seeing a positive difference in the way that parents interact with their baby's after attending Goslings. Staff at the University of Maryland NICU are thrilled with Goslings and hope to have it continue for a very long time!

specialists encourage premature babies to put their fingers in their mouths; the babies console themselves and find comfort in sucking on hands and fingers. It fosters the development of muscles needed for eating and talking. Because we *want* these babies to put their hands in their mouths, the final words can be changed from "But do not let them in" to "And then invite them in."

While giving an early literacy foundation to the youngest children, Goslings also teaches parents how to talk, sing, read, and play with their children. Through literacy, children's librarians want to help children be the best they can be. While hospitals may not have the time or funding to train staff to run Goslings programs, this may be an important outreach role for libraries and children's museums. It could occur once every two weeks or be a once-a-month program. Offering Goslings programs can be outreach at its finest, improving the lives of parents and our youngest children from all racial, cultural, and economic backgrounds.

Key Features

MGOL Goslings uses many traditional MGOL songs, but most of them are adapted in some way. Everything is recited or sung softly and slowly. All movements are slow and cautious. Each activity is accompanied by a description of how it should be used according to the signals the baby is giving. Songs and rhymes are adapted to include loving words as often as possible to promote bonding.

Tips for Success

NICU infants are extremely vulnerable; activities presented in the wrong way may cause harm. Therefore, it is imperative to only present programs in NICUs that have been vetted by qualified medical professionals, such as MGOL Goslings.

- The team that put Goslings together is working on creating a training program that includes appropriate early literacy activities, necessary medical information, and all the logistical information needed to run successful Goslings' programs. If you are interested in learning more about it, please contact Betsy at betsydc@mgol.org.
- Encourage the adults to learn by doing.
- Tell parents to modify the activities according to the medical status of the child that day. Match the level

Snapshot: Parents Speak

Jessica and Stan, the mother and father of twins who had been released from the hospital after a lengthy stay, shared the following:

These two guys were born at twenty-seven weeks earlier this year and were admitted to the NICU. We had a pretty lengthy stay. We were there every day, but we weren't really sure how to interact with them in that environment. We attended one of the very first Mother Goose on the Loose classes, and it was extremely helpful for us. It taught us to read their signs to see what kind of activities would be good for them that day; it gave us a book of songs that we could sing to them and told us how to read books that rhyme and to kind of turn them into songs. We still sing the same songs to them today. We use the toys, like the scarves and the rattles. And it also taught us how to incorporate new things as they progress from the isolette to the crib and eventually to home.

We would highly recommend this program for all the other NICU parents and especially those first-time parents like us.

of activity to the type of day the child is having; after a surgical procedure, it is often best to refrain from any activity and let the child sleep.
- Give adults the opportunity to talk about their child, but do not insist that they contribute. Some parents prefer to keep their situation private.
- Provide dolls for the parents of premature babies to use during your program so they can practice different ways to interact with their babies. Reflect the real multicultural world by choosing dolls with different skin colors and facial features such as "Tender Touch Baby Dolls" by Discount School Supply and "Feels Real Baby Dolls" by Lakeshore.
- Use a magnetic board in place of a flannelboard; laminate the characters so they can be wiped down after the program and attach a magnetic strip to the back.

- To listen or download free recordings of songs for use in the Goslings' program, visit the Goslings' dedicated page on the MGOL website (https://mgol.net/home/mother-goose-on-the-loose-goslings/songs).
- Adapt songs to remind parents of important behavior. For instance, singing "Two Little Goslings" reminds them that sleep is very important for the health and survival of their preemie. Rather than waking up their child to play when they arrive for a visit, these parents will understand that it is best to let their child sleep.
- Lyrics can be adapted to enable parents to at least give verbal hugs and expressions of love to their babies.

Hospital Programs for Staff and Volunteers

Many hospitals have volunteers who work with hospitalized children by talking, singing, and playing with them when parents are unavailable. These volunteers often benefit from trainings on appropriate ways to use books and share early literacy practices with children of different ages. As mentioned in the "Bedside Storytime" section, modified MGOL activities work well with bedridden children! Information sessions regarding library services can prove extraordinarily helpful to hospital staff and volunteers. Mobile library card sign-ups can encourage staff and volunteers to make use of your library's resources.

Key Features

Rather than focusing on a presented program, this adaptation teaches about MGOL so staff and volunteers will understand its value, encourage hospitalized children and parents to attend programs, and be able to use the MGOL activities with their patients if desired.

Tips for Success

- Check to see if your partner hospital has a program for volunteers.
- Find out who is in charge, and ask that person if you can attend a training session.
- Once you have observed the training, think about what you can contribute and ask your partner if you can be a presenter at the next training.
- Don't push to make changes too quickly; slow and steady wins the race!
- Give volunteers a pamphlet with a list of songs and rhymes that you typically use. Include short developmental tips that can be shared with parents.

NOTES

1. R. G. Pineda et al., "Alterations in Brain Structure and Neurodevelopmental Outcome in Preterm Infants Hospitalized in Different Neonatal Intensive Care Unit Environments," *Journal of Pediatrics* 164, no. 1 (2014): 52–60.
2. Z. Alipour et al., "Effects of Music on Physiological and Behavioral Responses of Premature Infants: A Randomized Controlled Trial," *Complementary Therapies in Clinical Practice* 19, no. 3 (2013): 128–32.
3. S. Arnon et al., "Live Music Is Beneficial to Preterm Infants in the Neonatal Intensive Care Unit Environment," *Birth* 33, no. 2 (2006): 131–36.
4. M. Bargiel, "Lullabies and Play Songs: Theoretical Considerations for an Early Attachment Music Therapy Intervention through Parental Singing for Developmentally At-Risk Infants," *Canadian Journal of Music Therapy* 9, no. 1 (2002); H. Blumenfeld and L. Eisenfeld, "Does a Mother Singing to Her Premature Baby Affect Feeding in the Neonatal Intensive Care Unit?" *Clinical Pediatrics* 45, no. 1 (2006): 65–70.

Adapting MGOL for Children of All Abilities

BECAUSE OF MOTHER GOOSE ON THE LOOSE'S (MGOL) accepting, nonjudgmental atmosphere, many adults feel comfortable bringing children who have difficulty sitting still or who have been diagnosed with conditions that impair their self-regulation skills. MGOL activities are designed to promote self-esteem for all children while helping their parents recognize and take pride in their children's simple achievements. Watching others applaud their child can provide sustenance to a parent who has been having a difficult day. Modeling positive reinforcement words gives parents language to celebrate even the smallest steps forward. And music is a universal language for everyone.

Any child with special needs should be able to participate in and benefit from attending a traditional MGOL session. However, with some modifications, sessions can run smoother and be even more beneficial by focusing on specific abilities. The first MGOL inclusive storytime took place at the Maryland State Library for the Blind and Physically Handicapped. Since then, different types of MGOL programs have been adapted for children with a wide range of abilities.

Key Features

Following the standard MGOL format, programs are modified to meet the needs and abilities of each specific audience.

Tips for Success

Attracting an Audience

- Before planning your program, decide if you are creating it for children with a specific diagnosis (e.g., children with autism or deaf children) or if it will be an inclusive program for everyone. When advertising, be sure to use the word *inclusive* or add the phrase "accommodations for people with disabilities available." If possible, include the name of someone who can answer questions (e.g., "Contact Betsy at this phone number"). Parents and caregivers are more likely to ask questions and share information with a specific person rather than just calling the library's main number or information desk.
- If looking to start a MGOL program for children with the same disability, you may want to seek a partner (e.g., a speech therapist or a physical therapist) to help.
- Since families of children with special needs often have many medical appointments, you may need personal contact, either with the families or the professionals who work with them, to convince them that the library is a valuable resource for their family.
- Try inviting community organizations to the program, and offer to present some sessions at their sites.

- Ask a parent of a child with special needs who visits the library to help inform others in the community of the upcoming program.
- Send a blurb about your program to health-based organizations, advocacy groups, and pediatricians. Follow it up with a phone call, asking them to encourage parents to bring their children.
- Remember that you are a facilitator of relationships and not a performer. Be a positive but not preachy role model. Encourage bonding between caregivers and their babies or children through the activities that you are modeling, whether it is blowing kisses to a child who can't look directly at you via a mirror, soothing an anxious child with a lullaby, or placating an ever-moving child with knee bounces.

Preparing the Library Staff

Be sure to inform the entire library staff about your upcoming program and stress the importance of making everyone feel welcome. Prepare the circulation staff to expect visitors who have not been in the library before and may not be familiar with typical library behaviors or procedures.

- Encourage *all* library staff to say a welcoming word to everyone.
- Request their patience for first-time library users who may request repeat explanations of procedures.
- Explain that children are not "behaving badly"; they are probably doing the best they can with their particular disability. Patience and a smile go a long way for the parents of these children.

Preparing for Your Sessions

- Practice speaking slowly in front of a mirror ahead of time if need be. Speaking slowly gives everyone more time to process what is being said—but don't speak too slowly!
- Consider adopting a policy of 90 percent repetition rather than 80 percent.
- Remember that gentle guidance and verbal encouragement can help when a child is not sure about something, but activities should always be voluntary with nothing forced.
- In some cases, you may be asked to run a MGOL program for a group of children with a specific disability. Be sensitive to physical capabilities and restrictions. Consider your audience, and list the types of adaptations needed.

  » Children with autism may feel uncomfortable with loud sounds (use soft-sounding shakers, not loud bells).
  » Children with low vision may need to sit near you and have tactile rhyme representations.
  » Children with physical disabilities may not be able to leave their wheelchairs.
  » Use bells that go around the wrist if the child can't grasp the handle.
  » Some children may consistently make noises (try to use a portable microphone and headset).
  » Some children may not be able to sit still at all (arrange the room in a way that gives them space to move but does not let them go running out of the room unsupervised).
  » Some children get overwhelmed by noise (encourage them to wear a headset that blocks out noise).

Snapshot: MGOL for Children of All Abilities

Dr. Jordan Sachse, an occupational therapist, ran a MGOL program with Betsy for children with developmental delays and their parents. She also used MGOL activities at home with her children.

I've run several programs: programs for mothers with disabilities and programs for children with a variety of developmental disabilities ranging from limb differences to spina bifida, hydrocephalus, and speech and language differences. One of the things that is most powerful and most special about MGOL is that it can be used as a treatment intervention where families and children can participate together. Families get this beautiful parent training piece built into the group. The beauty of MGOL is that it's fun, and children just naturally get this repetition and practice, not only within each session but from week to week. There is wonderful carryover.

(See also the "Together Time" snapshot.)

- If appropriate, cue children by stating their name or touching them lightly on the arm.
- If loud noise is distracting or uncomfortable for the children, tone down the music so it's not as loud as usual or use rain shakers, which aren't as noisy as egg shakers.
- Keep the flannelboard out the entire time, and display small pictures of each section (for example, rhymes and reads could be denoted by a picture of musical notes and a book) in the order in which they are presented during the session. As each section finishes, put the picture away to show that you are done with that activity and moving on to the next.
- Pay attention to the language you use, focusing on "person first" or strength-based language. For instance, instead of saying "Joe has ADD," use "Joe has a diagnosis of ADD." Instead of targeting Ryan's behavior problems, focus on the fact that he "needs behavioral support."

- When possible, invite parents to stay and play after the session has finished. Having the opportunity to socialize with other parents who may be dealing with similar issues can be beneficial for everyone.
- Take out toys such as sensory balls, cardboard books, and wooden puzzles for children to play with once the session has finished.

Modifications for Children on the Autism Spectrum

The autism spectrum encompasses a wide range of behaviors. It can include involuntary movements and noises, sensitivity to sound, and avoidance of eye contact. Volunteer Janet Shepherd brought MGOL to a school for children on the autism spectrum with Tammi, a Karma Dog who had been specially trained to work with children of all abilities. Janet modified the sessions by repeating songs numerous times and eliminating the loud

Snapshot: Attending MGOL with a Son on the Autism Spectrum

Roxanna is the mother of Luis, who was two when she began bringing him to Buena Casa, Buena Brasa (BCBB), a Spanish-language version of the original MGOL program.

My son has autism, and the library has helped our whole family in so many ways. I started going with my son to BCBB as soon as it started. I noticed that it always took a few weeks for the babies and children to get used to the BCBB routine; however, my one-and-a-half-year-old son never seemed to show the same behaviors as the other children his age. I got really worried about his development, so once I asked Miss Ellen what she thought. Miss Ellen and the other librarians referred me to an organization and made sure that my family received the services we needed to help my son. It is thanks to the library that I discovered my son has autism and can get the right treatment. Now my son is almost three years old. He participates in special programs and therapy sessions during the week, but I always make sure his schedule allows us to attend BCBB. It's so important for both of us. Luis loves to be at the library. It's a good opportunity for him to be around other children. It also helps him with his communication. Because he has autism,

he is behind in his communication skills. Right now, he has learned to say about five words, and one of them is Annie (the BCBB facilitator)! But he definitely understands what the library is. Every time we drive by the library, I say, "That's the library," and he always gets excited and points.

Sometimes in public I feel embarrassed that my son doesn't behave like other children. But I never feel that way at the library. The other participants and their children treat us like anyone else, and the librarians always make us feel welcome. They understand Luis's condition and why he acts like he does.

Going to the library has also helped me personally. It is challenging to care for Luis, so going to BCBB gives me a break and lets me socialize with other people. I have made so many friends at the library. The library has become such an important part of our lives. In a year and half of attending BCBB, I have only missed one week! We really look forward to Wednesdays.

musical instruments. Tammi enjoyed marching around the circle with all the boys and girls. Janet was delighted when a boy who had never spoken before began singing along to some song lyrics!

Key Features

Eye contact between the facilitator and participants may not be possible. Loud activities such as clapping or shaking maracas should be muted or eliminated. Extra time may be given for distributing and collecting props; rhymes may be repeated more than two times.

Tips for Success

Here are some tips from Janet and Deborah J. Margolis, a former librarian from the Maryland State Library for the Blind and Physically Handicapped.

Snapshot: A Teacher Talks about MGOL for Preschoolers on the Autism Spectrum

Robin Head is a preschool teacher from Rio Grande Elementary School in Terre Haute, Indiana. Her school is visited by the Vigo County Public Library's Goosemobile regularly.

MGOL is beneficial because it teaches the children so many things. They must listen, they must participate, they must sing and chant, and they hear stories being read to them. It incorporates fine motor and gross motor skills, language arts, memory, listening skills, and many more.

Our favorite part is the repetition of the chants. The children learn them, repeat them, and even request them. We use the rhythm of banging out syllables on a drum, tambourine, and rhythm sticks.

An example of the influence of MGOL is when a child with autism who is nonverbal can follow movements and rhythm to the songs and chants. When I see these children quietly sitting on a carpet square and listening and then participating in some way, it shows me that the program is making an impact.

- Consider limiting the number of attendees; too many people in a room can be overwhelming to some children.
- Be flexible with age restrictions. Although MGOL was designed for children from birth to age three, older children may enjoy and appreciate participating in the program. Welcome siblings to join in too.
- Be flexible with time since things don't always go the way you expected. For instance, when you don't have time to do all the rhymes you've planned, feel free to skip sections and go straight to your ending rhymes if necessary.
- It may take longer to pass objects around the circle. If so, just continue repeating the song until everyone has had a turn. The repetition, routine, and ritual in MGOL are especially important for children on the autism spectrum.
- Always use the same hello and good-bye songs.
- Depending on your audience, you may want to repeat rhymes more than twice. Children may not appear to be paying attention when they don't provide visual or verbal feedback, but they are often fully engaged in their own way.
- Minimize distractions in the room. Avoid background music and loud noises.
- Make sure no material is too sudden, too scary, or too loud. Children on the autism spectrum can become very easily frightened, even by things that other children love.
- Use lots of expression in your face and voice.
- Go slower (but not too slow!) with songs and rhymes, giving more time for language processing. Raising your voice does not help with understanding.
- Prepare children for transitions between activities by using a visual clue (e.g., the flannelboard piece) or by telling them.
- Try including some signs from American Sign Language—it's easy and fun!
- It's OK if a child wants to hold an object for the rest of the time, if everyone has had a chance to hold it. If using objects, try to have multiples to allow for this.
- Children on the autism spectrum often respond more to music and singing than anything (except maybe dogs!).
- See the rest of this chapter for additional tips.

Snapshot: About Programs for Children on the Autism Spectrum and with Sensory Processing Disorder

Maricela Leon-Barrera is the early learning coordinator at the San Francisco Public Library and the parent of a child on the autism spectrum.

Having a child on the spectrum can be bewildering for parents, and often getting a concise diagnosis is difficult and can take a long time. Observing how their children might or might not engage with others or how they engage in settings like play-grounds or library storytimes can be parents' first indicator that something might be amiss with their child. This might lead to parents asking librarians questions regarding resources or for ideas as to how to include their children. Imagine how welcoming it would be if the setting was appropriate for all children regardless of need. It is important to make sure that inclusivity is at the forefront of library program planning and to have an understanding of what can make the experience a good one for the parent, child, and provider.

In recent years, sensory processing disorder (SPD) has become better known terminology. Though it is often paired as a characteristic of children with autism, not all children with autism have sensory processing disorder, and conversely, not all persons with sensory processing disorder have autism. Sensory processing disorder is a person's inability to cope with environmental stimuli: sound, light, touch, and smell. Children with sensory processing disorder can find some situations disabling and painful. The ways they find to cope (such as rocking, vocalization, or avoidance) may cause concern.

Autism spectrum disorder (ASD) is a neurological disorder that affects one out of fifty-nine children in the United States, according to the Centers for Disease Control and Prevention.[1] Research on ASD offers a lot of information, so many parents find the description of what it looks like provided by Autism Speaks to be helpful. The organization offers a free downloadable 100 Day Kit, stating that "Autism spectrum disorder (ASD) and autism are both general terms for a group of complex disorders of brain development. These disorders are characterized, in varying degrees, by difficulties in: social interaction, verbal and nonverbal communication and repetitive behaviors."[2] Not all children with autism show "typical signs" such as lack of eye contact, perimeter walking, echolalia, hyperactivity, repetitive movements, fixation on objects or topics, and difficulty with changes in routine, but these are often seen as indicators.

When a library decides to develop programs for children on the spectrum or with sensory processing disorder, it is important to gauge the audience, support, training, and timing. Librarians should familiarize themselves with the needs of the children they are serving: Are there children who have a hard time sitting in storytime? Is the child seemingly disengaged, walking in circles? Is the parent constantly apologizing for his or her child's atypical behavior? If any of these are the case, therein may lie an opportunity to learn more about a particular family and child and modify an existing program such as MGOL.

A good first step is to look at the community to see if there are any agencies serving children with special needs that can provide support. A search using key terms such as "children with disabilities" and your location might yield names of parental support agencies that may be ecstatic to hear from the local librarian who wants to learn more. They may offer support on creating more inclusive programming. This can lead to training opportunities or tips on how to find trainings with other associations. The information might also become a valued resource to refer to parents seeking information and help.

A broader search might reveal links to websites that increase awareness of autism and SPD. Professional associations often offer webinars on inclusive programming and information via blog posts. Another great training resource is other libraries that are already pioneering storytimes for special needs children or holding sensory storytimes. Looking at their resources will surely spark ideas and may yield some names and points of contact. There is no need to recreate the wheel since many librarians are already trying to increase access and awareness. *(Continued on next page)*

Timing and preparation are key. When planning an inclusive program, there are many considerations. When is a program best for a family who might need a modified environment? What modifications are needed (softer lighting, softer sounding instruments, or more interactive elements or props that enhance the experience such as seating circles, fidget toys, and visuals)? When is the best time for a local classroom serving children with special needs to visit the library for an inclusive session? Creating appropriate programs may take a combination of time, flexibility, and patience on the part of the programming librarian. However, the investment of time and effort to offer safe and welcoming programs to families with children with special needs will lead to a treasured experience for families who need it most.

Modifications for Visually Impaired Children

Because using felt characters as visual reminders is a basic component of MGOL, modifications must be made for children with low vision or those who are blind. Deborah Margolis, a former children's librarian at the Maryland State Library for the Blind and Physically Handicapped, created the first MGOL program for working specifically with this population, and her programming has continued with subsequent librarians.

Key Features

Programs for visually impaired children include extensive verbal descriptions, tactile elements added to rhymes wherever possible, and larger pictures on felt pieces with uncluttered backgrounds. The facilitator speaks slower than usual. Parents are invited to tell the facilitator about their children's special need ahead of time. Rhymes may be repeated more than twice, which means that fewer rhymes will be used in the course of the thirty-minute program.

Tips for Success

- Children with low vision should be invited to sit close to the flannelboard.
- When visually impaired children are present, use words and describe what you are doing. For instance, while doing a fingerplay, clearly describe what your hands and fingers are doing. Try adding touch-and-feel books and silk or corduroy fabric.
- Think multisensory by using realia, fabric, or other tactile objects to enhance books, rhymes, and songs.

- Tactile elements work well for children with visual impairments. For instance, "Humpty Dumpty" is a popular MGOL activity, rich with practice of self-regulation skills. To modify it for blind children, use a plush Humpty Dumpty toy and a cardboard brick for his wall. Place the "wall" in front of the child with Humpty on the wall. Recite the rhyme and ask the child to help Humpty fall. A gentle tap will push Humpty over; it may even knock down the wall! Aides may be required to help, but don't skip over this fun activity!
- Pass around stuffed animals, puppets, and plastic animals. Be sure there are some defining characteristics of the actual animal. Audubon birds that make real bird sounds are great!
- Use kitchen instruments such as water bottle shakers, wooden spoons, and plastic plates. Match real objects with activities. For example, give everyone a wooden spoon to stir with for Bob Marley's "Stir It Up," or pass around carrots with the tops still on for "The Carrot Seed."
- Rain sticks make soft, soothing sounds that can be used to accompany a rhyme about rain.
- If possible, use silk scarves. Nylon is fine, but silk adds another level of richness for children who can't see the scarves.
- Check out Seedlings Braille Books for Children for print Braille books.
- Explore the American Printing House for the Blind's website, especially its tactile graphic image library for free templates.

- Make your own books by enlarging pages and laminating them, then adding tactile elements such as sandpaper or fake fur.
- Make and use very large felt pieces with discernible shapes and high-contrast colors such as sunshine yellow and royal blue.
- Choose picture books or Big Books with large illustrations and bold colors so they can be seen from anywhere in the circle.
- If it takes longer than expected to pass objects around the circle, just continue repeating the song until everyone has had a turn.
- If you don't have time to do all the rhymes you've planned, feel free to skip sections and go straight to your ending rhymes.
- Invite a volunteer reader with a disability or a Braille story reader to read a picture book aloud.
- Lori Guenthner, a former children's librarian at the Maryland State Library for the Blind and Physically Handicapped, recommends following MGOL sessions with accessible crafts such as Crayola Model Magic (clay), Wikki Stix, fabric collage, cookie decoration, fuzzy stickers (not coloring sheets!), and scented crayons or markers.
- See also the tips throughout the rest of this chapter.

SAMPLE PROGRAM

Inclusive MGOL

Deborah J. Margolis, a former children's librarian at the Maryland State Library for the Blind and Physically Handicapped, designed this program for inclusive story times. For a complete script with lyrics included, visit https://bit.ly/2P7mAoo.

Section 1: Welcoming Comments

"Greetings and Welcome! Please sit in a semicircle with your children on your laps if possible. If anyone needs to sit close to me or the interpreter, please come right up. I hope you will join me as I sing or chant the nursery rhymes. I will repeat each rhyme, so if you don't know it already, you can join in on the second round. Children this age don't sit perfectly still, so it's fine if they move

about. But if they come right in front of me or the sign language interpreter, please physically bring them back to your lap. Also, feel free to take your children out of the room for a change of scenery and bring them back whenever they are ready to rejoin the group. It doesn't interrupt us and may help your child feel more comfortable."

Section 2: Rhymes and Reads

"Old Mother Goose" *(Use a felt piece.)*
"Goosey, Goosey Gander" *(Use a felt piece.)*
"Two Little Pretty Birds" *(Teach the American Sign Language sign for bird, and use Audubon birds like a soft dove and a loud raven. When the rhyme is finished, pass around the birds and give everyone a chance to have them tweet.)*
"We Hit the Floor Together"
Book: Snappy Little Farm Yard by Dugald Steer (Act out animal noises or motions.)
Developmental/reading tip: You don't have to read the whole book; one or two pages is good enough. You don't need to read the exact words on the page.

Section 3: Body Rhymes

Head: "My Face Is Round"
Pass out handheld mirrors.
Face: "I Look in the Mirror, and Who Do I See?"
Face: "Mirrors Away"
Hands: "The Eency Weency Spider" / "The Great Big Spider"
Tickle Rhyme: "Round and Round the Garden"
Knee Bounce: "Seesaw Scaradown"
Knee Bounce: "Humpty Dumpty"
Knee Bounce: "Jack Be Nimble"
Leg Rhyme: "This Is Bill Anderson"

Section 4: The Drum Sequence

"Rum Pum Pum"

Section 5: Stand-Up / Sit-Down Activities

"We're Marching to the Drum"
"See the Ponies Galloping" *(with a big horse puppet or a hobbyhorse)*

Section 6: Animal Activities
"I Went to Visit the Farm One Day"
(show illustrations and pass around puppets)
"When the [Cow] Gets Up in the Morning" *(pass around plastic animals for tactile connections)*
"Hickory Dickory Dare"

Section 7: Musical Instruments and Scarves
Bells: "We Ring Our Bells Together" *(Have wrist or ankle bells available for children who can't grasp.)*
Bells: "Ring Your Bells" ("Jingle Bells" version)
Bells: "Are You Sleeping, Brother John?"
Bells: "Grandfather's Clock"
Bells: "Bells Away"
Scarves: "Wind, Oh Wind"
Scarves: "This Is the Way We Wash Our Knees"
Scarves: "Peek-a-Boo"
Scarves: "Scarves Away"

Section 8: Lullabies
"Twinkle, Twinkle" *(Becky Bailey version, accompanied by a rain stick)*

Section 9: Interactive Rhymes
"Humpty Dumpty" *(using plush toy Humpty Dumpty and cardboard brick for the wall)*

Section 10: Closing Ritual
"Can You Kick with Two Feet?"
"It's Time to Say Good-Bye"
"We're So Happy"

Modifications for the Deaf and Hearing-Impaired Child

The rich visual stimulation and movement in MGOL make it easily adaptable for children who have impaired hearing or are deaf. Children enjoy watching interpreters; they may find it easier to learn basic signs for communication before starting to talk. As the official US sign language, American Sign Language (ASL) should be used for any signing done during library programs. While deaf children may need an ASL interpreter, children who are hearing impaired should be invited to sit as close to the flannelboard as needed.

Key Features
MGOL sessions for the hearing impaired include ASL activities and more signing than usual.

Tips for Success
- Only use ASL. Avoid using picture books that feature signs created by their author that are not ASL.
- Try teaching one ASL sign per session related to a book, rhyme, or song. Easy signs are *more* (bring thumb under fingers to form an O, then touch fingers together), *bird* (make beak near your mouth with a thumb and pointer and tap your fingers together twice), *hat* (pat head twice); *monkey* (scratch sides under arms), *caterpillar* (flatten one hand to make a floor and let your index finger inch along it), and *spider* (cross one hand over the other at the wrist, wiggle your fingers, and have them crawl forward).
- Books with terrific suggestions for incorporating ASL into library programs are Kathy MacMillan's *Little Hands and Big Hands* (ALA Editions 2013) and *Try Your Hand at This!* (Scarecrow Press 2015).
- Use the board book *Nita's First Signs* (Familius Press 2018) by Kathy MacMillan.
- See also the tips throughout this chapter.

Modifications for Children with Physical Disabilities

Physical disabilities can include missing fingers, toes, arms, or legs. Children without these parts may not be able to do fingerplays, dance, shake maracas, hit a drum, and more. If running a session for a group of children with severe physical disabilities, those activities can be eliminated. When possible, however, activities are modified so everyone can participate in some way. For instance, a child without fingers who may not be able to grip a handbell might be able to ring a wrist or ankle bell. The goal of this program is to have everyone participate in the ways that they can, leading to feelings of success and enjoyment.

3 Snapshots of Inclusive Storytimes

"SenseSational Storytime"

Carolyn Brooks is the former library services manager and community/school liaison at the El Dorado Hills Branch Library and the current library programs consultant for the California State Library.

"SenseSational Storytime" is an hour-long interactive storytime program for children with sensory needs or who are on the autism spectrum that began as a modification of MGOL. The El Dorado Public Library in California received an IMLS (Institute of Museum and Library Services) grant funded through LSTA (administered through the CA State Library) and hired occupational therapist Robyn Chu (MOT, ORT/L) to help create a research-based program for on-the-move toddlers that was also modified for children with different needs. The entire manual for this program is freely available online at the El Dorado Public Library website, www.eldoradolibrary.org/0-to-5-year-olds.

"Together Time"

Occupational therapist Jordan Sachse (OTD, OTR/L) created "Together Time" to help parents and children facing enormous challenges both in their homes and in the community. It can be combined with MGOL in a library or museum setting to provide therapy for parents while creating positive play and literacy experiences for children with and without their parents.

The "Together Time" curriculum is strongly rooted in occupational and learning theory, focusing on everyday activities as a way of increasing caregiver-child attachment through daily routines. It develops social support for families, addresses gaps in families' knowledge and skills, teaches concrete strategies to improve parent-child interactions, and provides alternative interaction strategies aimed at extinguishing rough handling, yelling, hitting, or other aggressive and potentially abusive interactions.

Jordan and I (Betsy) created a five-week program that combined MGOL with "Together Time" for children with developmental delays from at-risk families. This program helped those children deal with separation anxiety; it also gave the parents a window into what would happen when their children entered pre-K. Lack of funding prevented us from continuing this program, but everyone involved agreed that combining "Together Time" with MGOL had led to an enriching, successful program. Jordan has made her curriculum available free of charge at https://togethertime1.wordpress.com/together-time-manual.

"Sensory Storytime"

Chicago Public Library's Josh Farnum is a children's librarian who has run Sensory Storytime programs.

The Chicago Public Library runs sensory storytimes for older children as well as for children with a wide range of developmental differences. Rather than doing a MGOL program per se, different elements are chosen and adapted to work for children with a wide range of abilities. For instance, children on the autism spectrum find the predictability of using "Wind, Oh Wind" regularly to be comforting, which helps their engagement in the program. According to Josh Farnum, each participant is encouraged to do it in their own way: "Nonverbal participants might just wave their scarves, some may just observe, and others might recite the rhyme but just hold their scarves in their laps." Josh's supershort logistical checklist for sensory storytime includes the following: (1) use a visual schedule, (2) provide fidgets, and (3) have open sensory play. Only half of the program time is used for directed activities like stories and songs; the other half is for open play. Check out Josh Farnum's sensory storytime script below.[3]

Key Features

After becoming familiar with the audience, standard sessions are planned to eliminate sections that are impossible for physical reasons. Similar instruments may be substituted. When only a few children are physically challenged, look for ways to modify the program so that they can participate, albeit in slightly different ways.

Tips for Success

- Choose only fingerplays to simple rhymes with a limited number of steps and easy movements, or modify the more complicated movements. For instance, the twisting hand spider movements used in "The Eency Weensy Spider" can be difficult to replicate, but you can modify the movement to only opening and shutting your thumbs and index fingers so the rhyme remains a favorite.
- Children like seeing representations of themselves. Use books with illustrations or felt board characters that depict children similar to those in your audience.
- Ask parents what their children's favorite rhymes or songs are and incorporate those into the program. The children will enjoy having beloved rhymes used during your session.
- Make sure there is plenty of room for doing circle activities with children in wheelchairs.

SAMPLE PROGRAM

Sensory Storytime

by Josh Farnum

In this bare-bones Sensory Storytime plan from the Chicago Public Library, everything repeats exactly for a six- or eight-week series except for new read-aloud books each week.

Section 1: Welcoming Comments

Section 2: Rhymes and Reads
"The Shirt Song"
"Peter Works with One Hammer"
Book: Kitten's First Full Moon *(with flashlights and cricket nighttime sounds)*

Section 3: Body Rhymes
Wiggle Break: Move your legs like an ocean and so on.

Section 4: The Drum Sequence *(not done)*

Section 6: Animal Activities *(not done)*

Section 7: Musical Instruments and Scarves
Scarves: "Wind, Oh Wind"
Scarves: "This Is the Way We Wash Our Knees"
Scarves: "Wind, Oh Wind"
Scarves: "Scarves Away"

Section 5: Stand-Up / Sit-Down Activities
(with Beanbags)
Beanbags: Play a recording of Hap Palmer's "Beanbag Song," *and follow along with the actions.*
"Handy Spandy"

Section 8: Lullabies *(not done)*

Section 9: Interactive Rhymes *(with Read-Aloud)*
Read aloud: Higher! Higher! *by Leslie Patricelli (Toss foam balls in the air.)*

Section 10: Closing Ritual
Open play with cloud dough, some other sensory exploration stations, blocks, and so on.

NOTES

1. Centers for Disease Control and Prevention, "Autism Spectrum Disorder (ASD)," 2018, https://www.cdc.gov/ncbddd/autism/research.html.

2. Autism Speaks, "About Autism, Diagnosis, Causes and Symptoms," 100 Day Kit, 2018, https://www.autismspeaks.org/sites/default/files/docs/about_autism_0.pdf.

3. For an additional sensory storytime playgroup script, check out this one by Jason Driver at the Chicago Public Library: https://bit.ly/2MBoMaQ.

Adapting MGOL to Include Different Cultures and Religions

CAN YOU IMAGINE HOW BORING THE WORLD WOULD be if we were all clones of each other? The world we live in is wonderfully composed of people with differences. Our families may come from different countries, speak languages other than English, and observe a variety of religious practices. They come in all shapes, sizes, sexes, and colors. This includes parents and children with disabilities, new immigrants, gay families, other minorities, foster parents, and grandparents raising grandchildren. A benefit of library programs is that they can bring together families of all backgrounds, including all races, genders, ages, and religions.

Although public libraries typically avoid religious activities, introducing different religious customs into Mother Goose on the Loose (MGOL) programs promotes understanding of other cultures and diversity. Keeping new traditions and cultural awareness in mind when planning sessions helps bring understanding to people who otherwise might not be exposed to these activities.

Although MGOL is designed to form a community, individuality should never be lost. As a vehicle for celebrating our differences, MGOL can be used to teach about one specific culture or to connect attendees with their heritage. It can promote multiculturalism within the United States. Singing songs and reciting rhymes throughout childhood connects generations. The treasures buried in handed-down words are endless. An appreciation for cultural heritage; an "ear" for the sound of the language; new words set in context so their meaning becomes easily known; familiarity with cultural, social, and geographical references; and knowledge of traditional rhymes enhance phonological awareness and increase linguistic benefits.

Key Features

Diverse MGOL programs can focus on a number of cultural and religious traditions or just one. They can specifically welcome LGBTQ couples and their children, be geared for grandparents, or engage teen parents. In these adapted programs, the activities are used as learning tools.

Tips for Success

Here are a few tips to keep in mind when tailoring your program to a widely diverse audience.

- Always remember that a welcoming atmosphere and nonjudgmental environment is the most important part of any MGOL program!
- People want to feel included. In addition to learning about others, they like seeing themselves reflected in the activities going on around them too.
- Do not share your own religious, cultural, or political leanings. Simply present the options as a learning experience.
- Choose a holiday, give a brief explanation, and create an activity to go along with it.

- Remember that not all children have a mother and a father. Reword rhymes if needed.
- *Mom* does not always describe the primary care-giver; sometimes that person is grandma, daddy, or a caretaker who is not a relative.
- Hold a MGOL celebration of "Generations Day" rather than "Grandparents Day."
- Ask attendees which pronouns they would like you to use.
- Refer to animals as *he*, *she*, *they* or *it* instead of just *he*.
- If appropriate, incorporate songs learned from session attendees. Try singing one verse of a song in a new language.
- It is impossible to identify the country or culture program attendees come from. Be careful not to put any participants in an uncomfortable situation by assuming they are Latino or came from another country based on their skin color, type of head wrap, or clothing. Your program should always be a welcoming, safe space for everyone.

MGOL for American Indians/ Native Americans

While Indian nations in the United States may share some common features, language, clothing, and customs, they are not homogenous. Each nation is a separate entity. Just as Italians and Germans are both Europeans but would require different MGOL adaptations, there is no "one size fits all" adaptation for Indian nations. The state libraries of Oklahoma, Arizona, and New Mexico have staff liaisons who work with the tribal librarians in their states. New Mexico State Library has a Tribal Libraries program.

Key Features

The standard MGOL program can be adapted to reflect the language and values of different American Indians. Depending on the nation, artifacts may or may not be incorporated into the program.

Tips for Success

- Ask a tribal elder or a native teacher from a Tribal school if there is a song, chant, or rhyme that you can learn to use in your MGOL program. Make sure that it is not a sacred song or something that should only be used during rituals.
- Find out the meaning of the song, chant, or rhyme, and make a felt piece to represent it visually. Think of a way to present the rhyme that involves some type of action that matches the meaning of the rhyme.
- Since children like to see themselves and objects they are familiar with as felt pieces during a MGOL program, look for picture books illustrated by a member of the local tribe. Make felt pieces from color photocopies of familiar images.

Snapshot: Cinco de Mayo Celebration

During sessions of Buena Casa, Buena Brasa (BCBB, a Spanish version of MGOL), librarian Edwin Perez found unique ways to incorporate celebration of traditional Spanish holidays.

Cinco de Mayo, the story of the Battle of Puebla, was told in my library. This holiday is not Mexican Independence Day, as many people mistakenly believe, but it celebrates an important battle for the Mexican people and marks the turning point when they were able to defeat French rule in Mexico. In the US, Cinco de Mayo is a big holiday; in fact, it is celebrated more in the US than in Mexico. At BCBB, we recounted and examined the roots of the holiday. People who were already celebrating the holiday were introduced to current information that helped them understand myths and misunderstandings that have arisen over the years. It cleared the air for some of the adults. Others who were unfamiliar with the holiday learned about it. The children celebrated too by enjoying piñatas, a traditional Mexican game. We sang a song to go along with it that involved counting and signing using our hands and motor skills. At the end, when the children broke the piñata, they got the candy, which was a reward in itself.

(Note: This module has been reviewed by a member of the Kickapoo Nation.)

MGOL in Navajo

Hear a version of "The Ants Go Marching" in Navajo at https://youtu.be/J_PfaaB3dRo (adapted from "When Johnny Comes Marching Home").

MGOL in Spanish

MGOL programs can include some Spanish, be presented mostly in Spanish, or use only Spanish. Two popular Spanish-language MGOL programs are BCBB and Escucha y Disfruta con Mama Gansa. In 2010, I wrote *Early Literacy Programming en Español: Mother Goose on the Loose Programs for Bilingual Learners* (Neal-Schuman) based on my own experiences with starting a Spanish-language MGOL program at the Enoch Pratt Free Library. Even though I do not speak fluent Spanish, a fruitful partnership with Dr. Annie Calderon led to this how-to manual. Designed to address the shortage of bilingual children's librarians working in areas with Latino communities, it describes how librarians can recruit community partners fluent in Spanish and prepare and present sessions together. It addresses challenges, provides tips, and contains a complete MGOL program in both English and Spanish. Because there is not one official or proper dialect of Spanish, the book's script was written in generic Spanish using grammar according to the Real Academia Española. The vocabulary is the most common variant for the majority of Spanish speakers and also universally inoffensive.

The "Escucha y Disfruta con Mama Gansa" CD with MGOL songs in English and Spanish with Rahel and tenor Evelio Mendez provides material for use in Spanish programs (now available for download at https://store.cdbaby.com/cd/rembdc). In addition to those specific MGOL-related resources, access to Spanish children's books, musical recordings, and rhymes will enable interested librarians to easily create their own Spanish versions of MGOL.

Key Features
Traditional Spanish children's songs as well as popular American children's songs translated into Spanish can be sung. Musical instruments are played to recorded music in Spanish. Participants can dance to salsa, mambo, or flamenco music. Illustrations drawn by illustrators from Spanish-speaking countries or from Spanish-language books can accompany songs and rhymes.

Tips for Success
- If you do not speak fluent Spanish, look for a community partner to help you present the program.
- Use the Spanish MGOL script in *Early Literacy Programming en Español: Mother Goose on the Loose Programs for Bilingual Learners* as a starting point.
- Ask your partner to retranslate the script if there is one predominant dialect spoken in your community.
- Check out Gloria Melchor's bilingual storytime script at https://bit.ly/2wu5IQU.

Building Cultural Competence via BCBB

Edwin Perez, a former Enoch Pratt librarian, developed his own version of BCBB. Adapted from MGOL, it was based on the five Cs, which are foreign language standards that help measure goals for foreign language education from ACTFL (American Council on the Teaching of Foreign Languages). Comprised of five goal areas—communication, cultures, connections, comparisons, and communities—the standards are used by K–12 schools throughout America. The five Cs and MGOL are a perfect match because the underlying principle of both is that people learn best through experiences and connection.

Edwin advises, "Choosing to come to a program in a language that is not spoken in the immediate community, returning the following week, and coming continuously in following weeks builds the program attendees' sense that they have also established their own community at the library where they can rely on each other." Edwin's sessions attracted immigrants from many countries in addition to Spanish speakers, so he created a celebration of all cultures. English speakers also attended, expanding their knowledge of other cultures and religious customs. More about the five Cs can be found on ACTFL's website.

According to Edwin, "If you are not comfortable with Spanish or if you don't know any Spanish, I still encourage you to set up a program in Spanish, because it will bring in Spanish speakers. You will be surprised by how quickly it will begin to draw an audience. Then the Spanish speakers will help you learn their language. They will help build up the program because, on the personal level, they want you to succeed. If your program succeeds, they will be able to come to the library and then pass on what they are learning through you. Don't be scared; give it a shot. If you build it, they will come."

Key Features

Sessions are based on communication, cultures, connections, comparisons, and communities. Traditional holidays and holy days from Spanish-speaking countries and other countries around the world are incorporated into sessions.

Tips for Success

- Don't stress if it takes a number of sessions before you start attracting a nice-sized audience. Simply start your program and be enthusiastic about it. Enthusiasm breeds enthusiasm.
- Don't let a lack of personal knowledge of another language stop you from starting a program, as participants will often be eager to help the program succeed.

Snapshot from the Field: BCBB

Rocío and her baby daughter regularly attended the first BCBB programs at the Patterson Park Branch of the Enoch Pratt Free Library in Baltimore.

Before, I didn't understand the concept of a library. In the countries we come from, it's very different. Libraries are not free. It is not free to check out books. A person has to buy books, and there is never money for that. Also, in our countries, places like the library never offer us any opportunities like they do here. Now I check out movies for me and books for my daughter in both Spanish and English.

I have seen a lot of changes in my daughter. I attended BCBB while I was pregnant with her, and as soon as she was born, I could tell she recognized the songs when I would sing them to her. Now she is six months old, and she is very active and responsive. I believe that this is because I have always brought her to BCBB. She has so much fun there.

I have learned more English than I knew before. We sing songs in English, and there are some Americans in the program. I always talk with them in English, even if it is just a few words. It benefits me a lot. A few months ago, I asked Annie if we could pair up with the American participants and read a story to each other every week before the program. So now I have an American friend. Her daughter is three months older than mine. She reads us a book in English, and I read them a book in Spanish. Then we lend each other the books for the week, and I practice reading it at home to Rachel (my daughter).

My library friends help me out and care about me. Going to the library has been great for me. It gives me a chance to socialize. We all share our stories. Now we also get together outside of the library. There is a pregnant Egyptian lady who attends BCBB every week. Even though we can't communicate that well, we wanted to celebrate the birth of her baby. A group of us got together and gave her a baby shower. Even though we don't speak the same language, we still have a lot to share, thanks to the library.

I don't know what I would do without the library. If the program ended, I think I would get together with a group of the participants and write letters trying to find some organization to help us out.

Snapshot: BCBB

Edwin Perez, a former children's librarian at the Southeast Anchor Branch of the Enoch Pratt Free Library, presented weekly BCBB sessions. He is now a Spanish teacher at Baltimore's City College High School.

The five Cs ensured that I stayed on the correct educational programming path that I believe BCBB and MGOL aim for: a welcoming, safe, and nurturing environment where individuality is celebrated and learning is done through personal connections and playful activities.

BCBB was a perfect vehicle for building a welcoming, nourishing environment that fostered language learning and encouraged multiculturalism. Most families attending spoke either Spanish or English, although the majority of participants were English speakers who wanted to learn Spanish. Two participating families spoke German. There were also some Japanese families. Throughout the course of the program, we had fourteen different languages spoken! Instead of trying to be a homogenous group of "traditional Americans," I viewed the variety of people speaking different languages and having different backgrounds as a beautiful representation of cultural competence.

By being a multilanguage presenter in BCBB, I was able to converse with library visitors in Spanish, which gave library access to the Spanish speakers. Being able to come into a place and have someone speak your own language, to hear that language in a taught program, and to be able to communicate with others is powerful. I also promoted early childhood learning as well as literacy to the English speakers and to audience members who did not speak English, the main language used in our library.

Incorporating the concepts behind MGOL with communication defines the idea of flexibility. Using felt characters to ask questions of young patrons and adult patrons enables them to truly interpret what is being asked; when you are only using one language, the lesson might be lost. Being able to interpret what each other is saying increases communication and the message of early literacy, regardless of access to language.

The underlying purpose injected into BCBB was to give attending families a chance to experience different perspectives. Introducing a book or flannelboard story was also used as a way to introduce an idea of culture and how things are seen by different people. For instance, I might have used a rhyme that mentioned a traditional type of dress or food item. Although it might be stereotypical, the concept of understanding could be fine-tuned through a "story" connected with that rhyme, and the families would leave with better understanding.

Low learners, midlevel learners, high learners, and different types of audiences can be addressed. Using Spanish and English at the same time provides "differentiated learning," where you create levels of learning in your program so all participants will leave with some understanding of the concepts or acquisition of the language. In addition to acquiring language, cultural competence also grows through learning different rhymes from various Spanish-speaking cultures.

For example, we sang "Bate, Bate, Chocolate" every week in BCBB to incorporate it into "Día de los Muertos" (Day of the Dead). That song has a special meaning on this day because of its focus on making hot chocolate. The concept of chocolate comes from the indigenous populations. Many people in South American and Mexico still have a connection with the cacao pod and bean. Traditionally, during the festival of Día de los Muertos, a chocolate bean is created. In "Bate, Bate, Chocolate," hands are rubbed together to move an imaginary wooden spoon back and forth between your palms. These are not made-up movements; this stirring technique is actually used to prepare hot chocolate in Mexico. When palms slide back and forth, a foam is created on top of the hot chocolate. Without the foam, the hot chocolate is not considered "good"! Stirring hot chocolate in this way indicates respect for your guests. As part of the tradition, some Day of the Dead bread (pan de muerto) is then dipped into the hot chocolate.

In BCBB, we sang "Bate, Bate, Chocolate" almost every week, using the correct motions. But on Día de los Muertos, we turned it into a celebration that included making hot   *(Continued on next page)* chocolate the Mexican way and inviting everyone to dip their bread into the same hot chocolate that they had been singing about together all year long. It was a great culmination activity!

While wanting to see how each country or cultural group celebrated birthdays, we learned that not everyone celebrates holidays in the same way. We heard about different kinds of cake. People told me that without this exchange of information, they would never have known that there was a difference between similar types of frosting and how they are made. BCBB moms and dads and nannies would sit down and speak to each other when they had these cultural items in front of them, such as food, drink, and piñatas. They would relate it to their own cultures, so there would be a cultural exchange. This exchange would not have been possible if people had not been allowed to express themselves culturally or been able to publicly identify their religion or ethnicity. The nonjudgmental atmosphere of MGOL was an integral part of allowing that to happen.

People were not scared to sit next to anyone, even someone they had not met before or someone who looked different. I am not from Baltimore, but I heard many stories about Baltimore City being very divided. I was told that no one would come to a library program in Spanish. But BCBB was an example of people from all over the city getting together, having a good time together, celebrating together, and leaving with wonderful memories. It certainly broke all the stereotypes that I heard about Baltimore. In my library, there really was a world community, and it was great to see. It was the highlight of my week. It was everyone's highlight of the week. Even other library staff wanted to be at BCBB because they knew they were going to have a good time.

Recently arrived immigrants attended the program—occasionally we would meet people who had just arrived in the US the night before! Through their contacts in the neighborhood, they knew that at the library, the English speakers would treat them as equals, regardless of status. Although I did not ask how the immigrants arrived in Baltimore, I heard some harrowing stories and gruesome tales. I could see the fear in their eyes but also noticed the appreciation and gratitude of being with someone who could speak their language. They compared where they came from to where they were now, and they were grateful to be in Baltimore.

Whatever is learned in MGOL and BCBB will be taken beyond the library walls and into each individual's community. There, community members will then interact with others in their communities. And wherever the BCBB families go around the world, they will carry the vision of MGOL, which is literacy and community and culture. They will be able to spread the message so others can learn in the same fashion they learned.

Incorporating Catholic Traditions into MGOL

Edwin Perez recommends sharing traditional Catholic holiday celebrations from Mexico. For example, Las Posadas recreates a very important story in the Catholic tradition. It is the story of Joseph and Mary with the unborn baby Jesus going from house to house and knocking on doors, looking for a place to stay. To celebrate this holiday, people living in Mexico walk from home to home, knocking on doors, but they are not allowed to enter. When introducing this holiday, Edwin displayed books about Cinco de Mayo together with Las Posadas to recreate the Mexican tradition. While everyone sat in the circle, he gave a brief explanation of the holiday. Then during the stand-up / sit-down section, he asked everyone to pretend they were walking from home to home, knocking at each door and being rejected. In the end, everyone found a place to stay and then a party was held to celebrate.

Key Features

This activity requires an explanation with illustrations, a movement rhyme, and a celebration. Since it takes more time than the usual standing-up rhymes, other sections of the session should be shortened. These activities can take place during the stand-up section or can be moved to the end of the session in order to end with a party!

Tips for Success
- Keep your explanation of the holiday short and sweet.
- If possible, show a photo or two of people celebrating the holiday in its country of origin.
- Create a felt piece with the written name of the holiday on it to display during the festivities, and mention the holiday's name at least three times.

Using MGOL during Sunday School Hours

Parents who bring children to Sunday school may have babies or toddlers home too. Instead of simply dropping off older children at Sunday school and picking them up a few hours later, parents can be invited to an on-site MGOL program. Many religious institutions are looking for ways to bring people together and attract new members; what better way is there than to offer activities for very young children and their parents? Parents get an opportunity to meet others who are at the same life stage, and dropping off and picking up their older child will only require one car ride. Once a Sunday morning tradition is formed that involves coming weekly, the parents will be more likely to join that faith community.

Key Features
Psalms and short songs that are part of that religion's repertoire can be used. A short Bible story may be read or told during rhymes and reads. Gospel songs, praise and worship music, and religious rock are some recorded music choices for use when playing along with musical instruments.

Tips for Success
- Send fliers home with older children attending Sunday school to remind parents of upcoming MGOL sessions.
- Unless the room where the program will be held is carpeted, invite parents to wear sweats or comfortable clothing in the area where the program will be held.

- Ask parents to bring music they enjoy listening to.

Incorporating Jewish Traditions into MGOL via Savta Goose on the Loose

Since MGOL was developed while I was living in Israel, there is a Hebrew version called "Savta Goose on the Loose" (*savta* means grandmother). It is a combination of children's songs in Hebrew as well as translations of many Barbara Cass-Beggs songs.

According to Jan Fabiyi, an experienced MGOL facilitator, there is a wide treasure trove of Jewish-focused musical and literary selections for children, including rhymes, songs, and books from a variety of areas: Jewish culture (specific to the country or region), Jewish history, Jewish languages (biblical Hebrew, Israeli Hebrew, Yiddish), and the Jewish holidays. For instance, making chicken soup for the Friday night Sabbath meal is common in Ashkenazi (the dominant Eastern European Jewish culture) homes. A simple song about this tradition sung to the tune of "London Bridge" features elements drawn from religion, culture (culinary and regional), and holidays: "Put a *chicken* in the pot. Boil it up, nice and hot. Get it ready for Shabbat. For Shabbat." The soup ingredients can be changed from verse to verse, with new ideas solicited from children by asking, "What else should be put in our soup for Shabbat?" Although "carrots," "onions," and "noodles" are some common answers, expect outlandish and funny answers as well.

Many simple Hebrew songs celebrate Jewish holidays. For instance, a dreidel is a top inscribed with Hebrew letters, each of which has a different meaning. To "play dreidel" during Hanukkah, children spin the top, see which letter it lands on, and win chocolate coins. The song "I Had a Little Dreidel" is fun to act out because it involves spinning around and falling down.

Yiddish, a common language among Eastern European Jews, was spoken by the grandparents and great-grandparents of many American Jews. It is still spoken today in many strictly religious communities (among Orthodox Jews of Eastern European background) and in some academic circles. Since Yiddish has a very catchy sound, it is fun and instructive to include a Yiddish rhyme or two. Try it; you'll like it!

Key Features

Rhymes are adapted to include Jewish holidays and cultural norms. Simple Israeli folk dances can be used in the stand-up session. Recorded music can include klezmer, simple Israeli folk dances and debkas, Yemenite songs, and modern Israeli music. Yiddish clapping and bouncing rhymes broaden the offerings.

Tips for Success

- Show an illustration or two from a Hebrew language book to illustrate that books open from right to left and Hebrew is read from right to left. Show that Hebrew letters look different from English letters.
- Use a few Hebrew words such as *shalom*, which means hello, good-bye, and peace.
- A Jewish flavor can also be added by playing musical instruments to the beat of traditional music such as Israeli folk dance and debka music, songs by Yemenite singers, klezmer music, and modern Israeli songs.
- Use a Yiddish version of "Pat-a-Cake"—either "Patshe, Patshe, Hentelach" or "Patshe, Patshe, Kikhelekh"—as a knee bounce as well as a clapping rhyme.
- A Hebrew-English MGOL CD with songs and rhymes in both English and Hebrew is available on CD Baby at https://store.cdbaby.com/cd/bdcr2.
- Check out a Savta Goose on the Loose script at https://bit.ly/2PDFKTU.

Incorporating Virtues and Diversity into MGOL

Katharine Phelps, a member of the Baha'i faith, taught one of my MGOL groups a verse from a lovely Baha'i song, "The Wind Is Singing in the Mountains." We sang this song while waving colored scarves. After learning the song, everyone loved it, so we added it to our repertoire. Although no one else in our group was affiliated with the Baha'i faith, knowing a beautiful song and being able to sing it together strengthened our sense of community. It also provided a glimpse into a smaller religious community.

I later learned that Katharine facilitated MGOL programs within the Baha'i community abroad. Some of her observations and experiences are shared below.

Key Features

Key features include the addition of songs and stories emphasizing virtues (e.g., love, kindness, gratitude), good manners and politeness toward others, and the beautiful diversity of people in the world around us. Examples of storybooks that emphasize these virtues are *We Share One World* by Jane E. Hoffelt, *Whoever You Are* by Mem Fox, and *All the Colors of the Earth* by Sheila Hamanaka. Developmentally appropriate art projects can be inserted at the end of the music and story portion.

Tips for Success

- Learn the song well before introducing it to your group.
- Think of an activity (e.g., waving scarves, ringing bells, doing a fingerplay) that will go along with the song if there is not already an established way to act it out or play with it.
- Write out the words ahead of time so your audience can follow along.
- Repetition of the materials is important. Don't be overly worried about adult participants getting bored. The children's learning needs should be at the center of your time together. At their stage of development, infants, toddlers, and preschoolers don't tire of hearing the same things over and over once a week. It's necessary for their absorption of the material, and their growing familiarity with the content and structure can be comforting.
- Define the success of your program not simply by the number of people who show up but by the joyful attitude you possess and the growth mind-set you maintain in carrying out this valuable service. So much is happening in that half hour. Literacy development, cultivating a love for music, nurturing the bond between parents and children, building friendships, and sharing ideas that promote happiness and joy.
- Great books with developmentally appropriate art projects and activities are *First Art for Toddlers and*

Snapshot: Parent-Run Multicultural MGOL

Katharine Phelps attended MGOL sessions in Baltimore with her nine-month-old daughter while visiting her family on holiday. At the time, she lived in Haifa, Israel. She visited again when her daughter was nineteen months old. She granted me an interview in which I recorded some of the cool things she had done with MGOL.

There are three things that attracted me to this program. One was the focus on children under the age of two. I had yet to come across a literacy-based program that was designed for infants and toddlers. The second thing that attracted me to the program was the use of music in developing their language skills. The final thing I liked was its simplicity and that it was relatively inexpensive to offer. Essentially, anyone can deliver the program.

It's accessible to a lot of different cultures, and you can see its effectiveness over a short period of time. An example of its effectiveness is my daughter's interest in music. She is instantly drawn to playing instruments. When she hears a familiar tune, she starts to sing along with it and clap to it.

I came to Baltimore in August of 2005 and attended two of the Mother Goose sessions offered at the Central Library. I instantly saw its value. So I asked Betsy for the materials, and I bought the CD online. Within two or three weeks, I felt comfortable enough with the materials, bought instruments at a local toy store, made a flier, and sent it to mothers in my community with toddlers. The program ran consistently for nine months!

I was able to put the program together for about twelve dollars per person because all they needed was a set of bells, a set of rattles, and some scarves. Each mother contributed to that, knowing that at the end of the program they would be able to keep their instruments—so essentially, they were just paying for their materials. I bought a flannelboard for myself and some monkey dolls. I borrowed books from the library (we had a copy of *The Very Busy Spider*), and we already had tapping sticks. (We had some dowels, so I had a workshop just trim them down.)

There was a family from Estonia, a family that was half Persian and half Russian, some from the United States, one that was half Japanese and half Persian, and a family from Britain; they all were English speakers, although English was not every-one's first language.

One of the things that makes the program adapt-able is that there is a basic structure. Wherever you may live and offer the program, you can use the nursery rhymes and songs from your culture and insert them into the program. For example, the mothers in this particular group were interested in things related to virtues. So when it seemed appro-priate, we would have a song that would illustrate a particular virtue. We would also use books, and the storybooks we used would be illustrative of the importance of diversity, since this was one of our interests and something that we felt was important to convey to the children.

Once the ball started rolling and I was inspired by all the possibilities that the MGOL script and CD offered, I started to become aware of all sorts of songs and books and nursery rhymes that could be used to develop certain concepts. There is so much a person or group can do. Whatever the interest of your community is, you can take it and run with it.

When I came back to Baltimore in February of 2006, I attended two or three other programs (one at a different library), to get a sense of how it was adopted depending on the community. Essentially, I learned that each person takes on the program and makes it his or her own. You're thinking about your audience and the parents and the children and their needs, yet the structure stays the same.

Twos by Mary Ann F. Kohl, *Things to Do with Toddlers and Twos* by Karen Miller, and *More Things to Do with Toddlers and Twos* by Karen Miller.

Multicultural and English as a New Language MGOL Program

According to Ellen Galinsky's *Mind in the Making: The Seven Essential Life Skills Every Child Needs*, all children need to be able to put themselves in the shoes of others in order to see a wide range of perspectives.[1] One way to learn to appreciate differences is by learning about them! Celebrating different cultures and religions in a nonreligious way familiarizes children with customs and beliefs that are not their own. The public library can be the perfect place to do this.

In safe places, you can be who you are regardless of opinions or conflicts back home. Participants may come from countries that have been warring or in conflict for years. You may get people whose religions are different and who would not normally sit next to each other. Yet being together in your program demonstrates that they can interact. Because of the safe and welcoming environment, they are able to sit together, sing together, and learn from each other.

Although content may be adapted to fit a target audience, it is always important to create a welcoming environment for all families and to remain a positive piece of their lives.

Key Features

This version was designed to bring immigrants into the library, validate cross-cultural experiences, teach English as a new language, and acclimate everyone to the public library setting.

Tips for Success

- Introduce other languages in greetings and good-byes.
- If you hear new participants speaking other languages, ask if they would be comfortable sharing their cultural traditions with the group. Do not assume they are from somewhere else. Give an open invitation by saying beforehand, "If anyone feels comfortable sharing their cultural tradition

Snapshot: MGOL in Egypt

Marwa Seifeldeen is the children's library specialist at the Bibliotheca Alexandrina in Egypt.

The MGOL program that is being tested in Egypt in both Arabic and English has shown great success. As for the Arabic version of the program, it incorporates traditional Egyptian rhymes and songs. The English version is just the same as the original program. This great program has shown great enhancement and improvement in the preliteracy skills of Egyptian children.

or their language with us today, please see me before the program starts." While meeting with you, help them practice saying something like "I identify as Pakistani, and we say 'Shab bakhair' to say good morning." Then during the program you can announce, "We have a family here today that is from [this country] and identifies with [this cultural group]. Can you please tell us how to say hello?" The person who spoke with you earlier can then say hello, and everyone will repeat it together.

- Remove as many distractions as possible until the children learn how to pay attention. Gloria Melchior from the Metropolitan Library System in Oklahoma presents her multicultural program in a tight space; she recommends moving the table and chairs and disabling the children's computers for the duration of the program.
- Different cultures have different norms of behavior. We may expect parents to keep an eye on their children; they may think it is fine for their children to roam unattended around the library. Some parents are not used to keeping their children confined to a program area. If your library has stairs, you may need to purchase a child gate and install it at the top of the stairs each week before the families arrive.
- Edwin Perez, who has provided much material for this section, recommends using activities that invite comparisons. For instance, sing "The Itsy

Bitsy Spider" in both English and another language. With the great big spider's verse added in, the song includes a comparison of size as well as of language.

- Choose activities that help children reflect on the concepts of size, sound, and color. For instance, ringing the bells combines the shaking of the bells with the idea of the sounds, which enables children to compare and contrast. This is like comparing their old language with the new language.
- Use colored scarves because they are so much fun. Compare different languages by waving colored scarves up and down while saying the words in English and another language—for example, *arriba* ("high") and *abajo* ("low").
- Since daily routines are a big deal in early child-hood, use everyday activities like washing the face, the ears, and the belly to introduce and practice other languages. English-speaking parents may enjoy learning how to translate a routine that they do every day into another language. They can then ask their children, "How do you wash your face in [Spanish/Amharic/Polish]? How do you wash your face in English?" Or they can demonstrate "This is how we wash our face in English."
- Try incorporating math into your multicultural program by purchasing carpet squares that have a number as well as the name of the number (e.g., "1" and "*uno*") on them.
- Inviting children to sit on carpet squares during the program teaches them how to sit, which is expected classroom behavior for kindergarten but is also needed in adulthood for sitting in an airplane or concert hall.
- Play games and do math activities with the squares.
- Use the squares to provide opportunities for physical activity, helping children use their bodies to learn by playing games like "Red Light, Green Light." Say the name of the color in Spanish (or another language), and ask the children to iden-tify the green, yellow, and red carpet squares. At red, they stop, and at green, they move forward. In addition to familiarizing children with a game often played in kindergarten (in English), this also builds problem-solving skills since the children need to decide whether or not to move based on what they see in front of them.
- Put the squares in numerical order, and read out the numbers. When you say "ten" in English and then in another language, the children jump or hop in place that number of times. Then do "nine," and continue counting down in this way to "one." By counting in English and another language, identi-fying the number on the carpet square, and moving at the same time, the children connect their bodies with their knowledge. Children who are too young to jump or hop can be bounced on knees.
- Use a MGOL activity where children identify ani-mals and their sounds to show them that in other languages, some animals make different sounds than in English. For instance, a cat in Spanish says "miau," and it sounds a bit different from "meow." A dog in Hebrew says "hav hav." Aural as well as oral skills are challenged when children discover

Snapshot: MGOL at the Alexandria Library

Valerie Kimble, the librarian/selector at the Pio-neer Library System in Oklahoma, visited Egypt in 2008 as a part of a storytelling delegation from People to People.

I was a little surprised that the library in Alexandria was a public library as well as a research facility and that it was organized in a similar way to public libraries in the United States, with children's departments, teen departments, and adult departments. All the staff spoke beautiful English. In discussing where storytelling fit in their services, they talked about storytime and mentioned the fact that they used MGOL in their storytimes. Since not all of us were librarians, my fellow dele-gates talked about other ways that storytelling occurs in the United States. But I was one of two children's librarians in the delegation, and we were the ones who primarily interacted with the Alexandrian librarians. They said that they had become familiar with MGOL while traveling abroad.

that animal sounds are not the same in different cultures. When singing "When the Cat Gets Up in the Morning," make a sound and then ask, "Is that a Spanish-speaking cat or an English-speaking cat?"

SAMPLE PROGRAM

Multicultural MGOL

This program is a combination of programs by Edwin Perez and Jan Fabiyi with one of the songs from Katharine Phelps.

Section 1: Welcoming Comments

Section 2: Rhymes and Reads
"Old Mother Goose"
"Alouette" *(French)*

Section 3: Body Rhymes
Hands: "Yadayim L'malah" *(Hebrew)*
Knee Bounces: "Patshe, Patshe, Hentelach" *(Yiddish)*

Section 4: The Drum Sequence
"Rum Pum Pum"

Section 5: Stand-Up / Sit-Down Activities
"Bate, Bate, Chocolate" *(Spanish)*
"I Had a Little Dreidel"

Section 6: Animal Activities
"Los pollitos dicen" *(Spanish)*

Section 7: Musical Instruments and Scarves
Bells (ring to music): "Mocher Prachim" by Ofra Haza (at https://youtu.be/puaRJOmcMSU)
Maracas (shake to music): "Bamboleo" by the Gipsy Kings (at https://youtu.be/puaRJOmcMSU)
Scarves: "The Wind Is Singing in the Mountains"

Section 8: Lullabies
"De Colores" by José-Luis Orozco (at https://www.youtube.com/watch?v=hR2oYik-aCA)

Section 9: Interactive Rhymes
"Las Posadas" *(Do the traditional walk and knock.)*

Section 10: Closing Ritual
"Can You Kick with Two Feet?"

NOTE

1. Ellen Galinsky, *Mind in the Making: The Seven Essential Life Skills Every Child Needs* (New York: Harper-Studio, 2010).

Snapshot: Using Songs and Rhymes in Different Languages

Jan Fabiyi is an experienced MGOL facilitator who uses different languages in her sessions.

I enjoy using songs and rhymes in different languages. However, I take time not only to sing the songs but to almost teach them first so that people feel comfortable joining in. I find that when people are faced with a rhyme in a different language, they often sit back and assume that part of the program is not for them. They tune out. In order to successfully use foreign languages, I review it line by line and go over it a number of times with fun hand motions to involve and entertain everybody.

Teaching Adults about MGOL

ALTHOUGH MOTHER GOOSE ON THE LOOSE (MGOL) IS advertised as an early literacy program, facilitators understand that it is designed to benefit adults as well as children. In recognition that parents are a child's first and best teacher, developmental tips about child development combined with nursery rhyme activities and modeling of healthy parenting behavior helps librarians inspire adult attendees to build early literacy skills in their children.

Yet adult involvement in MGOL can go much further than that! Parents can learn to be MGOL facilitators. The adult education part of MGOL can be extended into a parent education program. MGOL can also be used as a parenting program for teen moms and for women recovering from addiction. It can become a training program for parents and a mentoring program for preschool and kindergarten teachers. Intrigued? Read on!

Parents as MGOL Facilitators

If you are planning a vacation and need someone else to run MGOL in your absence, try asking a parent who has attended many MGOL sessions to substitute. Since MGOL follows the same structure and has quite a bit of repetition, caregivers who have been to several sessions are likely to express interest in facilitating programs. This has happened a number of times: anecdotal evidence shows that parents enjoy facilitating and participants enjoy parent-run sessions.

Key Features

Parents run the program rather than librarians. Many parent-led MGOL facilitators have their little ones sit on their lap throughout the program.

Tips for Success

- Look for the "more involved" participants; encourage them to take their participation a step further by becoming a parent facilitator. The longer they have attended the program with their children, the more familiar and comfortable they will be with presenting sessions.
- Let volunteer facilitators know that their children are welcome to attend while they run the program.
- Schedule a time to train together.
- Prepare a program script, and explain the structure.
- Go through each of the materials (felt pieces, puppets, books, instruments, and scarves), stating the library's expectations for loaning the materials to the parent volunteer. Consider how and when the materials should be returned; discuss the physical logistics of transferring the materials when the parent volunteer arrives.
- Supply felt, and encourage parent volunteers to make their own felt pieces for the program, choosing rhymes and songs to go along with them.
- Practice together until the parents feel comfortable presenting the program.

- If possible, train several parents at once, so all the responsibility doesn't rest on the shoulders of one. It also helps avoid burnout.
- Highlight the benefits of modeling community involvement and participation for children, even if the children are still babies.

Using MGOL to Highlight Library Resources—Talking about Tots

Parents who want to learn about their children's development may be too busy to read or go to lectures. A special parent-education component held once a month directly following MGOL sessions can fill this void. Informal ten- to fifteen-minute sessions can be presented by talking about an aspect of child development, describing a book you have just read on parenting or brain development, reporting on new research regarding some aspect of early

childhood, or talking about an article on the importance of bedtime routines. These topics can be connected to MGOL by dissecting activities and highlighting the skills being developed. This explains to parents how and why MGOL activities help build school readiness skills. Use this time to also promote library resources to families, emphasizing your parenting collection. Feel free to use the "How Nursery Rhyme Activities Help Children Develop School Readiness Skills" handout in resource C.

Key Features

Information regarding child development and parenting can be shared with busy parents through informal presentations. The presentations take place in the same room where the MGOL session is held immediately following the session. Children are playing; parents keep an eye on them while listening.

Snapshot: Voices from the Field

Miruna Patrascanu filled in as a parent MGOL facilitator during the summer months, when the regular facilitator at the Village Learning Place was needed elsewhere.

I first started taking my daughter to Mother Goose on the Loose at the Waverly Library when she was eight months old. I heard about the program from another parent I met in the neighborhood and checked it out. I was amazed at how engaged my young child became. At that point, she was awake and alert, and I didn't really know what to do with her. It was interesting to see her in that group setting. I learned to do rhymes and songs with her—things that I had no clue about doing on my own.

That was how I got started. I started taking her every week. The more I learned about MGOL, the more interesting it became. I was interested in the structure behind it. At first, I didn't realize that everything had a purpose. When I attended more and more, I wanted to learn more about the theory behind it, to understand what was actually going on with my child. I knew nothing about early childhood development.

I wanted to keep it going because it had been so valuable to our family. So I wanted to pitch in, and I made my daughter love it. At one time, she was going three times a week, and it didn't feel like enough! Even though we were going three times a week, it was always interesting. The people doing it changed, and those doing it changed 20 percent, so they kept it interesting. I never got bored.

About two years ago, during the summer of 2015, Mr. Cork (the usual facilitator) was going to be gone for six to eight weeks, so I subbed for him. It's funny—my daughter is now four and a half, and she asked just last week, "Can we go teach MGOL at the VLP again?" She remembers!

I would teach, and she would sit on my lap, and sometimes she would help pass out the scarves. I used a mouse puppet that I had at home, Mousie. He went around and gave belly tickles. The kids really liked Mousie. They would come up and ask for more tummy tickles at the end of the session.

Tips for Success

- Do not overplan. This is a great opportunity to give short talks on relevant books you have read, conferences you have attended, and resources you want to recommend. The key word is *informal.*
- Don't worry if the adults don't look at you when you are talking or if they follow their children around the room rather than remaining in one place. Parents only pay partial attention when also keeping an eye on their children (who have just finished a thirty-minute program!), but they often absorb what they hear and express gratitude for the informal nature of the presentation.
- You may want to teach a few simple ASL signs and talk about ways that babies communicate.

MGOL for Parents—Talking about Tots Using Speakers

For two years, I was responsible for a partnership between MGOL at Port Discovery and the Kennedy Krieger Center for Autism and Related Disorders, a local multifaceted, interdisciplinary program serving children, families, and professionals in the autism spectrum disorders (ASD) community. Since several hundred graduates and postgraduates receive training at Kennedy Krieger each year, we designed a program that invited a guest speaker to speak to our MGOL families about their research once each month. The target group for these talks was parents and caregivers of children from three to thirty-two months. Since the talks started as soon as our MGOL session ended, some toys were brought out, and children played while parents listened. The presentations covered a number of topics, all tied in somehow with child development.

This was *not* a quiet listening atmosphere. Parents often had to play with their children while semilistening to the talk. Sometimes parents had to follow their children around the room and it would seem as if they weren't paying attention, but they would suddenly comment on something the speaker was saying or ask a related question.

Key Features

Inviting outside speakers once a month to give presentations on different topics and to answer questions adds to MGOL's parent education component. During these informal talks, children play with educational toys that have been brought out immediately following the session.

Tips for Success

- Remind participants at the beginning of your MGOL session that a guest presenter will be talking about the topic for ten minutes after the session. Mention that you will be providing toys for the children, and encourage everyone to stay.
- Introduce your guest speaker immediately after the session, even before you bring out the toys, in order to prevent people from leaving. Be sure to also mention the name of your guest's affiliated institution.
- Ask graduate and doctoral students to present; they often love to talk about their research.
- Ask a doctoral student or a professor to be your partner. Since doctoral students know other doctoral students, assigning responsibility for setting up the talk to your partner will save you from looking for new presenters every month.
- See the "Talking about Tots" topic list with annotations in resource C.
- See also "How Nursery Rhyme Activities Help Children Develop School Readiness Skills" in resource C.

Using MGOL to Train Early Childhood Professionals

As the early literacy coordinator for the San Francisco Public Library (SFPL), Christy Estrovitz initiated a workshop series in order to support the professional development of San Francisco's early childhood educators. As part of library's early literacy initiative, the series was designed to intellectually support and connect infant, toddler, and preschool teachers as well as early childhood educators. Since rhymes and songs are the universal language of early childhood, MGOL was used as a part of the series to bring educators together to improve their skills and inspire them in the classroom.

For eight years, SFPL's monthly workshops provided the opportunity for professional networking and gave out free resources that attendees could take back with them to enhance programming and share with their colleagues, thus creating a ripple effect. It supported the daily work of enriching the lives of young children while inspiring their caregivers as professionals.

Key Features

The learning series is held monthly and requires a commitment from the library for program organization, scheduling, marketing, and space. Attendees register one month in advance for the Saturday professional develop-

ment training. The series features a variety of topics and guest speakers; sometimes themes will scaffold from one month to the next. Morning refreshments provide the opportunity for networking and are followed by professional development. Participants leave with resources in hand. Library books and media enhance each presentation. At least one session is devoted to MGOL; manuals, music, and tote bags are given to each attendee.

Tips for Success

- Start by having a miniature resource fair with your partners so you can spread the word to ensure they know about the library as a resource to the community.

Snapshot: Voices from the Field

Klaus Libertus was instrumental in creating the "Talking about Tots" speaker series while working as a postdoctoral fellow at the Kennedy Krieger Institute in Baltimore. He is now an assistant professor in the Department of Psychology at the University of Pittsburgh.

Fun fact: most scientists are parents as well. I myself have three children. Watching them grow has changed and challenged my understanding of child development. It is one thing to read about how children learn to share objects and quite another to see them actually do it. But being a new parent is also scary. Information on how to raise children, what to do and what not to do, pops up everywhere. How are parents to know what advice to take and what advice to ignore? This is mostly left up to our intuition. This is where science can help. While those Facebook posts you read and YouTube videos you watch are based on tips from other parents who experienced their own children, scientists try to establish general patterns that repeat across a large number of children.

Knowledge is power, and can be highly reassuring for new parents. For example, while all the babies of your friends may start walking at ten months, research shows that there is a wide range with some babies staring to walk only around eighteen months of age. As a parent, knowledge about research findings helped me stay calm, drown out the noise of advice, and know when to worry and start asking questions.

But I have to confess, talking to parents after the MGOL program also has some benefits for us

scientists. Why do we do research? Yes, we do want to find out how things work and how we can help if things go wrong. But most of all, we would like to generate new knowledge that is being used in the real world. In my work, I examine the relation between motor and cognitive development and write research reports about my findings. I know a lot about these things and love to write about them. But sadly, only a few people will ever read my articles. As a parent, I understand why you don't have time to read scientific reports. Talking about Tots gives scientists like me an opportunity to talk to parents about our findings and let them have an impact on your daily interactions with your child. Sure, you hear about some findings in the news. But chances are that the research that matters most to you will available only at a Talking about Tots program.

Talking about Tots is a great idea, and a program like this should be accessible to parents everywhere. It is hard to make time when you have children. This is why bringing science to parents and their children in an engaging context is important. It is important for science to make an impact on the next generation, and it is important for parents to better understand their child and foster growth and development during fun interactions.

- Have refreshments. If a morning series does not work for your library, you can easily modify it to an afternoon tea.
- Provide a space large enough to move around for activities.
- Utilize experts from the field, local leaders in early education, and your own in-house talent.
- Ask your guest speakers if they have resources they can provide during their session.
- If you cannot provide resources, offer prizes; if you do not have enough books for everyone, do a raffle.
- Ideas for free resources include books (for children or for professional development), puppets, flannelboard pieces, media (CDs with songs), and musical instruments.
- Thank the workshop attendees for choosing to be at the library to enhance their profession. Take time to celebrate them and what they do for the community. Offer them appreciation, because it is a choice. These teachers work early mornings and late evenings five days a week, and they choose to come in on a weekend to continue their learning.
- Show your appreciation by pulling and displaying books related to that session's topic from the library's resources in order to save the educators' time.
- Know who your partners are so they can spread the word and assist with marketing the series.
- Make sure everyone has a library card.
- If possible, offer a special "teacher card" or assist teachers by offering longer borrowing periods, lending small collections or activity boxes, and removing overdue fines.

MGOL Activities for Senior Citizens

Nicole Brown from the Buffalo and Erie County Public Library uses MGOL's format and layout to integrate traditional MGOL activities into a monthly program called "Journeys with Nicole," presented for the senior citizens she visits monthly with her library's bookmobile. In addition, each program includes a discussion in which participants are asked about things they remember and experiences they've had. For example, one program included a discussion on Elvis songs and trivia. The res-

idents enjoy puppets, musical instruments, and scarves. There are no interactive rhymes since residents of rehabilitation and nursing homes often have trouble standing up and sitting down.

Key Features

Nicole's program focuses on a time period, person, or holiday. The flannelboard is not used, and there are no interactive rhymes that require the older adults to get up and down. Each session has a discussion where participants are encouraged to share their life experiences and be heard. Books are discussed, and program themes are on a higher level more suitable for older adults rather than children. Picture books are not read, but a puppet is always used. Stand-up / sit-down activities are changed to stretches afterward. Bells or another musical instrument is used with a song or rhyme, and scarves are always used.

Tips for Success

- When working with adults who have dementia and other memory issues, keep your book short and simple, but make sure it has interesting content. For example, *Wild about Books* by Judy Sierra is not a good choice because the content is too low and the book is too long.
- Keep in mind that things will not always go as you planned, and you may not end up using all the sections that you intended. Go with the flow and relax. It is always good to overplan rather than underplan. Because you are working with adults rather than children, they may enjoy discussing one section of trivia more than singing or playing with the scarves. As long as they are enjoying themselves, that is all that matters.
- Nicole recommends, "Don't be afraid to be silly and put yourself out there! Seniors truly enjoy having you engage with them through singing and dancing. They may not be able to move the same way you can, but if you are involved, they will sing with you and do as much as they can!"
- It is important to let the seniors be heard and to share their life experiences.
- Use many of the same tools you would use in a MGOL storytime, and adjust as needed. Scarves,

puppets, and musical instruments are the key when engaging participants and having them invest in the program. Make sure the on-site activities director is involved too!

- Check out one of Nicole Brown's scripts for use with senior citizen at https://bit.ly/2LpbKYE.

MGOL Training for Childcare Providers, Pre-K, and Kindergarten Teachers

Created in response to the need for improved quality of childcare in Baltimore, this grant-funded program kicks off with a half day of MGOL training for teachers that highlights findings in brain research, describes the structure and philosophy of MGOL, and presents a sample program. Another half day of training involves practical instructions for planning and presenting a MGOL session with sample activities that give the participants hands-on experience.

Teachers are given a classroom "kit" with enough instruments and scarves to run their own MGOL program. For the next five weeks, the librarian presents a weekly MGOL program in each teacher's classroom or daycare group. The first three programs are presented solely by the librarian while the teachers participate along with their students. Teachers receive printed lesson plans and extension sheets containing rhyme resources, book recommendations, and early childhood activities to complement each session.

Following the first three sessions, teachers work with the librarian and choose a section or two to present, such as the rhymes and reads or the stand-up / sit-down activities and the drum sequence. During the week, they are responsible for preparing on their own and practicing. After having seen three sessions modeled, learning the songs and rhymes along with their students, and reading the written materials, the teacher presents the fourth program with the librarian by performing the chosen sections. The librarian provides written feedback, highlighting good practices and giving some suggestions. The same process takes place for the fifth and final sessions, helping teachers become comfortable presenting the entire program on their own. After using the rhymes in their circle times, teachers can also use them for tran-

sitions or classroom management such as cleaning up or putting things away. Following the fifth session, the librarian asks the teachers to plan an entire MGOL program that they would be comfortable presenting on their own, providing assistance if requested.

Evaluations at the end of the program sessions and at the end of the training ask for feedback. The librarian returns after several months to see what the teachers are still doing from the training.

This is an intensive intervention. Because the materials, staffing, and professional expertise that go into it can be costly, grant funding is often needed. But the contact with the teachers and the continuity provided is invaluable. This model presents a great opportunity for offering library support services beyond the sessions, as it includes readers' advisory with the handouts, referrals to the library for checking out books for use in programs, and personal assistance to teachers in program planning and presentation. This model involves at least seven separate contacts between librarians and teachers, enabling maximized library support for teachers.

Key Features

This rendition of MGOL features at least one training workshop for adults plus classroom programs, mentoring sessions, and a classroom "kit" for each teacher. Sessions differ slightly depending on ages. For example, the traditional MGOL program is used for infant classes. For pre-K or kindergarten children, the session is leveled up by reading two books aloud, eliminating the farm animals sounds because they have already passed that level, involving more extended rhymes because children have a capacity to learn the language easier, and extending the singing and rhyming. Activities such as clapping songs with a clapping routine (like a playground clap) may be added. Scarf time remains but includes more sophisticated activities than naming and pretending to wash body parts. Occasionally two different instruments like bells and castanets are used in place of scarves. All sessions last for forty-five minutes, even the sessions for infants and toddlers.

Tips for Success

- Work with your counterparts to decide when the original training is going to be offered; most teachers will want to do it during paid professional development time. Find out when the childcare center director will schedule this time for their staff; some centers may actually need to close for the training. Or you may be asked to train teachers in the evenings.

- Bring your own props for each session, but deliver a classroom kit to each teacher at the first session, equipping them from the beginning with read-aloud books, teacher resource books (rhyme collections and songs), props, and enough instruments for the entire class.

- Remind teachers during the training and also during the sessions that they will be presenting different segments during sessions four and five.

- Learn everyone's name by asking teachers to give you an attendance list with each student's first name, taking it home, and studying it. It is easier to match names with faces when the names are already familiar.

- As you will be in the classrooms for all five sessions, learn students' names right away. Using their names is a way of creating relationships quickly, recognizing individual children, and making them feel like they belong.

- Use students' names as much as possible, such as when passing out the bells: "Here, Jessie. Here, Lynn." If you really work at it for the first and second sessions, it gets easier. The more you use their names, the more they bond with you.

- Remember that you are teaching the teachers as well as the students, and be responsive to both audiences. Keep an eye on how the students are responding, and adjust to that while also watching the teachers or childcare providers in the same way.

- Young children learn songs quickly; by the second or third session, they are singing along. Teachers and childcare providers don't seem to absorb new songs as quickly. Impress on them that knowing the songs and rhymes is essential for running a program and that in order to learn the rhymes, they need to make it a priority.

- Open and explore all the items in the classroom kit with each teacher. Suggest that they use the items with their students right away and practice the songs with their students between sessions. This forces them to use MGOL activities even if they are not 100 percent confident. If the kits aren't explored as soon as possible, teachers delay digging in and the kits sit unopened in the corner for a week or two. Build administrative support by asking the childcare center director or fellow teachers to ensure the kits are being used.

- In addition to supplying program materials, focus on building relationships with the teachers. While the students benefit from your sessions, you want teachers to take advantage of your presence. Get administrative endorsement from the beginning by asking to meet with the principal and the teachers, including them directly in the scheduling of the training and the classroom sessions. Hold face-to-face meetings with the teachers ahead of time.

- Try spending time with teachers during lunchtime, after school, or at their center in the evening.

- After the third session, ask the teachers to tell you which section they want to lead and which rhymes they plan on using for the upcoming joint session. If they are having trouble deciding, feel free to offer suggestions. When it is the teacher's turn to present a segment or two during the fourth and fifth sessions, you will already know what rhymes to expect. When the teacher is presenting, you should observe and take notes. Ask questions like the following:

  » Does the teacher know the words?
  » Does the activity match the words?
  » Is the activity joyful?
  » Is the activity age appropriate?
  » Are the children engaged?

- When the session ends, ask the teacher "How did you feel?" and "How do you think it went?" Listen to the teacher's impressions. Provide positive feedback (there is always at least one good thing to say) and then add suggestions for making the presentation even better. You may prefer to type up your feedback and send it via e-mail rather than in person. Bring a physical copy of the feedback to the next session, go over it with the teacher, and see if your suggestions have been implemented.

Adaptations for Infants and Toddlers

- Limit the number of lap rhymes done and use more stand-up / sit-down activities, because with infants and toddlers, you are not working with one adult per child.
- Because toddlers are very active, encourage their teachers to participate but realize that they also have to manage the group.
- Plan on forty-five-minute sessions for infants, but be prepared for much of that time to be eaten up by teacher instruction. There may be three infants per teacher, and you will want to do the same rhyme with each infant. Some infants may have to be put in little booster seats for parts of the session, because teachers can't hold three infants on their lap at the same time.
- For infants, use lots of rotation and repetition.

Adaptations for Older Children

- As the sessions progress, let the students volunteer and take turns leading rhymes. For instance, look for students who are participating well, and ask one of them to stand up in front of the room and lead the hello rhymes. Be ready to assist when needed.
- When choosing volunteers for different sessions, remember that not everyone has to have a turn. Let older children volunteer to read a rhyme, to pass out and collect the instruments, and to turn the handle on the jack-in-the-box. You may want to ask the teacher "Who had a really good day today?" and choose that child to run an activity. The other children will follow his or her lead. This empowers the student leaders while giving them the chance to do a public presentation.
- During the drum sequence, start off with the traditional "Rum Pum Pum" activity. If it seems easy for them, ask them to tap out their first and last names during the second session. If that seems easy, during the third session, play other name games with or without instruments, such as "Jack Be Nimble," and say the child's name "jumps over the candlestick" while everyone claps. While the group

claps to the rhyme or claps to the syllables, each child still get individual attention by stepping out in front of the group, doing something with all eyes on them, and then returning to the group. This activity builds a sense of being responsible to the group as well as exercising self-regulation skills.

MGOL Use in Educating Future Librarians

Jamie Naidoo, Foster-EBSCO professor at the University of Alabama, School of Library and Information Studies, uses MGOL to teach students about varying aspects of children's librarianship. MGOL is introduced in relation to other readings about early literacy as an example of putting theory into practice; four of his classes have connections with MGOL.

When exploring early literacy initiatives and programs in his "Early Childhood Literacy Materials and Story Programs" course, students intensively dive into, explore, and pull out need-to-know resources from selected websites including MGOL. They are asked to think critically about ways to put the shared information into practice and report on how that relates to what they currently do or what they could do in terms of serving young children in their libraries.

During Jamie's "Youth Programming" course, guest speakers share stories about outreach programming in their communities. It is not unusual for speakers to mention MGOL adaptations; a recent speaker from Georgia mentioned it as a "great resource" and spoke enthusiastically about putting elements from MGOL into practice at his library.

After reading an interview with me about the Felt Board Mother Goose on the Loose app in Dr. Naidoo's book *Diversity Programming for Digital Youth: Promoting Cultural Competence in the Children's Library* (Libraries Unlimited 2014), "Cultural Literacy Programming" students watch a demonstration of different ways to use the MGOL app. They are asked to explain how they can incorporate the app into MGOL programs or another early literacy program they present.

In "Traditional and Digital Storytelling," the MGOL app is modeled via screen share and a webcam. Students see how the app can be used for storytelling purposes.

One student did an independent study project on early literacy relating to her library system. She looked at MGOL as part of various other programs that were out there and as a way to specifically put early literacy concepts, theory, and skills into practice; monitor success; and see if there was any change in her community.

Key Features

Using MGOL in master's of library and information science (MLIS) classes allows current and future librarians to connect their readings with a current research-based early literacy practice. It gives students an opportunity to learn about this practice, interact with librarians who have presented or participated in MGOL programs, explore the website, and learn about the MGOL app.

Snapshot: MGOL Training for Childcare Providers, Pre-K, and Kindergarten Teachers

Aiming to make MGOL practices sustainable in the classroom or childcare center while providing professional development credits and materials, Summer Rosswog, the early childhood and literacy manager at Port Discovery Children's Museum, developed this grant-funded MGOL training and mentoring program for home daycare providers, daycare center teachers, preschool teachers, and kindergarten teachers.

What's personally satisfying to me is watching kids play with language and have fun with it, because a lot of times, we don't think of play and early language and literacy as going together. MGOL is a program where you play with language. I noticed older kids starting to make up their own rhymes and lyrics. Or if they weren't sure, they would substitute their own words. I would say, "That's a great way of saying that," and we would all try it that way. A big joy for me was that they were playing with the words, having fun, and using language in different ways. It is like building with blocks and playing with animal figures. We generally think of play as involving tactile things, but using language is also a way of playing.

You can explore different cultures and try to integrate things that are culturally relevant into your programs. Almost 100 percent of the children who participate in my programs are African American, so I investigated playground songs and rhymes with a rich African American connection. There are playground rhymes that have been around for decades. That is language play! It is authentic for the environment in which I work, with urban, African American kids.

Integrating those rhymes into MGOL adds fun with the language, and it is fun to watch the children play with the language. I've added songs and playground rhymes that I used to do, such as hopscotch rhymes and skip rope rhymes. There are books on those, and they can be adapted to MGOL, enabling children to play with language. That is what MGOL is about. Children start to play with the words they are using. They start by repeating and singing back to you, and then they start by creating their own words, their own lyrics, their own tunes.

The other great experience is the progress you see in five short sessions with children and their teachers. Teachers engage with the materials and engage with their students in new ways. They learn how to get out of their comfort zones and try something new. They also get opportunities to demonstrate what they are good at. The children just absorb it.

Although you may have started out as a stranger, when you enter the classroom for session three, a student will start singing a song to you that you sang last week. When I arrived for the fourth session, there was a chorus of kids singing as I entered the classroom. That happens in most classrooms by session three or four; several children start singing as I am setting up or breaking things down. They'll sing songs we have just sung together. They are finding their voices; they are playing with language; they are bringing song into their classrooms. This usually happens with every series of this program!

Tips for Success

Using MGOL in the classroom can help students make deeper connections between their textbook readings and an actual literacy program.

- Since many student bodies consist of a national online cohort, one or more students may have attended a MGOL session. When this occurs, invite them to talk about their firsthand experience seeing MGOL in action.
- For early literacy classes, bring in guest speakers who have had personal experience with MGOL.
- Invite "Youth Programming" students who are interested to explore the outreach components of MGOL.
- Introduce your students to the MGOL app, and ask them to use it to find new ways to build children's literacy skills.

Conclusion

By reading about the many different directions in which people have taken MGOL and the wide variety of people it has positively impacted, I hope you will be inspired to use MGOL to help create a program that works for you and the communities that you serve. Whether you are working with infants, toddlers, preschoolers, school children, teens, adults, or senior citizens or are presenting programs in hospitals, prisons, Early Head Starts, libraries, museums, classrooms, school cafeterias, parks, living rooms, or churches, there should be plenty of ideas regarding what to expect and lots of suggestions for planning and executing programs suitable for different audiences. I am indebted to this book's many contributors for their wisdom, their creativity, and their willingness to share.

Snapshot: Using the MGOL Curriculum to Teach Future Librarians

Lisa G. Kropp is the director of the Lindenhurst Memorial Library in Lindenhurst, New York, and an adjunct professor at St. John's University in Queens, New York.

One of the reasons that I chose to be an adjunct at St. John's University was because they offered an early learning materials and services course (LIS 125). As an early learning librarian, I knew how important an area this was to devote an entire course. This fifteen-week, three-credit graduate course focuses on all things early learning, from child development charts to selecting materials, how to create age-appropriate programs, and community engagement. Students spend a significant amount of time learning about national early learning programs such as the Public Library Association and Association for Library Service to Children initiatives, Every Child Ready to Read, Middle County Public Library's Family Place Libraries, and MGOL. Very often, students taking LIS 125 come to the classroom with no experience in planning early learning programs. It is very easy to become overwhelmed by the many different areas of developmental needs to cover in a "simple" nursery rhyme program. This is where MGOL shows its strength—in its curriculum. It is designed to easily build on the different social-emotional, fine and gross motor, and early literacy skills needed for all children to enter school ready to learn. It has become an important component of our online discussion board, where students spend time working through the various components of the curriculum. As an educator, I am confident that my students are prepared to work in the field of early learning in a public library because of the high-quality curriculum MGOL offers them. One of the best aspects of it is the true practicality of the program. This isn't a theoretical program but rather a hands-on, evidenced-based approach that shows participants how to organize, design, and implement successful early learning programs at their library. We also spend time discussing how the program has evolved in an increasingly online world, with students downloading the MGOL app and coming up with ways to incorporate the app into their sample library programs.

I believe that the secret to MGOL's success is the fact that it is so versatile. Rather than being told to follow a script, each MGOL facilitator is given a flexible blueprint and then told to put his or her own individual stamp on it. Learning is all about connections; when the brain learns something new, a synapse or new connection is formed. People also learn best by connecting with other people, and joyous connections make a very strong impact. Thus the best MGOL programs are the ones that reflect the interests and personality of their presenter. There is no "one right way"; instead, there is a universe of uses for MGOL, and we have just touched the tip of the iceberg.

Someday, I hope to have a serious research study done on MGOL's impact, so we can say its impact is research-proven as well as research-based. But in the meantime, please take new ideas from this book, enjoy building on them, and let me know about the great new programs you have been creating. Happy singing!

Part IV
Mother Goose on the Loose Resources

The Mother Goose on the Loose Songbook and Rhyme Book

Stage directions are italicized throughout the songs. All songs are traditional, public-domain songs unless otherwise noted.

A

ABC Song

A, B, C, D, E, D, G,
H, I, J, K, L, M, N, O, P,
Q, R, S, T, U, V,
W, X, Y, and Z.
Now I know my ABCs
I love you, and you love me.

Abracadabra *(a call-and-response song)*

Abracadabra ickity boo!
Participants repeat.
This scarf's gonna turn into…
Participants repeat.
a horn on a unicorn…a very, very, very long horn!
Stretch scarf out from your forehead.
(Repeat the first two lines each time you do a different action.)
a snake slithering in the grass like that!
Wave the scarf around on the floor.
a flag waving on a pole!
Say the Pledge of Allegiance if you like; wave scarf back and forth in the air.
a ghost…woooooo…woooooo…boo!
Cover your head with the scarf.

a flute…toodley doot, toodley doot!
Hold the scarf out to the side of your mouth and make flute sounds.
a butterfly…flying high in the sky, a beautiful butterfly!
Hold the scarf in the middle to make a butterfly shape, and move it through the air.
a guitar!
Strum scarf, and make musical sounds.
a blindfold…Oh, no! I can't see!
Hold the scarf over your eyes.
a ball! Roll it up into a ball. Make it very, very small… one, two, three, wheeeee!
Throw scarf up into the air.

—Adapted by Gloria Bartas
(A video can be viewed at https://youtu.be/1e8ivrpyhug.)

Alligator, Alligator

Alligator, alligator, sitting on a log.
Down in the water, he sees a frog.
Down goes the alligator, around goes the log.
Away swims the frog.

(A video can be viewed at https://www.youtube.com/watch?v=bH9HZ8ArxvU.)

Alouette

Alouette, gentille alouette
Alouette, je te plumerai.
Alouette, gentille alouette
Alouette, je te plumerai.

Je te plumerai la tête.

Je te plumerai la tête.

Et la tête

Et la tête

Alouette

Alouette

Are You Sleeping, Brother John? / Frère Jacques

Are you sleeping? Are you sleeping? Brother John? Brother John?

Morning bells are ringing. Morning bells are ringing.

Ding, ding, dong. Ding, ding, dong.

Frère Jacques, Frère Jacques, dormez-vous? Dormez-vous?

Sonnez les matines. Sonnez les matines.

Ding, ding, dong. Ding, ding, dong

—By Alain le Lait

B

Baa Baa Black Sheep

Baa baa black sheep, have you any wool?

Yes, I do, here are four bags full.

One for my mommy, and one for my dad,

One for the little girl and one for the lad.

Baa baa black sheep, have you any wool?

Yes, I do, here are four bags full.

Repeat, substituting different colors.

(A video can be viewed at https://youtu.be/juMWGV29 hvY.)

Baby Shark (*This is a favorite of children and adults. They love Grandma Shark!*)

Make a small shark mouth with two fingers.

Baby Shark, doo doo, doo doo doo doo. (3x)

Baby Shark.

Make a bigger shark mouth with hands connected at the wrist.

Mummy Shark, doo doo, doo doo doo doo. (3x)

Mummy Shark.

Make a large shark mouth using whole arms.

Daddy Shark, doo doo, doo doo doo doo. (3x)

Daddy Shark.

Make a small shark mouth with wrinkled gums using knuckles on fists.

Grandma Shark, doo doo, doo doo doo doo. (3x)

Grandma Shark.

(A video can be viewed at https://youtu.be/vlnM3Lc71Pk.)

Bat under My Hat

(*Flannelboard: Put a felt bat under a felt hat*)

Bat, bat, come under my hat

And I'll give a piece of bacon.

And when I wake, I'll bake you a cake

If I am not mistaken.

(A video can be viewed at https://youtu.be/qSGsK9JL6oE.)

Bate, Bate, Chocolate

Bate, bate, chocolate,

Tu nariz de cacahuate,

Uno, dos, tres, CHO!

Uno, dos, tres, CO!

Uno, dos, tres, LA!

Uno, dos, tres, TE!

Chocolate, chocolate!

Bate, bate, chocolate!

Bate, bate, chocolate!

Bate, bate, bate, bate.

Baje la voz y el cuerpo [Lower your voice and body].

Bate, Bate, CHOCOLATE!

Brinque y grite [Jump up and shout].

—Traditional

Bears

The bear family. (3x)

Wild about bears. (3x)

Hibernate. Hibernate. Go to sleep for a long time. Go to sleep for a long time. (2x)

Bears have fur. (3x)

Bears have claws. (3x)

Baby bears are cubs. (3x)

Bears live in caves. (3x)

Bears eat lots of honey. (3x)

Hibernate. Hibernate. Go to sleep for a long time. Go to sleep for a long time.

Bears!

—By Gloria Bartas

(A video can be viewed at https://bit.ly/2CB8HNK.)

Bells Away

Bells away, bells away,
Put your bells away today.
Walk around with an open canvas bag, and sing this song while children put their bells back into the bag. (Note: This song can be used to clean up many items!)

—By Barbara Cass-Beggs
(A video can be viewed at https://youtu.be/WiMlKBtvZFc.)

C

Can You Kick with Two Feet?

Can you kick with two feet, two feet, two feet?
Can you kick with two feet? Kick, kick, kick, kick…
Continue with more verses: clap with two hands, wave with two arms, nod with one head, kiss with two lips, and sway from side to side.

—Words and music by Barbara Cass-Beggs
(A video can be viewed at https://youtu.be/iuX21Rlr4eY.)

Chewy, Chewy Bubble Gum

Chewy, chewy, chewy, chewy, bubble gum, bubble gum, bubble gum.
Chewy, chewy, chewy, chewy, bubble gum, stick your _____ to your _____.
Unstick….

Chicken Soup for Shabbat *(tune of "London Bridge")*

Put a chicken in the pot.
Stir it up, nice and hot.
Get it ready for Shabbat,
For Shabbat.
Repeat these lyrics over and over, asking the children what else to put into the pot. You may get some funny answers!

Cobbler, Cobbler, Mend My Shoe

Sit on the floor with your legs outstretched and feet together.
Cobbler, cobbler, mend my shoe.
Have them done by half past two.
Move to the beat by opening your feet to form a V and then bringing them together.
Stitch them up
Lean back and lift one leg up.

and stitch them down.
Lean back and lift the other leg up.
Make the finest shoes in town.
Make your hands into fists, and tap them together twice (this is the word shoes in ASL) to the beat.

—Adapted by Gloria Bartas
(A video can be viewed at https://youtu.be/q2MBx5VnAJw.)

D

Dance Your Fingers Up

Dance your fingers up, dance your fingers down.
Dance them to the side, and dance them all around.
Dance them on your shoulders, dance them on your head.
Dance them on your tummy, and put them all to bed.

(A video can be viewed at https://youtu.be/clobiGT8V2A.)

Do You Know the Ice Cream Man? *(Tune: "Do You Know the Muffin Man?")*

Do you know the ice cream man, the ice cream man, the ice cream man?
Do you know the ice-cream man, who lives down on our street?
His bell goes tingle, tingle, ting [3x]
As he goes down our street.

—Traditional English; words adapted by Barbara Cass-Beggs

E

The Eency Weency Spider *(Variation: The Great Big Spider; perform with puppet kisses)*

The eency weency spider went up the waterspout.
Put your thumb to your index finger on the other hand and vice versa; "walk" your fingers up in the air.
Down came the rain and washed the spider out.
Push down and out with your hands.
Out came the sun and dried up all the rain.
Raise hands above your head, and touch your fingers together to form a circle.
So the eency weency spider climbed up the spout again.
Repeat the initial walking motion with fingers.
The GREAT BIG spider went up the waterspout…
Repeat the song using a deep voice and large hand movements.

The Elephant

> The elephant moves very slowly.
> Oh, so very slowly.
> He doesn't like to move too fast.
> Because he is so big and heavy.
>
> But should he see a tiger
> Or spy a mean old hunter
> He will start to run and shake the ground
> And make them all fall down.
>
> Rumble, rumble, rumble.
> Hear the jungle rumble.
> Rumble, rumble, rumble.
> Hear the jungle rumble.
>
> Trees shake and sway
> As the birdies fly away.
> Lions run and hide
> With their babies by their side.
>
> Rumble, rumble, rumble.
> Hear the jungle rumble.
> Rumble, rumble, rumble.
> Hear the jungle rumble.
>
> *Repeat.*
>
> The elephant moves very slowly.
> Oh, so very slowly.
> He doesn't like to move too fast
> Because he is so big and heavy.

—Words and music by Hap Palmer (from the album Early Childhood Classics, ©Hap-Pal Music, www.happalmer.com)

Elephants Have Wrinkles

Lyrics can be found at www.songsforteaching.com/animalsongs/elephantshavewrinkles.htm.

(A video can be viewed at https://youtu.be/Zs3dwkqJ898.)

Everybody Loves Saturday Night

> Everybody loves Saturday night. (2x)
> Everybody, everybody, everybody, everybody,
> Everybody loves Saturday night.
> *Repeat in different languages.*

(Videos can be viewed at www.songsforteaching.com/folk/everybodylovesasatnight.php.)

Eye Winker, Tom Tinker

> Eye winker, Tom tinker.
> *Point to one eye, then the other.*
> Nose smeller, mouth eater.
> *Beep nose, tap mouth.*
> Chin chopper, chin chopper, chin chopper.
> *Tap chin per syllable.*
> Guzzle whopper!
> *Tickle baby's belly.*

(A video can be viewed at https://youtu.be/uWy_P3dRfuc.)

F

Farm Animals Song (Tune: "Where Is Thumbkin?")

> *Pull stuffed animals or puppets out of a tote bag or pillow case and sing this call and response song about each one. Demonstrate the ASL sign for each animal.*
> Where is cow? *(librarian)*
> Where is cow? *(audience)*
> Here she is. *(librarian)*
> Here she is. *(audience)*
> What does cow say? *(librarian)*
> What does cow say? *(audience)*
> Moo! Moo! Moo! *(librarian)*
> Moo! Moo! Moo! *(audience)*
> Moo! Moo! Moo! *(librarian)*
> Moo! Moo! Moo! *(audience)*
> *Repeat with rooster, pig, duck, horse, frog, dog, sheep, bumblebee, fish, and chicken.*

—Adapted by Gloria Bartas

Fee, Fie, Fo, Fum

> *Start with hand rolled into a fist.*
> Fee, fie, fo, fum,
> *Uncurl fingers one at a time.*
> See my fingers, see my thumb.
> *Wiggle fingers and thumb.*
> Fee, fie, fo, fum,
> *Curl up fingers one at a time.*
> Good-bye fingers, good-bye thumb.
> *Wave "bye-bye" with your other hand.*

(A video can be viewed at https://youtu.be/ry50-5Hj86k.)

Fingers Like to Wiggle Waggle

Fingers like to wiggle waggle, wiggle waggle, wiggle
waggle.
Wiggle fingers of both hands in front of you.
Fingers like to wiggle waggle way up high!
*Wiggle fingers as you raise your hands, saying "up
high" in a very high voice.*
Fingers like to wiggle waggle, wiggle waggle, wiggle
waggle.
Wiggle fingers of both hands in front of you.
Fingers like to wiggle waggle way down low!
*Wiggle fingers as you lower hands to the floor, saying
"way down low" in a very low voice.*
Fingers like to wiggle waggle, wiggle waggle, wiggle
waggle.
Wiggle fingers of both hands in front of you.
Fingers like to wiggle waggle on my knee!
*Place fingers on your knee without changing your tone
of voice.*

—By Barbara Cass-Beggs
(A video can be viewed at https://youtu.be/Z8kKQHYZt7c.)

Five Fat Peas

Five fat peas in a pea pod pressed.
One grew, two grew, and so did all the rest.
They grew and they grew, and they did not stop.
They got so big that the pod went *pop!*

(A video can be viewed at https://youtu.be/enZsxF18Fzs.)

Five Fat Sausages

Five fat sausages frying in a pan,
The oil was hot so one went *bang! (Clap your hands.)*
Four fat sausages…three….two…one…and there
were no sausages left!

(A video can be viewed at https://youtu.be/DDhk2cAVM8k.)

Five Little Apples

Five little apples in the apple tree.
Five little apples smiled down on me.
I shook that tree as hard as I could.
Down fell the apples, mmmmmmm, they were good.

Five Little Pumpkins

Five little pumpkins sitting on a gate.
The first one said, "Oh my, it's getting late."
The second one said, "There are witches in the air."
The third one said, "But we don't care."
The fourth one said, "Let's run. Let's run!"
The fifth one said, "Isn't Halloween fun?"
Then "woo" went the wind
And out went the lights.
And five little pumpkins rolled out of sight.

(A video can be viewed at https://youtu.be/dBvc-Kp-rGQ.)

Five Little Speckled Frogs

Five little speckled frogs sat on a speckled log,
Eating some most delicious flies: yum, yum!
One jumped into the pool, where it is nice and cool,
And now there are four green speckled frogs: ribbit,
ribbit!
Continue counting down until there are none.

(A video can be viewed at https://youtu.be/i5PSaQoHZ2A.)

G
Good-Bye Song

Good-bye, good-bye, good-bye to you.
Sing good-bye. Sing good-bye.
Good-bye, good-bye, good-bye to you…sing good-
bye to you.
Good-bye, [name of child].
*Hold out the drum so each child can hit his or her
name to the beat of the syllables.*

—By Norman Hogeland
(A video can be viewed at https://bit.ly/2NoWos6.)

Good Morning Medley *(call-and-response song)*

Leader: Good morning! *Group:* Good morning!
Leader: Good morning! *Group:* Good morning!
Leader: Good morning! *Group:* Good morning!
Leader: To you!

Wash your face in the morning, scrub, scrub, scrub,
scrub, scrub, scrub.
Brush your teeth in the morning, swish, swish, swish,
swish, swish, swish.
Eat your breakfast in the morning, chew, chew, chew,
chew, chew, chew.
Good morning, good morning to you.

Kiss your mommy in the morning, kiss, kiss, kiss,
kiss, kiss, kiss.

Hug your daddy in the morning, hug, hug, hug, hug.
Walk your doggie in the morning, woof, woof, woof,
    woof, woof, woof.
Good morning, good morning to you.

Read a book in the morning, open shut, open shut.
Do your exercises in the morning, one, two, three,
    four, five, six, seven, eight.
Come to the library in the morning!
Good morning, good morning to you.

Put your clothes on in the morning, whoop…whoop!
(Don't forget your shoes!)
Pet your kitty cat in the morning, meow, meow.
Watch cartoons in the morning, look left and right
    with big eyes.
Good morning, good morning to you!

—Adapted by Gloria Bartas
(A video can be viewed at https://youtu.be/O8za0El403o.)

Good Morning Song

Good morning to Nina. How are you?
Good morning to Abigail. Yay!
Good morning to James. Hi, there.
Good morning to Daniel. Hi, there.
Good morning to Hank. How are ya doing today?
Good morning. Is that Laila? Hooray!
Good morning to Mickey. How are ya doing over
    there?
Good morning to Jaden. Nice hair!
Good morning to Leon, who's with his grandma
    today.
Good morning, to Luka. He's sitting over there.
Good morning, Maxine. Hi!
Good morning, good morning to you.

—Adapted by Gloria Bartas
(A video version can be viewed at https://youtu.be/Ldr-TyJ
CqII.)

Goosey, Goosey Gander

Goosey, goosey gander,
Demonstrate patting your knees.
Where do you wander?
Upstairs
Reach up.

and downstairs
Reach down.
And in my lady's chamber.
Demonstrate hugging yourself.

(A video can be viewed at https://youtu.be/j15Gi24LUoQ.)

The Grand Old Duke of York (*Do knee bounces.*)

Oh, the Grand Old Duke Of York,
He had ten thousand men.
He marched them up to the top of the hill,
And marched them down again.
And when they were up, they were up.
And when they were down, they were down.
And when they were only half way up,
They were neither up nor down!

(A video can be viewed at https://www.youtube.com/watch
?v=NaL7ghS1eUM.)

Grandfather's Clock

Grandfather's clock goes tick tock, tick tock, tick tock.
Play instrument slowly.
Mother's kitchen clock goes tick tock, tick tock, tick
    tock, tick tock.
Play instrument at a medium tempo.
Brother's little watch goes tick tick, tick tick, tick tick,
    tick tick, tick tick, tick tick—stop!
Play instrument very quickly and then stop.

—By Barbara Cass-Beggs
(A video can be viewed at https://youtu.be/-pu66fHvvao.)

Grey Squirrel

Grey squirrel, grey squirrel, shake your bushy tail.
Grey squirrel, grey squirrel, shake your bushy tail.
Hold a nut between your toes, wrinkle up your little
    nose.
Grey squirrel, grey squirrel, shake your bushy tail.

(The music can be found at https://youtu.be/Fb_wYmRK
jmM, sung by Shari Stone on *Singing with Shari: Oldies but
Goodies.*)

H

Handy Spandy

(This song helps everyone sit down after standing up.)

Handy Spandy, sugar and candy, we all jump in.
Jump into the circle.
Handy Spandy, sugar and candy, we all jump out.
Jump out of the circle.
Handy Spandy, sugar and candy, we all jump up.
Jump up.
Handy Spandy, sugar and candy, we all sit down.
Sit down.

(A video can be viewed at https://youtu.be/-potc0sNq2s.)

Hello Everybody, Yes, Indeed

Hello, everybody, yes, indeed, yes, indeed, yes, indeed.
Hello, everybody, yes, indeed, yes, indeed, my darling.
Hello, everybody, tu la la, tu la la, tu la la.
Hello, everybody, tu la la, tu la la, my darling.
Welcome each child and acknowledge something about them to make a personal connection.

(A video can be viewed at https://youtu.be/ALGubtHDnTQ.)

Here We Go Upperty Up

Here we go upperty up. Here we go downerdy down.
Stand in a circle, lift baby up and bring baby down.
Here we go upperty up with the sweetest baby in town.
Lift baby up and give her a kiss.
Here we go in, in, in, in. Here we go out, out, out, out.
Walk into the center of the circle. Go backwards to original circle.
Here we go in, in, in, in. And we turn ourselves about.
Walk into the center of the circle. Turn around while hugging baby.

—By Barbara Cass-Beggs
(A video version can be viewed at https://youtu.be/PMob2soBcFE.)

Hey Diddle Diddle

Hey diddle diddle, the cat and the fiddle,
The cow jumped over the moon.
The little dog laughed to see such sport,
And the dish ran away with the spoon.

(A video can be viewed at https://youtu.be/5FjHZX-pbmQ.)

Hickory Dickory Dare

Hickory dickory dare. The pig flew up in the air.
Farmer Brown soon brought her down. Hickory, dickory dare.
Before reciting, explain that each child will get a chance to throw the puppet or stuffed animal up in the air and you will help if needed. Any animal can be substituted for the pig.

(A video can be viewed at https://youtu.be/BVnid6cfGpg.)

Hickory Dickory Dock

Stand up straight, dangle your hands, and clasp them together in front of you like a pendulum.
Hickory dickory dock,
Swing the pendulum from side to side.
The mouse ran up the clock.
Walk your fingers up from your toes to your head.
The clock struck one.
Clap hands once over your head.
And down she run.
Run your fingers down your body.
Hickory dickory dock.
Swing the pendulum.

(A video can be viewed at https://youtu.be/xbXbNpcCu9Y.)

The Hokey Pokey

You put your hand in.
Put your hand in front of you.
You take your hand out.
Put your hand behind you.
You put your hand in,
Move your hand forward.
And you shake it all about.
Shake your hand.
You do the hokey pokey
Point the index finger of each hand, and sway slightly from side to side while shrugging your shoulders.

And you turn yourself around.
Turn in a circle.
That's what it's all about.
Clap to the beat.
Hey!
Jump up.
(*Repeat with your foot, head, backside, and whole self.*)

The Hokey Pokey

(*revised; naming body parts and what they can do*)

You put your foot in, you take your foot out,
You put your foot in, and you kick it all about.
You do the hokey pokey, and you turn yourself
around.
That's what it's all about. Hey!
(*Repeat: fingers wiggle, hands clap, head nods, and
arms swing.*)

(A video can be viewed at https://youtu.be/eplRk7Pbc5g.)

Horsey, Horsey, on Your Way (with bells)

Horsey, horsey, on your way,
We've been together for many a day.
So let your tail go swish and your wheels go 'round,
Giddyap, we're homeward bound.

(A video can be viewed at https://youtu.be/CwGvcaBD
m7E.)

How Does the Busy Bee

(*interactive rhyme: put the bee on top of the flower*)

How does the little busy bee improve each shining
hour
and gather honey all the day, from every opening
flower?

Humpty Dumpty (Do knee bounces.)

Humpty Dumpty sat on a wall.
Lean gently from side to side.
Humpty Dumpty had a great fall…
"Fall" over onto one side.
All the king's horses and all the king's men
Bounce legs up and down rapidly.
Couldn't put Humpty together again.

(A video can be viewed at https://youtu.be/iJPEKxDJk54.)

Humpty Dumpty (as an interactive activity)

*Recite the rhyme, and invite children to take turns pulling
the felt Humpty off of his wall. Alternatively, use a plush
toy Humpty and a cardboard brick for the wall. Recite the
rhyme, and give each child a chance to push Humpty off of
his wall, rewarding his or her efforts with applause.*

(A video can be viewed at https://youtu.be/pqh5_Zc_0gY.)

Hurry, Hurry, Drive the Firetruck (ring bells)

Hurry, hurry, drive the firetruck. (3x)
Ding, ding, ding, ding, ding.

I

If You're Happy and You Know It

If you're happy and you know it, clap your hands.
If you're happy and you know it, clap your hands.
If you're happy and you know it and you really want
to show it,
If you're happy and you know it, clap your hands.
*One modification is "If You're Thankful and You Know
It, Clap Your Hands."*

(A video can be viewed at https://youtu.be/UkM_ajiHKMo
or https://youtu.be/_HbMFxog5cA.)

I Had a Little Dreidel

I had a little dreidel. I made it out of clay.
And when it's dry and ready, then dreidel I shall play.
Oh dreidel, dreidel, dreidel, I made it out of clay.
Spin while singing.
And when it's dry and ready, then dreidel I shall play.
It has a lovely body, with legs so short and thin,
And when it gets all tired, it drops and then I win!
Oh dreidel, dreidel, dreidel, with legs so short and
thin,
Spin while singing.
And when it gets all tired, it drops and then I win!
Fall down.

I Love You, You Love Me

(The lyrics and music to this song can be viewed at https://
kids.niehs.nih.gov/games/songs/childrens/i-love-you/index
.htm.)

I Look in the Mirror, and Who Do I See?

I look in the mirror, and who do I see?
I see [mommy / daddy / nana / Susie] looking at me.
Variations: I see ___ smiling at me, waving to me, or
  blowing kisses to me.
*Give each adult a handheld mirror to use with his or
  her child. This rhyme is particularly good for children who have difficulty making direct eye contact.*

I'm a Little Teapot

(A video can be viewed at https://youtu.be/_HbMFxog
5cA. The variation, "I'm a Little Airplane" is a great song
for large crowds who need get some exercise where
there is not enough space to move around the room.
This video can be viewed at https://www.youtube.com/
watch?v=Yv76PtdM4BU.)

I'm Driving in My Car

I'm driving in my car. I'm driving in my car.
Beep, beep, toot, toot, I'm driving in my car.
I'm driving very fast, I'm driving very fast.
Beep, beep, toot, toot, I'm driving very fast.
I'm driving very slowly. I'm driving very slowly.
Beep, beep, toot, toot, I'm driving very slowly.
I'm driving in my car. I'm driving in my car.
Beep, beep, toot, toot, I'm driving in my car.

(A video can be viewed at https://youtu.be/aDKsofGxxMo.)

It's Time to Say Good-Bye

It's time to say good-bye…but
I'm so happy, I'm so happy,
I'm so happy that everyone is here.

—By Barbara Cass-Beggs

I Went to Visit the Farm One Day

I went to visit a farm one day. I saw a [cow] along the
  way.
And what do you think the [cow] did say? [Moo,
  moo, moo.]
Suggest other animals and their sounds.

(A video can be viewed at https://youtu.be/BaMZoi4c-pg.)

J

Jack and Jill

Jack and Jill went up the hill to fetch a pail of water.
Jack fell down and rolled all around, and Jill came
  tumbling after.

(A video can be viewed at https://youtu.be/80t4ZLHw-jo/
and in Hawaiian at https://youtu.be/GvMav76Mpos.)

Jack Be Nimble *(interactive rhyme)*

Jack be nimble, Jack be quick.
Jack jump over the candlestick.
*Give each child a chance to jump over the candlestick,
  using his or her name in place of "Jack." Reward
  each jump with a positive word or clapping.*

(A video can be viewed at https://youtu.be/0buoF8kDVqY.)

Jack Be Nimble *(knee bounces)*

Jack be nimble, Jack be quick.
Bounce your child up and down on your legs.
Jack jump over the candlestick.
*Lift your child up or lean to the side and then continue
  bouncing.*

Jack-in-the-Box *(Show a real jack-in-the-box before doing the rhyme.)*

*As a standing-up rhyme, before you begin reciting this
  rhyme, pretend to climb into a box and shut the lid.*
Jack-in-the-box
Recite the rhyme while squatting.
Sitting so still. Won't you come out?
Yes, I will!
Jump up.

(A video can be viewed at https://youtu.be/NApWp8_Sof0.)

Jack-in-the-Box *(Bells)*

*One variation is to use bells instead. Because this rhyme
was demonstrated during the standing-up rhymes, you are
showing that the same rhyme can be used for multiple purposes. Instead of pretending to climb into a box, place
the prop on the floor and let go of it. Mime shutting the lid and
turning the handle. Recite the rhyme, and during the last
line, lift up the prop and vigorously shake it.*

Jack-in-the-Box *(Scarves)*
Another variation uses scarves. Children ball up the scarves in their hands and then throw them in the air.

L
Little Jack Horner
>Little Jack Horner sat in the corner,
>Eating his pumpkin pie.
>He stuck in a thumb and pulled out a plum
>And said, "What a good boy am I!"

London Bridge
>*Hold hands and dance around in a circle.*
>London Bridge is falling down, falling down, falling down.
>London Bridge is falling down, my fair lady.
>Build it up with sticks and stones, sticks and stones, sticks and stones.
>Build it up with sticks and stones, my fair lady.

(A different version of this can be viewed at https://youtu.be/QdUNyy6DuDs.)

M
Milkshake
>You take a little milk.
>*Pour some milk.*
>And you take a little cream.
>*Scoop the ice cream.*
>You stir it all up.
>You shake it and you sing:
>Milkshake, milkshake
>Shake it up, shake it up!
>Milkshake, milkshake
>Shake it all up!

—Copyright 1998 by Anne-Marie Akin, found on the CD "Songs for Wiggleworms"
(A version of this can be viewed at https://youtu.be/v_HBkvdAwXo.)

Miss Mary Mack
>Miss Mary Mack, Mack, Mack,
>All dressed in black, black, black,
>With silver buttons, buttons, buttons,
>All down her back, back, back.

>She asked her mother, mother, mother,
>For fifty cents, cents, cents,
>To see the elephant, elephant, elephant,
>Jump the fence, fence, fence.
>He jumped so high, high, high.
>He reached the sky, sky, sky,
>And never came back, back, back,
>Till the fourth of July, July, July.

(This can be viewed as a knee bounce at https://youtu.be/C-ans8IloCw.)

The More We Get Together
>The more we get together, together, together.
>The more we get together, the happier we'll be.
>For your friends are my friends, and my friends are your friends.
>The more we get together, the happier we'll be.

(A video can be viewed at https://youtu.be/ylrg6U2b8xU.)

Mother and Father and Uncle John
>Mother and father and Uncle John went to market one by one.
>*Gently bounce your outstretched legs as your child sits on them.*
>Mother fell off!
>*Lean to one side as far as you can.*
>Father fell off!
>*Lean to other side as far as you can.*
>But Uncle John went on and on and on…
>*Sit up straight, and bounce as quickly as you can.*

(A video can be viewed at https://youtu.be/7IuKcqVw0tE.)

Mother and Father and Uncle John *(adapted)*
>Mother and father and Uncle John went to town on a big, white swan.
>*Gently bounce your outstretched legs as your child sits on them.*
>Mother fell off!
>*Lean to one side as far as you can.*
>Father fell off!
>*Lean to other side as far as you can.*
>But Uncle John went on and on and on…
>*Sit up straight and bounce as quickly as you can.*

—Adapted by Jan Fabiyi
(A video can be viewed at https://youtu.be/9M7aIqiLWoI.)

Mrs. Turkey and Mrs. Duck

Start with both hands behind your back. One is Mrs. Turkey; the other is Mrs. Duck.

Mrs. Turkey went out in some very fine weather.

"Walk" fingers from one hand out to the front.

Along came Mrs. Duck, and they talked together.

"Walk" fingers from the other handout to the front.

"Gobble, gobble, gobble." "Quack, quack, quack."

Have hands "talk" to each other.

"Good-bye." "Good-bye."

Wave bye-bye

And they both ran back.

Hands go back behind back.

(A video can be viewed at https://youtu.be/5OTJ7iPJClU.)

My Face Is Round

My face is round.

I have two eyes, a nose, and a mouth.

Deborah Margolis suggests using a large photocopy of a child's face from Can You Say Peace *by Karen Katz.*

—By Regina Wade

(A video can be viewed at https://www.youtube.com/watch?v=kikymgO7xic.)

O

Oh Where, Oh Where Has My Little Head Gone?

(Tune: "Oh Where, Oh Where Has My Little Dog Gone?")

Place a scarf over your head.

Oh where, oh where has my little head gone? Oh where, oh where can it be? *(2x)*

One…two…three…*(Pull scarf off.)* Here it is!

Continue covering different body parts such as hand, knee, and leg.

(A video can be viewed at: https://youtu.be/kUiUj_uRQ5k.)

Old King Cole

Old King Cole was a merry old soul,

And a merry old soul was he.

He called for his pipe, and he called for his bowl,

And he called for his fiddlers three.

(A video can be viewed at https://youtu.be/gsn9MGIl-0U.)

Old MacDonald

Give all the children felt animals. Ask them to place their piece on the flannelboard when their animal's name is mentioned.

Old MacDonald had a farm, E I E I O.

And on that farm he had a cow, E-I-E-I-O.

With a moo moo here, and a moo moo there.

Here a moo, there a moo, everywhere a moo moo.

Old MacDonald had a farm, E-I-E-I-O.

Old Mother Goose

Old Mother Goose when she wanted to wander,

Tap your hands on the top of your legs.

Would fly through the air on a very fine gander.

Lift both hands up in the air, and move them in an arc over your head.

(A video can be viewed at https://youtu.be/p7LkuyFvf4A.)

Old Mother Goose *(alternate version)*

Old Mother Goose when she wanted to wander

Flapped her wings into the wild, blue yonder.

—Adapted by Lisa Tyson

One, Two, Buckle My Shoe

One, two, buckle my shoe.

Pretend to buckle a shoe.

Three, four, open the door.

Pretend to open a door.

Five, six, pick up sticks.

Pretend to pick up sticks.

Seven, eight, lay them straight.

Pretend to lay the sticks straight.

Nine, ten, a big red hen.

Hold hands together in front of you.

(A video can be viewed at https://youtu.be/_fSFv9rvVsE.)

One Yellow Fish Swimming in the Water

One little yellow fish swimming in the water,

Swimming in the water, swimming in the water.

One little yellow fish swimming in the water,

Bubble, bubble, bubble, bubble…pop!

Blue fish…

Red fish…

(Do the motions with your hands. Change colors each time.)

(A video can be viewed at https://youtu.be/QTlbZL8XKa8.)

Open Them, Shut Them

Open them, shut them. Open them, shut them.
Give them a great big clap.
Open them, shut them. Open them, shut them.
Put them in your lap.
Creep them, creep them, creep them, creep them,
Right up to your chin.
Open up your little mouth,
But…do not let them in!

(A video can be viewed at https://youtu.be/A_1terSLS9I.)

P

Pat-a-Cake

Pat-a-cake, pat-a-cake, baker's man,
Bake me a cake as fast as you can.
Roll it, and knead it, and mark it with a *B*,
And put it in the oven for baby and me!
(Substitute the letter, and use the name of your baby.)

(A video can be viewed at https://bit.ly/2PDFKTU.)

Patshe, Patshe Hentelach / Kikhelekh

*This Yiddish clapping rhyme or knee bounce ends with
the adult gently caressing the baby's cheeks.*
Patshe, patshe hentelach / kikhelekh.
Tate't koyfn shikhelekh.
Mame't shtrikn zekelekh.
a gezunt in deine bekelekh!
Translation:
Clap, clap, little children / cookies (hands)
Papa will buy little shoes.
Mama will knit little socks.
And good health in your cheeks!

(A video can be viewed at https://youtu.be/BM7c2BpaR5M.)

Peek-a-Boo

*Place a scarf over your head, and play peek-a-boo with
each child individually.*
Peek-a-boo, I see you, I see you hiding there.
Peek-a-boo, I see you. I see you smiling in there.

(A video can be viewed at https://youtu.be/SyGhJIjgzS4.)

Peter, Peter, Pumpkin Eater

*Lie on your tummy. Bend your knees so your feet are
pointed in the air.*
Peter, Peter, pumpkin eater, had a wife and couldn't
keep her.
Move your feet up and down to the beat.
Put her in a pumpkin shell, and there he kept her
very well.
Kick quickly.
*When finished singing the song a second time, do the
pumpkin roll to the right. Sing the song again, and
do the pumpkin roll to the left.*

—Activities designed by Gloria Bartas

(A video can be viewed at https://youtu.be/4R6yahpTYLs.)

Peter Works with One Hammer

Peter hammers with one hammer,
Pound one fist on a leg or on the floor.
One hammer, one hammer.
Peter hammers with one hammer,
All day long.

More verses:
Two hammers.
Pound two fists.
Three hammers.
Pound two fists, and stomp one foot.
Four hammers.
Pound two fists, and stomp two feet.
Five hammers.
Pound two fists, stomp two feet, and nod your head.
Peter's very tired now…
Rub eyes, and put your head on your hands.

(A video showing an adaptation of this rhyme with sticks
can be viewed at https://www.youtube.com/watch?v=jcLjO
IWRO24.)

Pitter Patter

Pitter patter, pitter patter, gently falls the rain.
Pitter patter, pitter patter, on my window pane.
Dropping, dropping, dropping, dropping, dropping,
Dropping to the ground.
Dripping, dripping, dripping, dripping,
Listen to the sound.

(A video can be viewed at: https://youtu.be/jECJkXZ4Yjc.)

Pizza, Pizza, Hot

Clap to the beat.

Pizza, pizza, hot. Pizza, pizza, cold.

Pizza, pizza in the box, nine days old.

Some like it hot. Some like it cold.

Some like it in the box, nine days old.

(A video can be viewed at https://youtu.be/wJjIMHpD
MRw.)

Los pollitos dicen

Los pollitos dicen pío, pío, pío,

Abra y cierre las manos.

Cuando tienen hambre, Cuando tienen frio.

Frótese la barriga, abrácese y tiembla.

La gallina busca el maíz el trigo.

Haga gestos con las manos que parezcan picotazos.

Les da la comida, les presta abrigo.

Tóquese la boca, abrácese.

Baja sus alas, acurrucaditos.

Estire los brazos como si estuviera meciendo a un bebe.

Duermen los pollitos, hasta el otro día.

*Cierre los ojos y acueste la cabeza para el lado sobre
    las manos.*

¡Despiértense!

Abra los ojos, siéntese derecho.

—Traditional

(A video can be viewed at: https://youtu.be/iRiPCS4g__0.)

Popcorn

Pop, pop, pop, pour the oil in the pot.

Pop, pop, pop, bake and shake it till it's hot.

Pop, pop, pop, pour it out, and what have you got?

Pop, pop, pop…POPCORN!

(A video can be viewed at https://youtu.be/JXJ1vMsgM
_Y.)

Popcorn *(Variation: the old fashioned way to make
popcorn)*

Popcorn, popcorn,

Motion pouring with one hand.

Pour it in the pan.

Pretend pouring with the other hand.

Stir it up, stir it up…

Make stirring motions with both hands.

Bam, bam, bam!

*Clap your hands together hard! Repeat this part three
    times loudly.*

Popcorn Kernels *(Tune: "Are You Sleeping, Brother
John?")*

Popcorn kernels, popcorn kernels,

In the pot. In the pot.

Shake them, shake them, shake them,

'Til they pop.

(A video can be viewed at: https://youtu.be/zQscnkpoejE.)

Put Your Fingers in the Air

Put your fingers in the air, in the air. Put your fingers
    in the air, in the air.

Put your fingers in the air, and wave them away up
    there.

Put your fingers in the air, in the air.

Put your fingers on your nose, on your nose. Put
    your fingers on your nose, on your nose.

Put your fingers on your nose and then drop them to
    your toes.

Put your fingers on your nose, on your nose.

Put your fingers on your knee, on your knee. Put
    your fingers on your knee, on your knee.

Put your fingers on your knee, and count together,
    one…two…three…

Put your fingers on your knee, on your knee.

—Original song by Woody Guthrie, adapted by Betsy
Diamant-Cohen

(Woody Guthrie's version of this can be viewed at https://
youtu.be/ZjTBqsI1wHE.)

R
Rain on the Green Grass

Rain on the green grass,

Rain on the tree,

Rain on the rooftops,

But not on me.

End with a hug, as if the parent is the child's umbrella.

(A video can be viewed at https://youtu.be/jWWVVfCy9
IQ.)

Ring around the Rosie

Ring around the rosie, a pocket full of posies.
Hold hands, and walk around in a circle.
Ashes, ashes, we all fall down!
Kneel or squat.
The cows are in the meadow, lying fast asleep.
Tap both hands on the floor in a rhythmic beat.
Along came a bee, buzz.
Wiggle your fingers in the air.
They all jumped up!

(A video of a different version can be viewed at https://youtu.be/o5DEUEa2Iuw.)

Ring Your Bells (Tune: "Jingle Bells")

Ring your bells, ring your bells, ring your bells today.
Oh, what fun it is to ring, to ring your bells today-ay!

—Music by James Pierpoint; words by Barbara Cass-Beggs
(A video can be viewed at https://youtu.be/inW7qAA0Ync.)

Ring Your Bells Today (Tune: "Lightly Row")

Ring your bells, ring your bells, you can ring your
    bells today.
Ring your bells, ring your bells, ring your bells today.
Ring them around and around and around.
Listen to their pretty sound!
Ring your bells, ring your bells, ring your bells today.

—Adapted by Barbara Cass-Beggs
(A video can be viewed at https://youtu.be/DiAwVPJUN
PQ.)

Round and Round the Garden

Round and round the garden goes the teddy bear.
One step, two steps, tickle him under there!

(A video can be viewed at https://youtu.be/-X_1AF_
-KOA.)

Row, Row, Row Your Boat (*Do knee bounces—fast and slow.*)

Row, row, row your boat, gently down the stream.
Merrily, merrily, merrily, merrily, life is but a dream.

*(Put your child on your outstretched legs, facing you. Hold
each hand in one of your hands. Lean back and forth, pulling in a gentle rocking motion. Sing at a normal speed,
then very quickly, then slowly, and then back to normal
speed. Match your movements to the tempo.)*

(A video can be viewed at https://youtu.be/hJmLI1WpaIw.)

Row, Row, Row Your Boat (*for preschoolers*)

Rock, rock, rock your boat
Mightily down the stream.
Rock your body side to side.
If you see a crocodile,
Don't forget to scream!
Put hands on face and "scream."
Row, row, row your boat
Gently to the shore.
"Row" with your arms.
If you see a lion,
Don't forget to roar!
"Roar."

Rum Pum Pum

Rum pum pum, this is my drum.
Hit a drum to the beat.
Rum pum pum, this is my drum.
My name is [Betsy]. What's your name?
*Tap your name with syllables on the drum. Then take
    the drum around the circle, and let each child tap
    out his or her own name with syllables. Give a per-
    sonal greeting after each name.*

—By Barbara Cass-Beggs
(A video can be viewed at https://youtu.be/5Sjjjg0guT0.)

S

Scarves Away

Scarves away, scarves away,
Put your scarves away today.
*Use this song to collect scarves in a canvas bag or a
    basket.*

—Words and music by Barbara Cass-Beggs
(A video can be viewed at https://youtu.be/AO7HB7p
gv1c.)

Scrunch Your Scarves into a Ball

Scrunch your scarf into a ball.
Scrunch your scarf into a tiny ball.

Make it very, very small.
Recite rather than sing the following lines.
On the count of three, throw them in the air, and watch all the beautiful colors fly down.
One, two, three, THROW!
Throw the scarves into the air and watch them float down.

—Regina Wade
(A video can be viewed at https://youtu.be/b-Cgg0we E9M.)

See the Ponies Galloping

Use a big horse puppet or a hobbyhorse for the inclusive version.
See the ponies galloping, galloping, down the country lane.
Repeat the above line faster and faster for as many times as you can.
See the ponies coming home, all tired out. All tired out.

(A video can be viewed at https://www.youtube.com/watch ?v=8WiMN7SBrO8.)

Seesaw Scaradown

Seesaw scaradown, this is the way to Londontown.
One knee up and the other knee down, this is the way to Londontown.
Repeat and fill in the name of your town.

(A video can be viewed at https://www.youtube.com/watch ?v=RFOUi5yQqgQ.)

The Shirt Song

[Name of a child] is wearing a *[color]* shirt, a *[color]* shirt, a *[color]* shirt.
[Name] is wearing a *[color]* shirt, all day long.
Repeat and sing with the name of another child, using the color of his or her shirt.
Continue until you have sung the song to each child present.

Smooth Road, Bumpy Road *(knee bounce)*

Children should sit on a parent's outstretched legs.
Let's get in the car. Let's put on our seat belts: click, click.
Let's start the engine: vroom, vroom.

Let's honk the horn: beep, beep.
Let's go!
We're going driving on a…
Smooth road, a smooth road, a smooth road, a smooth road.
Gently rock child back and forth with a small bounce.
A rough road, a rough road, a rough road, a rough road.
Bounce legs up and down gently.
A bumpy road, a bumpy road, a bumpy road, a bumpy road!
Bounce legs up and down vigorously.
Up the hill.
Knees up.
Down the hill.
Knees down.
Up the hill.
Knees up.
Down the hill.
Knees down.
A bumpy road, a bumpy road, a bumpy road, a bumpy road!
Bounce legs up and down vigorously.
A rough road, a rough road, a rough road, a rough road.
Bounce legs up and down gently.
A smooth road, a smooth road, a smooth road, a smooth road.
Gently rock child back and forth with a small bounce.
And back home again.
Give child a great big hug and kiss.

(A video can be viewed at: https://youtu.be/RJQ8f9I vIm8.)

T

Ten Horses Galloping

Sit with legs crossed, and tap your knees to the beat.
Ten horses galloping, galloping, all through the town.
Ten horses galloping, galloping, all through the town.
Five were white,
Show five fingers on one hand.
And five were brown.
Show five fingers on the other hand.
Ten horses galloping, galloping, all through the town.
Tap your knees to the beat.

They galloped to the left,
Lean left.
They galloped to the right,
Lean right.
They galloped so fast that they galloped out of sight.
Tap your knees very quickly.
Neigh!

—Adapted by Gloria Bartas
(A similar version can be viewed at https://youtu.be/iexFs2
AIyvs.)

This Is Bill Anderson

Place baby on your outstretched legs, facing you. Hold
each leg (at the ankle).
This is Bill Anderson.
Lift one of baby's legs and gently bounce it up and
down.
And this is Tom Trim.
Lift up baby's other leg and gently bounce it.
And Bill
Shake one leg.
Asked Tom
Shake the other leg.
To play with him.
Shake both legs.
Bill over Tom, Tom over Bill…
Cross one leg over the other and then reverse.
Bill over Tom, Tom over Bill…
Repeat, going a bit faster.
Bill over Tom, Tom over Bill…
Continue repeating and increasing tempo until…
Over and over as they fell down the hill!
Leg movements are all mushed together.

This Is the Way We Wash Our Knees

This is the way we wash our knees, wash our knees,
wash our knees.
Gently rub the scrunched scarf on your knees.
This is the way we wash our knees so early in the
morning.
Sing more verses, substituting other body parts.

(A video can be viewed at https://youtu.be/1mdtIHvvDLs.)

This Little Piggy

This little piggy went to market,
Gently tug your child's pinky.
This little piggy stayed home.
Gently tug on your child's ring finger.
This little piggy had roast beef.
Gently tug on your child's middle finger.
This little piggy had none.
Gently tug on your child's index finger.
And this little piggy cried,
Gently tug on your child's thumb.
Wee wee wee wee—all the way home!
Give your child a big tummy tickle!
Repeat using other the hand or toes.

(A video can be viewed at https://youtu.be/pmyGha_j8Yc.)

Tick Tock, Tick Tock, Where's That Cuckoo Bird?

Tick tock, tick tock, where's that cuckoo bird?
Tick tock, tick tock, when will he be heard?
Tick tock, tick tock, the minutes tick away,
Tick tock, tick tock, listen and he'll say, "CUCKOO!
CUCKOO! CUCKOO!"

(A video can be viewed at https://youtu.be/LXsdB0IoxyY.)

To Market, To Market

To market, to market, to buy a fat pig,
Home again, home again, jiggety jig.
To market, to market, to buy a fat hog.
Home again, home again, jiggety jog!
To market, to market, to buy a currant bun.
Home again, home again, market is done.
To market to market, to buy a pound of butter,
Home again, home again, throw it in the gutter!

(A video can be viewed at https://youtu.be/Zqt5ddwRcHo.)

Twinkle, Twinkle

Twinkle, twinkle, little star. How I wonder what you
are.
Up above the world so high, like a diamond in the
sky.
Twinkle, twinkle, little star. How I wonder what you
are.

For the inclusive version, use a rain stick to make a special sound to quiet down, like using a whisper to get attention.

—By Jane Taylor

(A video can be viewed at https://youtu.be/AeB2x8vQe9w.)

Twinkle, Twinkle *(alternate version)*

Twinkle, twinkle, little star. What a wonderful child you are.

With big bright eyes and nice round cheeks,

Talented person from head to feet.

Twinkle, twinkle, little star. What a wonderful child you are.

—Adapted by Becky Bailey, courtesy of *I Love You Rituals*; see www.consciousdiscipline.com.

(Listen to an adaptation at https://mgol.net/home/mother -goose-on-the-loose-goslings/songs/.)

Two Little Apples

Two little apples hanging in a tree,

Lift both arms up high.

Two little apples smiling down at me.

I shook that tree as hard as I could.

Shake arms quickly.

Make a falling sound or use a slide whistle.

Down came those apples…yum, yum, good!

Slowly lower arms and rub tummy.

—Adapted by Gloria Bartas

(A version of this can be viewed at https://youtu.be/ M3GKhADxxBM.)

Two Little Dickey Birds

Two little dickey birds sitting on a cloud.

Make two fists; each index finger points out. Bounce both hands up and down in front of you.

One named Soft

Whisper this as you bounce one hand up and down.

And the other named Loud!

Shout this as you bounce your other hand up and down.

Fly away, Soft.

Whisper as you put your first hand behind your back.

Fly away, Loud!

Shout as you put your other hand behind your back.

Come back, Soft.

Whisper as you bring your first hand to the front.

Come back, Loud!

Shout as you bring your other hand to the front.

—Words adapted by Barbara Cass-Beggs

(This can be modified for an international theme as "Two Little Kookaburras." A video can be viewed at https:// youtu.be/D-Ip4A8TGKY.)

Two Little Goslings *(Tune: "Hush Little Baby," a lullaby for NICU babies)*

Two little goslings safe in their nest.

One was awake and the other at rest.

One fell asleep, and the other did too,

And they slept and they slept the whole night through.

—By Betsy Diamant-Cohen

(The song can be heard at www.mgol.net/home/mother -goose-on-the-loose-goslings/songs. A video can be viewed at https://youtu.be/cGcSLc7RIsQ.)

Two Little Penguins

Two little penguins playing in the snow.

One named Fast, and the other named…Slow…

Move hands quickly and then slowly.

Fly away, Fast! Fly away, Slow.

Come back, Fast! Come back, Slow.

(A video can be viewed at https://youtu.be/M_t_RXxuzv0.)

Two Little Pretty Birds

Start by teaching the American Sign Language sign for bird by tapping pointer finger and thumb together near lips for "tweet, tweet." Then introduce two Audubon birds by name and the sounds they make. Put both birds behind your back and begin.

Two little pretty birds sitting on a cloud.

One named Soft

Bring one Audubon bird—a soft dove—from behind your back.

and the other named Loud!

Bring another Audubon bird—a loud raven—from behind your back.

Fly away, Soft.

Put the soft dove behind your back.

Fly away, Loud!

Put the loud raven behind your back.

Come back, Soft.
Bring the soft dove back to front.
Come back, Loud!
Bring the loud raven back to front.

—Words adapted by Deborah J. Margolis
(A video can be viewed at https://youtu.be/4mXRB5jfV
8Q.)

Two Little Puppy Dogs

Two little puppy dogs
Hold up two fingers.
Lying in a heap.
Let two fingers fall down.
Soft and wooly
Pet two fingers with opposite hand.
And fast asleep.
Lay hands against the side of your face and close eyes.

W

Way Up High in the Banana Tree (knee bounce)

Way up high in the banana tree, I saw a banana smile
   at me.
I rocked that tree as hard as I could.
Gently rock child back and forth.
Down came the banana.
Lower child back on lap.
Mmmm, it was good.
Give child a kiss.

(A video can be viewed at https://youtu.be/AoO0thQMA
to.)

We Hit the Floor Together

We hit the floor together, we hit the floor together,
Hit the floor with your hands.
We hit the floor together because it's fun to do!
*Sing more verses with other movements, such as
   "smack our knees," "clap our hands," "wave our
   arms," "wiggle our fingers," "wiggle our toes," "nod
   our heads," or "sway from side to side." (Note that
   "wiggle our toes" can only be sung if the children
   are barefoot; "nod heads" only works with older
   children who have muscle control of their heads.)*

—Traditional; words by Barbara Cass-Beggs
(A video can be viewed at https://youtu.be/AfRFiw4-lNs.)

We Ring Our Bells Together

We ring our bells together. (3x)
Ring bells.
Because it's fun to do.
Ring them up high,
Ring the bells up high.
Ring them down low,
Ring the bells down low.
And ring them in the middle.
Ring the bells in the middle.
*You can substitute "shake our shakers," "tap our sticks,"
   "play our instruments," and so forth.*

—Traditional; words by Barbara Cass-Beggs
(A video can be viewed at https://youtu.be/AB6KYxMqx
lE.)

Wee Willie Winkie

Wee Willie Winkie ran through the town.
Lay on your back and kick your feet in the air.
Upstairs (*feet go way up*), downstairs (*feet go down*),
   in his nightgown.
Tapping at the window,
Clap three times.
Hollering through the lock,
Cluck tongue three times.
"Are all the children in their beds? It's now eight
   o'clock!"
*Hold up ten fingers and then hide your thumbs to
   make eight.*

—Movements by Gloria Bartas
(A video can be viewed at https://youtu.be/FJwOe8juM
FY.)

We're Going to Kentucky

We're going to Kentucky, we're going to the fair.
We'll meet a señorita with flowers in her hair.
Oh, shake it, shake it, shake it.
Shake it if you can.
Shake it like a milkshake.
And drop it in a can.
Drop maraca.
Plop!

(A video can be viewed at https://tiny.cc/q7kgzy.)

We're Marching to the Drum *(Tune: "The Farmer in the Dell")*

> *(Hit the drum to a steady beat while everyone marches around in a circle.)*
>
> We're marching to the drum, we're marching to the drum.
>
> Hi-ho the derri-o, we're marching to the drum.
>
> We're marching 'round the room. We're marching 'round the room.
>
> Hi-ho the derri-o, we're marching 'round the room.
>
> We're marching to the drum, we're marching to the drum.
>
> Hi-ho the derri-o, we're marching to the drum.
>
> And the drum says, "Stop!"
>
> Can you hit "stop"?
>
> *(Walk around the circle, asking each individual child to hit the drum. Try to use a different positive word each time one of the children hits the drum.)*
>
> We're running to the drum, we're running to the drum.
>
> Hi-ho the derri-o, we're running to the drum.
>
> We're running 'round the room. we're running 'round the room.
>
> Hi-ho the derri-o, we're running 'round the room.
>
> We're running to the drum, we're running to the drum.
>
> Hi-ho the derri-o, we're running to the drum.
>
> And the drum says, "Stop!"
>
> Can you hit "stop"?
>
> *(Repeat having children hit drum.)*
>
> We're creeping to the drum, we're creeping to the drum.
>
> Hi-ho the derri-o, we're creeping to the drum.
>
> We're creeping 'round the room. we're creeping 'round the room.
>
> Hi-ho the derri-o, we're creeping 'round the room.
>
> We're creeping to the drum, we're creeping to the drum.
>
> Hi-ho the derri-o, we're creeping to the drum.
>
> And the drum says, "Stop!" Can you hit "stop"?
>
> *(Repeat having children hit drum.)*

—Traditional; words by Barbara Cass-Beggs
(A video can be viewed at https://youtu.be/8FMY1vG-KyM.)

We're So Happy

> We're so happy, we're so happy,
>
> We're so happy that everybody's here!

—By Barbara Cass-Beggs
(A video can be viewed at https://youtu.be/FuZ5MEQ PikU.)

The Wheels on the Bus *(adapted version; scarf song)*

> The wheels on the bus go 'round and 'round, 'round and 'round, 'round and 'round.
>
> The wheels on the bus go 'round and 'round, all through the town.
>
> *(Sing next verse slowly, moving a scarf in the air above your head in a circular motion.)*
>
> The wheels on the tractor go 'round and 'round, 'round and 'round, 'round and 'round.
>
> The wheels on the tractor go 'round and 'round, all through the farm.
>
> *(Sing the next verse quickly, moving the scarf in the air above your head in a circular motion.)*
>
> The wheels on the bike go 'round and 'round, 'round and 'round, 'round and 'round.
>
> The wheels on the bike go 'round and 'round, all through the city.
>
> *Repeat first verse and sing normally.*

—Adapted by Gloria Bartas
(Gloria's version with scarves can be viewed at https://youtu.be/yqlMPvTS5TA. A version with bells can be viewed at https://youtu.be/7ZNJ2N1Fp3k.)

When the Cows Get Up in the Morning *(use puppets or plastic animals)*

> When the cows get up in the morning, they always say moo.
>
> When the cows get up in the morning, they say moo, moo.
>
> *Suggest other animals and their sounds.*

(A video can be viewed at https://youtu.be/S6__rb0ikc0.)

Wiggle It High, Wiggle It Low

> Wiggle it high, wiggle it low,
>
> Wiggle your scarf in the middle just so!

The Wind Is Singing in the Mountains
The wind is singing in the mountains,
Over the valleys and the plains.
The wind is singing in the mountains,
Let love and unity reign.

—Adapted from *The Singing Wind* by Mrs. Jerald Day
(The music can be heard at https://youtu.be/MFyIGU3zDuI.)

Wind, Oh Wind
Wind, oh wind, oh wind, I say.
What are you blowing away today?
Scarves, oh scarves, oh scarves, I say.
I am blowing the scarves away.
Wave scarves from side to side.

—By Barbara Cass-Beggs
(A video can be viewed at https://youtu.be/QJogs0cIzrA.)

With My Little Hands I Go Clap, Clap, Clap
With my little hands I go clap, clap, clap.
With my little feet I go tap, tap, tap.
With my little arms I wave bye, bye, bye.
With my little legs I kick high, high, high.
With my little eyes I go, peek-a-boo.
With my little lips I say, "I love you."

(A video can be viewed at https://www.youtube.com/watch
?v=VvGfLgqEr5M.)

Y

Yadayim L'malah (*"Raise Your Hands" in Hebrew*)
Yadayim l'malah al ha rosh.
Raise your hands up onto your head.
Al hak'tafayim, echad shtayim, shelosh.
And onto your shoulders, one, two, three.
Yadayim l'malah al ha rosh.
Raise your hands up onto your head.
Al haraglayim, echad shtayim, shelosh.
On your legs, one, two, three.

(An audio version can be heard at https://youtu.be/Gua
_G3_131Y.)

You Are My Sunshine
You are my sunshine, my only sunshine.
You make me happy when skies are grey.
You'll always know, dear, how much I love you.
So enjoy the sunshine today.

(A video can be viewed at https://www.youtube.com/watch
?v=h57AbR4IxEw.)

Z
Zoom, Zoom, Zoom
Zoom, Zoom, Zoom, we're going to the moon. (2x)
If you want to take a trip, climb aboard my rocket
    ship.
Zoom, Zoom, Zoom, we're going to the moon.
Five, four, three, two, one…. Blast off!
*Try "Fun, fun, fun, we're going to the sun" and "Far,
    far, far, we're going to the stars."*

(A video can be viewed at https://youtu.be/Qi-v_ofXoiM.)

Using Digital Media

ACCORDING TO THE 2018 "MOBILE FACT SHEET" FROM a Pew Research Center study, 95 percent of Americans own cell phones and 100 percent of eighteen- to twenty-nine-year-olds own a cell phone.[1] Young parents rely on digital media for communication, and social media is a free marketing tool. Using social media casts a wider net and allows us to interface with families that may not otherwise have access to information about our programs. Social media can notify families about changes immediately and can also be used as an evaluation tool. It thus makes sense to use digital media to manage information, create community, and market programs.

Using Social Media Messaging for MGOL

- Create simple forms for capturing attendees' contact information with QR codes. Google Forms works well because it stores information in easy-to-read spreadsheets that can easily be downloaded to other systems or programs. It can also be used for feedback surveys. Google also easily creates QR codes.
- Print out and bring the QR code to your programs. By scanning the QR code with their phones, parents will be taken directly to the form or survey.
- Bring an iPad with the sign-up sheet and playlists ready for use.
- Social media can be used as a predictive tool to

announce new events and estimate attendance beforehand.
- Look at your statistics regularly, and make changes as necessary. Check to see how many people see your posts. How many are sharing them? How many are interacting with them? For instance, if posts with videos are more popular, you may decide to include more videos to increase viewership.
- Once you have a captive audience through social media, you can provide people with other valuable resources and information outside of your program offerings, such as developmental tips and relevant community events.

Marketing Your Program Using Social Media

- Instead of relying on just one form of social media, use them all! Many people use just one platform—for instance, the Jones family might use Facebook, but the Brown family might use Twitter. You will can contact both families, reaching much wider audience by using different forms of social media.
- Subscribe to an app to collect participants' contact information, which is kept private.
- Look for an app such as Remind, a user-friendly tool created for teachers by teachers, where subscribed users can send mass texts to large groups of

people while keeping all phone numbers blocked from view. Messages can be scheduled and translated into multiple languages.

- Send messages electronically to give weekly reminders and location updates if necessary.
- Create a Facebook page as a business (rather than a personal page). Draw followers through weekly posts and events. Invite parents and families to also share MGOL stories and photographs there.
- Hashtags can be used across all social media. Identify and create hashtags that have yet not been used, and ask families to use those hashtags when they are posting to social media regarding one of your programs. Use these hashtags to alert families to upcoming sessions as well as other exciting local educational opportunities.
- MGOL uses the hashtag #MGotL. Including this in your social media blasts will help bring the larger MGOL community together.
- There are multiple programs designed to help make the social media process easier by putting them all in one central location and pushing out information to all the different platforms. Hootsuite, for instance, is used by many educators. You only have

to create one message, but it is then disseminated through all the platforms.

About the MGOL App

With encouragement from Cen Campbell, a friend and colleague, I joined forces with Software Smoothie and created the Felt Board Mother Goose on the Loose app. It is currently available for download on iTunes and is only for use on the iPad. It looks like felt pieces on a flannelboard, uses many of the MGOL activities, and has characters that match the templates in this book. It was designed to build early literacy skills, encourage playful interactions between children and the adults in their lives, and support the use of narrative skills and imagination.

First, children choose a nursery rhyme and its related characters. Then they press an icon for sound and manipulate the characters as the rhyme is recited. (This improves fine motor skills—a first step to writing.) Once they learn the words to the rhyme (vocabulary!), they no longer need to use the icon; they can recite the rhyme on their own. (This emphasizes using words and communicating.) When they are ready to advance to the next

Snapshot: Using the App during MGOL Sessions

While working as the branch librarian and youth services coordinator of the Kent Island branch of Queen Anne's County Library in Stevensville, Maryland, Julie Ranelli was one of the first children's librarians to use the Software Smoothie Felt Board Mother Goose on the Loose app during MGOL sessions.

We had the greatest success when we projected the iPad onto a screen so that all the children could see and appreciate the efforts of others as each child uncovered a sheep for Little Bo Peep. Most children were able to manipulate the sheep and bushes with ease and responded with proud smiles—very similar to their responses to the traditional flannelboard. A few children had never used a touch screen before and required some adult guidance. I emphasized taking turns and social skills.

The first time I used the app and projector for

"Five Fat Sausages," the children were all interested in the images. However, instead of participating in the rhyme as they usually would (counting on fingers, clapping for "bam!"), their eyes were riveted to the projection screen. The next time I used the app for "Five Fat Sausages" and when I introduced it for "The Grand Old Duke of York," I reminded children and caregivers to continue the same motions we would use with the flannelboard. That simple reminder worked, and they laughed when the duke's men turned upside down!

Using the MGOL app during the session with a small group.

step, they can use the characters to create their own stories, even combining characters from different rhymes. (This exercises imagination, play, and narrative skills.) Instructions for parents state that the app is meant to be used for communication and play between parents and their children, not for babysitting. Descriptions of how the app can be used on the iPad and suggestions of ways to extend the rhyme play through activities at home are included.

Key Features

The app uses MGOL felt templates as digital felt board pieces and includes MGOL songs. In-app guidance regarding appropriate use of technology with young children is available for parents, librarians, and educators. Rhymes in Spanish are included in addition to the traditional MGOL rhymes in English. Rhymes can be listened to or recited and "acted out" with the felt characters. The characters can be combined to create and tell stories.

Using the App during Library Programs

According to *Young Children, New Media, and Libraries*, edited by Amy Koester,[2] the best way to mirror a tablet to a television or large screen is to use an HDMI cable and iPad adapter. If the librarian wants to walk around, make sure to have a secure Wi-Fi connection, and use a streaming device such as Google Chromecast or Apple TV with your iPad.

Tips for Success

- Choose apps that present rhymes in active, engaging ways, allowing for children's hands-on participation. For instance, when using "Little Bo Peep" from Software Smoothie's Felt Board Mother Goose on the Loose app, put Little Bo Peep and the sheep on the screen and then cover the sheep with the bushes, leaving just a tiny bit of the sheep visible. Recite the rhyme, and tap the visible part of the sheep. The entire sheep will instantly appear! Tap the bush, and the sheep will be hidden again. Then either walk around the room and give each child a chance to "find the sheep" or, if the app is being projected onto a screen, invite children to come up to where you are sitting to tap the device.
- For large groups, project the iPad's images to a bigger screen that everyone can see. With small groups, walking around and giving each child a chance to move items around on the tablet gives firsthand experience with using iPads and apps.

Using the MGOL App in Schools

Libraries that run book clubs for schools can use the Felt Board Mother Goose on the Loose app to stimulate creative thinking via an "Extreme Makeover" program. According to Beth Munk, the children's services manager at the Kendallville Public Library in Indiana, students should first listen to the various nursery rhymes, learning the words and familiarizing themselves with the "felt" pieces and where they are to be placed. Once a level of comfort has been reached, children can be challenged to recite the rhymes without using the available sound.

Snapshot: Aligning the MGOL App to the STEM/STEAM/Maker Movements

MGOL can be used during school visits to increase literacy skills while aligning students with the STEM/STEAM/Maker movement via use of the Felt Board Mother Goose on the Loose app. According to children's services manager Beth Munk at the Kendallville Library in Indiana, the MGOL app has been used during her visits to the East Noble School Corporation to ignite imagination, encourage writing, and stimulate creative problem solving.

This app has become the cornerstone of our weekly kindergarten (and sometimes third-grade) classroom visits as we work to increase literacy skills while aligning them with the STEM/STEAM/Maker movements. Each week, we cover a different rhyme, reading and playing with the rhymes within the app. Next, students are encouraged to deconstruct the rhyme and identify all the parts, characters, problems, and solutions. After much discussion, they "rebuild the rhyme," coming up with a new approach to solving the problems they identified. This is first done on paper and in open discussion and then physically done using "maker" materials provided for them.

Last week, our focus was on the rhyme "Jack and Jill." After listening to the rhyme and discussing it in groups, the students were asked, "What problem should we address?" We had students who wanted to solve the danger of walking up and down the hill and others who wanted to eliminate the hill and dig a new well or design a machine to get the water down from the current well without requiring you to walk up the hill at all. We were able to incorporate discussions about force and motion, simple versus complex machines, soil and water, and many other things. Did we find a new solution? Yes and no. Some students were satisfied with cutting steps into the hill, while others still didn't think this was fixing the problem. As a group, we tabled the lesson for a week so they could think about new ways to attack the problem and be creative in their solutions.

Why nursery rhymes? Well, they're short, easy, familiar, and fun while still presenting a variety of "problems" that enable us to work with them in new and exciting ways—creating connections between reading, writing, singing, talking, and playing.

From there, give children the unique opportunity to play with words, retell stories, and use their imaginations by asking them to make up their own stories using the felt characters. After all, who needs a waterspout when it can become a cell phone tower instead?

Key Features

Use the Software Smoothie Felt Board Mother Goose on the Loose app to engage older children, teaching them nursery rhymes while also igniting their imaginations and giving them the opportunity to practice narrative skills.

Tips for Success

- Even if there are iPads in the classroom, bring a number of them with you to the school with the app that you want to use already installed.
- With the teacher's permission, use your camera or phone to record some of the final presentations. These can be played back on subsequent visits and used as starting points for continuing the adventure.
- Depending on the ages of the students, oral stories can be turned into written compositions.

NOTES

1. Pew Research Center, "Mobile Fact Sheet," February 5, 2018, www.pewinternet.org/fact-sheet/mobile/.
2. Amy Koester, ed., *Young Children, New Media, and Libraries: A Guide for Incorporating New Media into Library Collections, Services, and Programs for Families and Children Ages 0-5* (self-pub., Little eLit, 2015), https://littleelit.files.wordpress.com/2015/06/final-young-children-new-media-and-libraries-full-pdf.pdf.

Printable Resources

Mother Goose on the Loose Session Planning Sheet

Section 1: Welcoming comments
Introduce yourself and welcome everyone.
State expectations ("Children this age don't sit perfectly still").
Set guidelines ("If they come within this invisible circle, please come and get them").
Explain how it works ("I'm going to say things twice").

Section 2: Rhymes and reads

Section	Rhyme/Read	Prop
Opening	"Old Mother Goose"	
Opening rhyme		
General rhyme		
Puppet kisses		
Book to read aloud		
Tickle rhyme		
General rhyme		

Section 3: Body rhymes

Head		
Head		
Fingers		
Tickle		
Hands		
Knee bounces		
Knee bounces		
Knee bounces		

Section 4: The drum sequence

Children tap out names with syllables

Section 5: Stand-up / sit-down activities

Stand-up action 1		
Stand-up action 2		
Stand-up action 3		

Section 6: Animal activities		
Book		
Puppets		
Puppets		
Section 7: Musical instruments and scarves		
Musical instrument		
Musical instrument		
Musical instrument		
Musical instrument		
Musical instrument		
Colored scarves		
Colored scarves		
Colored scarves		
Colored scarves		
Colored scarves		
Section 8: Lullabies		
Lullaby		
Section 9: Interactive rhymes		
Interactive rhyme		
Section 10: Closing ritual		
Closing rhyme		
Closing rhyme		

Developmental Tip #1: _____

Developmental Tip #2: _____

Observations: _____

Betsy Diamant-Cohen, Mother Goose on the Loose: Here, There, and Everywhere (Chicago: ALA Editions, 2019).

Mother Goose on the Loose Intake Form

Name of agency: _____ Education rating (if possible) _____

Day of month: _____ Time: _____

Address: _____ Phone number:_____

Contact person: _____ E-mail: _____

Number of classrooms: _____ Number of children per classroom: _____

Age range: _____ Quality rating or level (if applicable): _____

Any topics you can't read: _____

Policies for weather school closing and holidays: _____

Is there a last day for presenting programs? If so, when? _____

Notes (door codes, where to enter the building, if shoes need to be removed at the door, if sign-in is necessary, which classroom to go to first):

_____

_____

_____

Directions:

_____

_____

_____

Minutes/miles from library:_____ Minutes/miles from previous daycare: _____

Monthly attendance (for keeping statistics) / books given out:

September _____   January _____   May _____

October _____   February_____   June_____

November _____   March_____   July _____

December _____   April _____

(Created by Dora Garraton, Vigo County Public Library)

Mother Goose on the Loose Teacher Survey

Teacher's / provider's name: _____ School or center name: _____

Questions for teachers regarding the series:

What have you learned from the Mother Goose on the Loose program?

_____

_____

_____

Will you use any of the Mother Goose on the Loose activities or tips in your classroom? If so, please describe.

_____

_____

_____

What do you think was the most important part of Mother Goose on the Loose? Why?

_____

_____

_____

If you could change anything about Mother Goose on the Loose, what would it be? Why?

_____

_____

_____

Any other comments?

_____

_____

_____

Thank you for filling out this survey!

Talking about Tots Topics

Talking about Tots was developed and administered through a partnership between Port Discovery Children's Museum and the Kennedy Krieger Center for Autism and Related Disorders in Baltimore. The topics that follow were all successfully used during monthly spots immediately after an MGOL session. Choose the titles that are relevant to your MGOL families, and look for local resource people to give the presentations.

- **"Enhancing Your Child's Skills through Connection-Based Play"** provided information on the benefits and how-tos of playtime that specially focused on bonding and connecting with young children.

- In **"Routine Based Language: Enhancing Your Child's Language during Routines,"** a speech-language pathologist spoke about ways to incorporate predictable language into everyday routines. Parents learned strategies to pair language with bath time, bedtime, snack time, and so forth. The routines operate in a predictable way in order to enhance their children's understanding and use of language.

- During **"Why Sensory Play Makes Sense,"** parents learned how activities that encourage a child to explore using his or her senses (e.g., touch) can be used to enhance a child's receptive language, teach new vocabulary, and refine motor skills, as well as develop other important learning and social skills.

- **"Run, Dance, and Play! Establishing Physical Activity Habits to Last a Lifetime"** discussed development of physical skills, included practical tips to encourage unstructured and structured physical activity, and highlighted various benefits of maintaining a healthy lifestyle.

- **"Big Fun…Homemade Toys for You and Your Child's Development, Birth to Age Three"** offered information on toy materials and ideas for play. The presentation concluded with opportunity to build a toy.

- During **"Motor Milestones: How to Enhance Your Child's Gross and Fine Motor Skills through Play,"** an occupational therapist gave parents strategies for encouraging motor development through play and children's exploration of their environment. She also discussed how successful participation in motor activities can impact engagement and attention.

- **"Kids Kitchen: Enhancing Child Nutrition through Interactive Cooking"** highlighted the short-term and long-term benefits of encouraging children to help cook in the kitchen. The speaker offered age-appropriate cooking tasks and tips, enabling parents to promote their child's involvement in mealtime and initiate a lifelong interest in cooking.

- **"This Book Is Too Long"** discussed how to creatively cut down books so that they will be interesting and maintain children's attention.

- **"Why Buy It When You Can Make It!"** discussed how parents can creatively make toys and engaging activities out of common household items.

- Since sleep deprivation is one of the toughest challenges that parents face when their children do not sleep well, **"Lullaby and Goodnight: Fostering Sleep for Infants and Toddlers"** discussed bedtime routines, techniques for putting children to bed, and sleep training to help children sleep through the night.

- **"Do You See What I'm Saying? Nonverbal Communication in Infants and Toddlers"** described the many ways that infants and toddlers use their eyes, hands, and bodies to communicate with those around them before they can speak and into toddlerhood.

- Since research studies have shown that signing with babies accelerates language acquisition, reduces frustration, and deepens the bond between parent and child, during **"Sign Language Is for Everyone,"** parents were shown core signs and taught how to integrate them into everyday routines.

- **"Babies and Toddlers with Tablets: Tools to Enhance Development versus Electronic Babysitter"** discussed positive and negative impacts that exposure to tablets may have on infant and toddler development.

Snapshot: Parent Comments

Parents appreciated the relaxed atmosphere and the up-to-date information provided during Talking about Tots segments. Surveys following this program included comments such as "I was motivated to attend this morning because I saw the feeding/mealtime talk advertised on the website. I think it's a great value for my child to be able to play/enjoy music time and for me as a 1st time mom to hear about a very timely topic! :) (I am the mother of a 12-month-old). Thanks!" and "I enjoyed the talk from Krieger. I saw that he would be here and thought it might be impossible to attend a 'lecture' with 3 kids on a 'fun trip.' The format of having an informal discussion in the tot zone while the kids played worked great! Mothers are great at multi-tasking and listening while watching their kids." As a result of "Talking about Tots," some parents said that when they returned home, they created opportunities for their children to paint, share books, help in the kitchen, cook, and play homemade musical instruments. Tha's the type of response we like to hear!

- **"Movers and Shakers: Incorporating Music and Movement into Your Daily Routines"** outlined the advantages of music and movement in children's cognitive development and provided examples of how to best utilize music and movement as teaching tools.

- **"Strengthen Your Child's Early Literacy Skills with Nursery Rhymes"** involved adults and caregivers singing and playing with their children while learning the value of what they were doing in MGOL and how it aided in their child's development.

- **"Beyond Yes or No: The Power of Your Child's Choices"** outlined why it is important for children to have choices and explained benefits and strategies for incorporating choice-making opportunities into everyday activities.

- **"Thinking Outside the Book: Book-Linked Activities to Support Motor and Sensory Development in Toddlers"** discussed and provided models and ideas of sensory-based activities and sensory-play ideas that correspond with a variety of popular children's books.

- **"The Stages of Brain Development—An Overview for Parents"** described the important role of experiences for shaping the developing brains of children.

- **"Using Touch to Promote Your Baby's Development"** taught parents about the benefits of infant massage for relaxing babies and promoting development across multiple areas, including motor, language, and social development.

- **"ABCs and 123s: Understanding Behavior and How It Adds Up"** discussed some of the negative behaviors children may show (such as screaming or throwing things) and how to effectively address them as a parent.

How Nursery Rhyme Activities Help Children Develop School Readiness Skills

by Dr. Betsy Diamant-Cohen

NURSERY RHYMES ARE PERFECT FOR BABIES AND toddlers. They are short and simple to recite or sing. They include words that begin and end with the same sounds, helping children's brains to recognize syllables and hear patterns. Familiarity with nursery rhymes can lead to phonological awareness. The repetition in nursery rhymes helps increase a child's vocabulary. Research shows that children who enter kindergarten knowing nursery rhymes will have an easier time learning how to read. MGOL is based on nursery rhymes that are presented in a variety of different ways.

Nursery rhyme activities can be easily used to teach children skills needed for school readiness, including social and emotional skills, language and literacy, math and science, physical development, and general knowledge of the world around them, while also helping them develop a positive approach to language, books, and learning.

- Exposure to rhythm instruments such as shakers, tambourines, bells, and maracas helps children learn scientific observation. They are experimenting and learning from their experiences, answering questions about each items' properties: "What does this do when I shake it? What happens when I play it quickly? What does it taste like?"
- While singing songs with actions, children learn to follow directions, concentrate, and gain new vocabulary.
- While clapping to rhymes, children learn to listen for the syllables in each word. Hearing the sounds in words and being able to break them down into syllables is called "phonological awareness," and it is an important step in learning how to read.

Using Nursery Rhyme Books with Children

When books are read aloud in a joyous way, children will absorb the happy feeling related to books and carry it on later in life—one of the values that is now associated with school readiness!

- When you read nursery rhymes aloud from a book, children are seeing "book reading behavior." They notice that there is a front cover to the book and a back cover; they see how you turn the pages and read from left to right. This exposure to books in a lighthearted way leads to positive feelings about books and reading.
- Seeing rhymes being read aloud connects written words with spoken words.
- Looking at pictures of nursery rhyme characters (such as Humpty Dumpty) encourages children to increase their visual literacy. Talk about what you see, and ask your child to point to different things in the picture. Use the picture to create fun interactions with your child.
- Another time, look at pictures of Humpty drawn by different illustrators. Seeing the same character being drawn in different ways introduces children to abstract concepts; they realize that the same thing can have different visual representations.
- Exposure to illustrations also encourages aesthetic appreciation of art.

Examples:
Reciting Nursery Rhymes with Children

Rhymes about everyday occurrences and familiar animals may spark a child's general interest in the world around him or her.

> I had a little turtle. He lived in a box.
> He swam in the water, and he climbed on the rocks.
> He snapped at a minnow, he snapped at a flea, he snapped at a mosquito, and he snapped at me.
> He caught the minnow, he caught the flea, he caught the mosquito, but he didn't catch me!

Learn how to count with a fun rhyme!

> Five fat sausages frying in a pan, the oil was hot so one went *bang*!
> Four fat sausages...three...two...one...
> And there were no sausages left!

Research shows that hand-clapping songs improve motor and cognitive skills.

> If you're happy and you know it, clap your hands.
> If you're happy and you know it, clap your hands.
> If you're happy and you know it and you really want to show it,
> If you're happy and you know it, clap your hands.

A video about the value of sharing nursery rhymes with your children can be viewed at www.youtube.com/watch?v=rj3HwKpxMMY&feature=related.

Books and Websites for Planning Programs for Children with Special Needs

Books

Banks, Carrie Scott, Sandra Feinberg, Barbara A. Jordan, Kathleen Deerr, and Michelle Langa. 2014. *Including Families of Children with Special Needs: A How-To-Do-It Manual for Librarians.* Chicago: ALA Neal-Schuman.

MacMillan, Kathy. 2013. *Little Hands and Big Hands: Children and Adults Signing Together.* Chicago: Huron Street Press.

Naidoo, Jamie Campbell. 2014. *Diversity Programming for Digital Youth.* Santa Barbara: Libraries Unlimited.

Prendergast, Tess, and Rhea Lazar. 2010. "Language Fun Storytime: Serving Children with Speech and Language Delays" in *Children's Services: Partnerships for Success*, edited by Betsy Diamant-Cohen. Chicago: ALA Editions.

Websites and Articles

ALSC Association for Library Service to Children. 2015. *Library Services to Special Population Children and Their Caregivers: A Toolkit for Librarians and Library Workers.* January 2015. www.ala.org/alsc/sites/ala.org.alsc/files/content/professional-tools/lsspcc-toolkit-2015.pdf.

Burgstahler, Sheryl. 2018. "A Checklist for Making Libraries Welcoming, Accessible, and Usable." Equal Access: Universal Design of Libraries. www.washington.edu/doit/equal-access-universal-design-libraries.

Collaborative Summer Library Program. 2018. "Inclusive Programming." Inclusion Resources. 2018. https://www.cslpreads.org/inclusion-resources/inclusive-programming.

Diamant-Cohen, Betsy, Tess Prendergast, Christy

Estrovitz, Carrie Banks, and Kim Van der Veen. 2012. "We Play Here! Bringing the Power of Play into Children's Libraries." *Children and Libraries* 10 (1): 3–10, 52.

Harman, Teri. 2015. "Tips for Reading to Children with Special Needs." KSL, December 18, 2015. www.ksl.com/?sid=22953662.

Humphrey, Jennifer. 2015. "Sensory/Special Needs Storytime." Pinterest. December 17, 2015. www.pinterest.com/jelander74/sensory-special-needs-storytime.

Library Connections. 2015. "Programming Strategies That Work." Libraries and Autism. December 17, 2015. www.librariesandautism.org/strategies.htm.

National Library Service for the Blind and Physically Handicapped Kids Zone. https://goo.gl/xpk1ch.

Autism Resources

Autism Speaks. 2018. "100 Day Kit for Young Children." https://www.autismspeaks.org/sites/default/files/docs/about_autism_0.pdf.
The 100 Day Kit for Newly Diagnosed Families of Young Children *helps families with children ages four and under make the best possible use of the hundred days following a diagnosis of autism.*

Bennie, Maureen. 2010. "The DSM-V and Sensory Processing Disorder." *Autism Awareness Centre Inc.* (blog), March 13, 2010. https://autismawarenesscentre.com/the-dsm-v-and-sensory-processing-disorder/.
Maureen Bennie created the Autism Awareness Centre in 2003 to address what she saw as a gap in support and advocacy for those struggling with autism.

Subject Index

Title Index